D1241388

John Reed

John Reed

Eric Homberger

Manchester University Press
Manchester and New York

Distributed exclusively in the USA and Canada by St. Martin's Press, New York

Copyright © Eric Homberger 1990

Published by Manchester University Press,
Oxford Road, Manchester, M13 9PL, UK
and Room 400, 175 Fifth Avenue, New York, NY 10010, USA

Distributed exclusively in the USA and Canada
by St. Martin's Press, Inc., 175 Fifth Avenue, New York, NY 10010, USA

British Library cataloguing in publication data
Homberger, Eric
  John Reed. — (Lives of the left)
  1. United States. Journalism. Reed, John, 1887—1920
  I. Title   II. Series
  070.92

Library of Congress cataloging in publication data applied for

ISBN 0 7190 2194 4 *hardback*

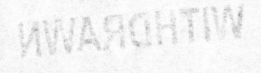

Set in Perpetua
by Koinonia Ltd, Manchester

Printed in Great Britain
by Biddles Ltd, Guildford and King's Lynn

Contents

Acknowledgements

Professor Scott Sanders of the University of Indiana, Mr George Abbott White of Brookline, Massachusetts and Dr Bill Albert of the University of East Anglia, Norwich, were kind enough to read various sections of this manuscript. Their discriminating interest in Reed has helped me to sharpen certain aspects of my own argument.

For John Marshall Harris

'... among our people we have gallant fore, main, and mizzen top-men aloft, who, well treated or ill, still trim our craft to the blast'.

Melville, White-Jacket, 1850

Introduction

'The main task', wrote Anatoli Rybakov in his novel *Children of the Arbat*,

> was to build a mighty socialist state. For that mighty power was needed. Stalin was at the head of that power, which meant that he stood at its source with Lenin. Together with Lenin he had led the October Revolution. John Reed had presented the history of October differently. That wasn't the John Reed we needed.[1]

Each generation since Reed's death has felt the need to recreate a 'John Reed' in accordance with the spirit of the age. In the 1920s, in a period of repression and defeat for radicalism, Reed was a link with revolutionary tradition:

> I remember standing at his grave under the Kremlin wall [in 1926], as six years earlier in Paris I had stood before Heine's grave in the Père Lachaise; and I could not help reflecting that there was a continuity in socialist revolutionary tradition, and that for my generation the American had replaced the German poet.[2]

He was also seen as part of the 'missing generation', a tragic model of youth destroyed:

> Bartering all else for some adventurous deed—
>   Now here, now there, in thickest of the fray—
> That was the glory of your life, John Reed,
>   Your short life spent in flinging life away.[3]

In the 1930s he became a model for young radical writers, his name given to the clubs formed by the editors of the *New Masses* and the

Communist Party to encourage proletarian literature and ideologi-
cal struggle in the sphere of culture. John Reed was one of the
revolutionary heroes whose life story was told in John Dos Passos's
influential novel *USA*.[4] A leading Communist Party literary critic,
Granville Hicks, wrote an illustrated biography of Reed for
teenagers which was published in 1935, in which Reed was seen
as an inspiration for revolutionary struggle:

> the revolutionary workers of America, in crowded mass meetings,
> pledged themselves with upraised fists to a harder fight in John Reed's
> name. And in America's prisons, in Leavenworth and Atlanta and San
> Quentin, and in the penitentiaries of forty-eight states, comrades,
> awaiting trial, serving their ten or twenty year sentences, perhaps
> awaiting death, thought of John Reed and steeled themselves once
> more for the final conflict.[5]

In his major biography of Reed which was published in 1936, Hicks
presented an exemplary story of a Greenwich Village bohemian
who was transformed by his experience of class struggle and
revolution into a revolutionary.

Interest in Reed waned in the dark period of the Cold War in
the 1940s and 1950s. It was perhaps not surprising that in the era
of 'the end of ideology' attention now shifted towards Reed as a
Greenwich Village bohemian and as an 'idealist-radical' who was
to exert a considerable influence over the student generation in the
1960s and the New Left. He was uniquely a role-model of the
intellectual who transcended the division between thinking and
doing:

> The importance of John Reed lies, then, in this: that he acted
> physically, the turmoil that most of the activist-intellectuals confined
> to paper in journalistic, literary or critical form. Reed lived his
> turmoil. In a sense that he did not live longer – to recant his communist
> heresy, or to eat humble pie in America, or to follow a new ideal –
> is beneficial to the student of the second decade of the century in
> America, for he is provided with a dramatic reference point and a

picture of the inner agony of many in the observable life of John Reed [who was] actually [the] only one of the intellectuals of his time to reach the very limits of idealism – but one of the only ones to reach it in the physical absolute.[6]

The 1960s saw the return to print of most of Reed's books. But for the wider reading public a softer, less exemplary John Reed was available: the 'romantic revolutionary'. The title of Robert Rosenstone's detailed and scholarly life of Reed, *Romantic Revolutionary* (1975), and the film which Warren Beatty made about Reed, fixed the 'John Reed' for our generation. People who were interested in Reed wanted to talk about his role in the Paterson Strike Pageant, the Provincetown Players, and his relations with Mabel Dodge Luhan and Louise Bryant. Reed's complex friendship with Eugene O'Neill, and the playwright's affair with Bryant, omitted from Hicks's biography, were described in detail for the first time in Arthur and Barbara Gelb's substantial biography of O'Neill (1962). Following the publication of the second volume of Eastman's autobiography (*Love and Revolution*, 1964) and William L. O'Neill's substantial anthology of the *Masses* in 1966, there was renewed interest in the magazine which embodied the rebellious spirit of the younger writers and artists in New York between 1913 and 1917. And equally predictably, a counter-current of scholarship, hostile to the naïvety of the Villagers, has emerged.

Despite the skirmishing back and forth of scholars seeking to praise or bury the Villagers' free-wheeling style of cultural rebelliousness, interest in Reed as a writer has generally lagged behind the many fascinations of his biography. John Reed was a working journalist during the decade between his graduation from Harvard and his death in 1920. He was also the author of numerous plays, poems, dozens of essays and some of the best reporting of the age. He published three books of prose during his lifetime (several additional volumes appeared posthumously). Nevertheless, Reed remains an anomalous figure, a 'writer' ignored by students of literature, and, once labelled a 'romantic revolution-ary', denied serious attention either as an observer of the Bolshevik revolution or as an actor in the politics of the Left.

There are many reasons why we should be interested in Reed. By the time he died in 1920, at the age of thirty-three, he had met and commanded the respect of Lenin, Trotsky, President Woodrow Wilson, William Jennings Bryan, Bill Haywood and the Mexican revolutionary Pancho Villa. Reed had been a member of the distinguished Harvard class of 1910, which included T. S. Eliot and Walter Lippmann; he numbered among his friends Lincoln Steffens, Eugene O'Neill and Max Eastman; he organised one of the most original pieces of political theatre in American history and was a leading contributor to the *Masses*. Reed witnessed two of the most stirring revolutionary upheavals of the century; travelled widely throughout Europe during the First World War; was a founding member and leader of the Communist Party in the United States. When he died, he was a member of the Executive Committee of the Communist International. He had earned the hatred of Teddy Roosevelt, been repeatedly arrested, put on trial for espionage in America and held as a spy in Norway; he was the object of a massive surveillance operation by the United States government and intelligence services, and was (briefly) appointed Consul in the United States for the Bolshevik government.

But above all he could write, and if his books survive it will be because Reed possessed the energy, talent and commitment to become an observer without equal of the decade from 1910 to 1920. As Louis Fischer put it in his biography of Lenin, Reed 'had eyes that saw and a pen that recorded vividly what he saw and what he heard...'[7]

This book was finished on the day the Romanian tyrant Ceausescu was driven from power, culminating a year in which the communist regimes in Eastern Europe came at last to submit to the will of the people. Though Reed was a communist, he was no defender of tyranny and it is part of his enduring legacy that we can see him as someone who would have been a supporter of Dubček and Gorbachev. At the time of his death he had not broken with the Communist International, but I suspect he would have done so. To see him as a potential Stalinist, or as a cynical, self-seeking defender of the totalitarian system which was established in the Soviet Union, and imposed upon Communist Parties throughout the world, is profoundly to misunderstand Reed. The tragedy for the American left is that the courage which enabled him to break with his class was gone, and an icon of revolutionary idealism remained. No one who knew Reed was prepared to accept his canonisation, nor should we. Nevertheless, I find his political itinerary the most remarkable of any American writer in this century.

The aim of the present biography is to introduce Reed, as writer and political activist, to contemporary readers for whom many of the details of his world will be unfamiliar. Everyone who proposes to write about Reed will eternally be in the debt of the Harvard Alumni John Reed Committee, whose Secretary-Treasurer was Corliss Lamont. They sent John Stuart to Paris to organise the John Reed papers which Louise Bryant had with her in Paris, and to return them to America where they were used by Granville Hicks in writing his biography of Reed in the 1930s, and which were subsequently donated to the Houghton Library at Harvard. Without Reed's papers, it is doubtful whether biographies of the quality of Hicks's and Rosenstone's could have been written. The Reed manuscripts, in all their confusing abundance, have also during the course of my own research, led me to attempt a revaluation of a figure who transcends the roles of playboy and 'romantic revolutionary' which our time seems most comfortable to assign to Reed.

Eric Homberger
Norwich

1 Early years and education 1887-1910

In the 1870s Henry D. Green, a leading citizen of Portland, Oregon, built a grand mansion, Cedar Hill, in a five-acre tract of land adjacent to the City Park. Modelled after a French château, with formal gardens and elegant grounds, it affirmed his eminence and economic success. Green arrived in Portland in 1856 and made his fortune in the provision of gas and water to the growing community. He was a partner in the Portland Water Company between 1862 and 1885, when it was bought for nearly half a million dollars by a committee created by the state legislature.[1] Green was also a founder of the gas company which from 1860 provided Portland with heat and light made from coal shipped down from Vancouver. (His brother and partner carried on the gas business until it was sold in 1892 for $850,000.) Green was engaged in the manufacture of pig iron. Many local fortunes were built upon 'frontier' economic activity, centred upon land speculation, the railroads and the timber trade, but Portlanders thought their community was more governed by propriety and decorum than other western towns; indeed, the wealthy thought that Portland was not really 'western' at all, and behaved accordingly. An outwardly measured, conservative style was cultivated. The elite built their homes far from the bars, gambling dens and prostitutes of the Willamette River dockside. No one cared to look too carefully at the way fortunes were made in the early years of Portland. Western economic life in the gilded age was robust, and not overly burdened with scruples.

Henry Green and his wife Charlotte came originally from upper New York State. All that talk about Henry James's cautionary tale *Daisy Miller* persuaded many such proper matrons not to trust their children to local schools. The Greens sent their daughters east, to be educated at a proper New York finishing school. After Henry Green's death, in 1885, Cedar Hill became noted for the extravagance of Charlotte Green's social life. She was rich and headstrong, and travelled widely around the world after she became a widow. The Greens had four children. Of the two girls, one married an army officer who was soon posted back east. The other, Margaret, became a busy socialite in Portland before marrying Charles Jerome Reed in 1886. He was recently arrived in the west, where he represented the D. M. Osborn Company, an eastern manufacturer of agricultural machinery. C.J., as he was called, had a ready wit and soon won broad acceptance within the local business community. His social and economic standing was reflected in his election to membership and then to the presidency of the Arlington Club, and his election to the exclusive Bohemian Club in San Francisco. With his sharp tongue and observant eye, C.J. dominated the Arlington's daily lunchtable and came to understand much of what lay behind the respectable façade of Portland.

The Reed's first child, John Silas, was born in Cedar Hill on 20 October 1887. Another boy, Harry, was born two years later. Both were petted and looked after by relays of nurses and servants. When they grew old enough to play with other children, their companions were carefully selected from the offspring of the better families. It was the way such things had always been done among the wealthy. C.J. and Margaret Reed lived in Charlotte Green's house for Jack's first nine years. Reed's autobiographical essay 'After Thirty' gives an account of some of his childhood memories, and of the riches around him which fed his imagination. A disorder in Jack's left kidney persuaded the family that he needed a particularly careful regimen. He was a 'delicate' child and when he began to read was encouraged to substitute the imaginative adventures of romantic tales for the more normal ways little boys explore the world. Blackmore's *Lorna Doone* and *The Thousand and One Nights* were childhood favourites. 'My head was full of fairy stories and tales of giants, witches and dragons...'[2] From the family's Chinese servants he heard stories of ghosts, superstitions, strange customs and bloody feuds. His mother's brothers, Ray and Hal (the latter a suicide when Jack was eight), brought into the household hints of exotic travels and adventures. A visit with Harry and his mother to relatives in Massachusetts in 1898, which coincided with the final victory of America in the war with Spain, left an unforgettable memory of national celebration.

Jack, as he was universally called, was sent at the age of nine to the Portland Academy, a recently established private school. The discipline required by the school stultified his interest, and he scarcely bothered to do well. Boredom was intermingled with spells of rebellious misbehaviour. Taunting his teachers, disrupting classes, studied inattention, and then an occasional spell of excellent work when a topic appealed to him, left his parents frustrated and his teachers impatient. His uncertain health made it easy to persuade his grandmother, Charlotte, and his mother to allow him frequent days home from school. He enjoyed composition best of all, and some teachers recognised potential talent behind his waywardness. But what he learned at the Portland Academy was that it was not necessary to be a good boy. He could safely challenge authority and manipulate the system when he wanted to. His mother's protectiveness kept him from things he wished to avoid. The threat of low marks could be shrugged off. Cedar Hill was not a good place to train a young boy in docility, and his grandmother's impulsiveness was there to be observed. He became notably more stubborn and restless within an educational

9

system whose modest aims were to tame its students and make them tolerably good citizens. It is doubtful whether any American school in the 1890s could have served him better.

He was not popular with the other pupils. In the playground different values prevailed from those of Cedar Hill, and he found himself temperamentally and physically an outsider. He was frail, of quick wit and could hold his own in class. In the playground he was lost, and began to dread bigger and stronger boys. When his parents moved down the hill closer to Portland Academy, he had to walk through a rough neighborhood to school. The memory of a series of fights in Goose Hollow stayed with him, as did his fear of pain. His gift for story-telling and an audacious imagination in time helped him find a place in a boyhood world which contained much that was threatening. He was producer, director and business-manager of a theatre built in the attic with his brother Harry. As with his early response to his kidney illness, the imagination was his ally, his weapon. He knew early on that he wanted to become a writer. When his health improved, he worked on the school paper, the *Troubador*, and demonstrated gifts which would make him something of a personality among the small circle of chums which he gathered about him in the Portland Academy. But, where it counted on the streets and playgrounds, Reed felt himself to have been a failure. He thought of himself as a physical coward who was largely without friends. He felt intensely that he had failed his father.

In September 1904 Reed was sent to Morristown School, New Jersey, to prepare for college. C.J. had not had a college education and was determined that his boys would have every opportunity. He wanted them to go to Harvard. Morristown was a fresh start, a wiping clean of much that made Jack unhappy in Portland. He tried out for football, determined not to carry with him to the east the memories of his sickly childhood. He made the team. Reed even scored the winning touchdown in one of his first games. He was a skinny near-six-footer, with an agreeable slightly lopsided face, heavy chin and, as his new schoolmates were to learn, a considerable gift for mayhem, practical jokes and merriment. He admired the self-conscious sense of tradition in the school; it seemed to belong, he recalled in 1917, to a 'long settled and established civilization' remote from the 'raw, pretentious west'. (In *USA* John Dos Passos presented an unforgettable portrait of Reed as a westerner, a young man who carried his integrity held high against the wiles and compromises of the deceitful east. But, in truth, Reed never felt like he belonged in the west. He came home when he came east.) And he was able to use the school's snobbery and traditionalism as a foil for his cultivated japes. Reed was outspoken about sex, and was regarded at Morristown as a notorious teller of tall tales. What was a form of rebellion by a young boy at the Portland Academy became the social style which a sixteen-year-old hoped to use in a campaign to win favour in a new environment. He played up to his fellow students, and was prepared for whatever consequences the authorities might devise. Sometimes the punishments were swift and severe, but Reed's misbehaviour and clownish high spirits made him something of a hero to his contemporaries. The school was neither amused nor impressed; a teacher at the school remembered years later that Reed's 'powers as a boy were turned toward mischief and disorder. He was a difficult and rather disturbing influence in the school.'[3] His attitude towards academic work suggested that it was no more than something to be tolerated. What meant the most to him were the many ways to impose John Reed, 'legendary John Reed' as he was later called, upon the world.

He soon became a contributor to the school magazine, the *Morristonian*, and published vapid late-romantic verse and short stories on exotic topics (one on the destruction of Atlantis). He also revived a Morristown School comic paper, the *Rooster*, which he largely wrote for twelve numbers through the year. It contained

a vein of schoolboy humour which long persisted in his work. Reed
soon received the nickname 'Rooster'. His first year at Morristown, which had seen the usual array of academic disappoint-
ments (he did poorly in Greek and algebra, and failed geometry
and Latin), ended on a high point when he won a prize for a
historical essay, and in school-wide elections was successful across
the board, winning positions on the Athletic Association Committee, the *Morristonian* and the student annual, the *Salmagundi*.

Returning to Portland at the end of the school year, Reed found
his father embroiled in a political crisis.[4] C.J. had sold insurance
after the depression of the 1890s had destroyed the Osborn
Company, and the strain upon him to maintain the family position
was carefully hidden behind the façade of a moustachioed man of
dignified plumpness. C.J. was appointed United States Marshal in
May 1905 as part of an expanding effort by a special prosecutor,
Francis J. Heney, to break the Oregon timber frauds. The lumber
companies and railroads, notorious for their rapacity, had forged
relationships with state and federal officials, elected representatives, political machines and a range of private commercial
interests. These connections made it easy for them corruptly to
claim and despoil large tracts of federal woodland. Heney's
activities had been discreetly obstructed by the 'best people' as well
as by the United States Marshal, Jack Mathews, who was also the
Republican boss of Portland. Heney appealed directly to President
Roosevelt, and obtained Mathews's dismissal. Sensing a streak of
idealism in the normally witty and cynical leader of the Arlington
Club, he asked C.J. to accept the appointment. When Reed came
home he found his father proudly engaged in betraying his class.

There was heady talk nationally of busting trusts and slinging the
malefactors into jail. C. J. Reed's activities in Portland in 1905
were part of a wider Progressive attack upon corruption in public
life. The crusade began with articles in *McClure's* by Lincoln Steffens
on political and civic corruption ('Tweed Days in St Louis',

October 1902); Ida Tarbell's researches into the making of the Standard Oil Company trust (her articles began to appear in November 1902); Ray Stannard Baker's 'The Reign of Lawlessness: Anarchy and Despotism in Colorado' (May 1904), and 'The Railroads on Trial' (October 1905); and Samuel Hopkins Adams's articles on the dangers to public health of an unsupervised drug industry (October and November 1905). Soon the Hearst press, *Collier's* under the editorship of Norman Hapgood, the *Cosmopolitan, Munsey's* and *Everybody's,* competed with each other to publish ever more startling exposures of social problems. Novelists were no less busy in the service of reform. David Graham Phillips's novels of these years, *The Cost* (1904), *The Deluge* and *The Plum Tree* (both 1905), were concerned with financial manipulation and political bosses. His powerful articles on political corruption, 'The Treason of the Senate', appeared in the *Cosmopolitan Magazine* in 1906. Ernest Poole was sent to Chicago in the summer of 1904 by the *Outlook* to write about a bitter strike in the stockyards. Upton Sinclair spent seven weeks in the stockyards in the immediate aftermath of the strike, investigating conditions in the abbatoirs and meat-packing industry on a commission from the socialist magazine the *Appeal to Reason*. Sinclair's novel about conditions in the stockyards, *The Jungle*, was published in February 1906. Its most immediate political impact was to strengthen public support for President Roosevelt's proposed Pure Food and Drug Act. The movement reached its apogee with Roosevelt's speech on 14 April 1906, denouncing 'muckrake' excesses. (Sinclair's book, and other revelations of corruption, threatened to create more pressure for reform than he wished to deal with.) The swell of public opinion, which had boosted sales of *McClure's* and made *The Jungle* a bestseller, was for the moment reversed; the brilliant staff of *McClure's* dispersed.

John Reed's career was intertwined with some of the leading figures among the muckrakers. Steffens—a friend and admirer of

Francis J. Heney and C. J. Reed, and chronicler of their struggle in the September and October 1907 issues of the *American Magazine* – became Jack's adviser and patron; like Norman Hapgood, Reed supported Woodrow Wilson for re-election in 1916, and (for somewhat different reasons) favoured an early end to American military intervention in Russia in 1919. He became a close friend of Hapgood's brother Hutchins. Reed and Sinclair shared a revulsion at the tactics employed by John D. Rockefeller in the mining strike in Colorado in 1914. They passionately disagreed about the decision to enter the war in Europe in 1917, and debated the conduct of the Bolshevik revolution in 1918. Despite seeing eye to eye with such men over many issues during the next decade, as we shall see in chapter 2, he did not share their fundamental assumptions about American society, the city or political reform.

The collapse of the muckraking movement after 1906 had important consequences for Reed. Like so many other young writers, he might have been inclined to follow their lead in the pursuit of reforms within the political system. Steffens's colleagues hoped to awaken the Christian conscience of the nation (his *McClure's* articles were collected under the title *The Shame of the Cities* in 1904), but with public opinion in 1906 satiated with such material, magazine editors became increasingly wary of offending advertisers. The changing public sentiment was soon reflected in the political fortunes of reform. While Roosevelt was off shooting animals in Africa, his successor, Taft, largely ignored the radical reformers' agenda and, in the November 1909 elections, reform candidates went down to defeat. Heney was beaten for the District Attorney in San Francisco. The strategy of exposing wrongdoing, and the progressives' belief in the need for reform to be rooted in ethical values, seemed somehow naïve to young writers of Reed's generation. Walter Lippmann's *A Preface to Politics* in 1913, showed how Freudian theories of personality, and not the small-town Progressive mentality which saw an ethic of civic virtue at war against vice and corruption, embodied the new perspective of their generation.

Portland did not take kindly to C.J.'s enthusiastic pursuit of the land and timber frauds. Heney was simply regarded as an enemy, but C.J. posed a different and more malign threat. Many of Portland's civic leaders were involved in the frauds. Rooting out the corrupt men would require an attack upon precisely those people who constituted the backbone of the Republican Party and the city's commercial elite. Consequences for C.J. soon followed: he was socially ostracised, and a new president of the Arlington Club was elected. 'There was no doubt', wrote a historian of Portland, 'that Reed took a real beating from the Portland establishment.'[5] As the ramifications of the case spread, C.J. became more boldly determined to expose the hypocrisy of the Portland rich. Returning from Morristown, Reed saw his father in a new light. He was a now a crusader for the right, a hero. He never forgot the way C.J. bravely faced the disapproval of his peers. It was a lesson which remained with him in 1917.

Back at Morristown for his senior year, the distractions which had weakened his academic performance were even more insistent. He was again in conflict with the school authorities, and his academic record remained patchy. Jack was short of credits to graduate, and botched the Harvard entrance examinations. In that easy-going era, a C in English, D in history and French, and a pass in Chemistry (he failed Latin and geometry) were sufficient to be allowed to retake the exam. A summer working with a tutor in Portland did the trick, and he passed the entrance exam on his second try.

In September 1906 he enrolled at Harvard, a member of the class of 1910. 'I was thrilled with the immensity of Harvard, its infinite opportunities, its august history and traditions', he wrote in 'Almost Thirty', but, feeling himself lost in the huge freshman class of seven hundred men, he remembered feeling 'desperately lonely'. He was in very good company. The memoirs of Harvard students, particularly of the literary sort, are filled with recollections of loneliness, of the misery of social isolation. Harvard could make even intelligent, hard-working men feel shabby. Although in Portland Jack was from the aristocracy and he had made an undoubted success (on his own terms) at Morristown, Harvard made all his achievements and qualities feel mean and irrelevant. It was a humiliating experience. Officially, the university stood for independence of thought. In practice, the dining clubs on the 'Gold Coast' of Mt Auburn Street were bastions of snobbery and anti-Semitism. The social tone of Harvard was as unkind to outsiders as any college in the country. Two-thirds of the student body came from private schools, and his classmates were drawn from the oldest and richest families in America. As Reed was soon to learn, social life was largely arranged to confirm their supremacy. His fellow classmates seemed all to have been educated at private schools like St Marks or Groton. The college was filled with men whom they had known at school. Reed was just another face in the lecture halls, another hunched figure scurrying across the Yard at dusk. He was scarcely noticed. At Harvard he experienced a particularly disturbing form of self-doubt. In reflective moments it would return in later years. Reed's Harvard years left him with a wound, an alienation, which gnawed at his self-esteem.

He sought to get a foot on the ladder through athletics, as he had done at Morristown, by going out for football. He did not make the team. Nor did he make the freshman crew, despite extracurricular sessions on the rowing machine in an empty boathouse. (Lippmann became second assistant manager of the freshman track team, for the same purpose.) Reed was more successful with low-prestige sports like swimming and water polo, at which he excelled. His literary efforts seemed to win easy approval. Jokes were accepted by the *Lampoon*, and poetry and romantic prose appeared in the *Monthly*. The latter, founded in 1885, was an important vehicle for Harvard littérateurs. Santayana had been on the founding editorial board; Berenson was its fourth editor. the *Harvard Monthly* traditionally was the place where students in Barrett Wendell's expository writing course, English 12, had published. When Charles Copeland took over the course from Wendell in 1905, the tradition of Harvard writing entered its greatest era. Reed was to become one of the most glittering of Copeland's stars, but not yet, not in his first year at Harvard. He turned to writing out of the unhappiness he felt in 1906; it was also a way to make a name for himself.

The President of Harvard, Charles W. Eliot, was nearing the end of his revolutionary tenure of four decades when Reed entered the freshman class. Eliot's modernising reforms had greatly enlarged the college's endowment, and encouraged influential experiments in undergraduate education (such as the elective system, the introduction of laboratory sciences, sociology and much else besides) which brought the intellectual life of Cambridge into the industrial age. Eliot's Harvard attracted some of the finest minds and most distinguished scholars in late nineteenth-century America to the faculty: William James, Josiah Royce and Santayana in philosophy; Taussig in economics; Kittredge in literature; Babbitt in French culture. But Harvard was inevitably more than its presiding eminences. Some of the most influential teachers were far from being the most impressive scholars in Cambridge. The Harvard literary tradition, which in Reed's day still remembered Transcendental Boston, was seldom comfortable with the President's modernising reforms. The literary tradition as it was understood at Harvard, and as it was transmitted through figures like Wendell and Copeland, was profoundly Anglophile and respectful of a conservative version of culture. Literature ultimately mattered because it was a chief custodian of humanistic values.

Wendell had worked as a lawyer in New York before returning

to Harvard to teach, and had written two novels. He had perhaps an overly generous admiration for men of affairs, and was impatient with writers who seemed too introspective or self-preoccupied. His ideal of a clear prose style, as he explained in a series of lectures on English composition at the Lowell Institute in Boston in 1890, was something 'adapted to the understanding of the average man'.[6] 'My task as a Harvard teacher', he wrote, 'was to give glimpses of literature to men who would generally not be concerned with it in practical life... Any scholar can help make scholars; but lots fail in the process to humanize. My real duty, as I saw it, was not scholarly but humane.'[7] In effect, what Wendell wished to show was that a concern for literature was not soft or effeminate, but was something useful for a businessman. He cultivated an 'English' accent, parted his hair in the middle and carried his walking-stick on his little finger. While Wendell lectured he strode across the podium, habitually twirling his watch-chain. 'No student of Wendell will ever forget that great literature is the fit and therefore the beautiful expression of great thinking.'[8]

They were not the only influences upon student writing, not necessarily even the most important for some Harvard students. Walter Lippmann was regularly invited to tea with William James, and absorbed from him the revolutionary doctrine that thought must take into account will and the emotions, and that individuality was nourished in 'the recesses of feeling, the darker, blinder strata of character'.[9] No less powerful an influence on Lippmann was Irving Babbitt's classicism, and the subtle interrogations of reason and essence of Santayana, who called himself a 'cynic and Tory in philosophy'. Babbitt, a provocative and inspiring teacher, challenged his student's attitude towards the sentimental and the romantic, and in *Literature and the American College* (1908) unhesitatingly attacked popular taste and the American passion for democracy and size. Babbitt's defence of tradition and classical values appealed to T. S. Eliot, while Copeland's more emphatic ideals in composition did not.[10] There were many competing influnces for the allegiance of the bright young men of Harvard between 1906 and 1910.

Frantic to make a name for himself at Harvard, Reed threw himself into competition for every office, every team. He soon found that enthusiasm was never quite enough. He was passed over in preference for wealthier men, and responded with anger and aggression. He seemed too raw to the Harvard aristocrats; it was as though he did not know the rules of the game. The idea got around that Reed was a pusher, and people openly avoided him. A potential room-mate for his second year begged off. He began to affect something of the snobbery around him, and in turn dropped a bright New York Jew, Carl Binger, fearing that their friendship might have irrevocably barred him from the 'rich splendor' of Harvard life. As he was going through this desolating introduction to Harvard, his father was experiencing his own isolation in Portland as a result of his and Heney's investigations.[11]

There were successes in his second year (election to the staff of the *Lampoon* and the *Monthly*) but he failed to make the staff of the influential Harvard daily, the *Crimson*, and – more seriously – was passed over for selection to the 'waiting clubs' from which members of the elite 'final clubs' in the last two years at Harvard were drawn. Only 100 men were invited by the Institute of 1770 (the Hasty Pudding) to join the waiting clubs, and, as Walter Lippmann found, 'the clubs were not interested in Jews, or for that matter in those who did not "fit" – who were from public high schools or the hinterlands, or were obviously intellectual, or in some way "odd". Rejection was also part of the game.'[12] Reed's efforts to win social acceptibility were none the less undercut by something, in Hicks's words, 'defiant, belligerent, mocking' in his nature (*Reed*, p.30).

The Harvard of artists, writers and radicals responded to their social exclusion in Reed's second year with a manifesto by Lee

Simonson attacking the widespread indifference in Cambridge to the larger social issues of the day. Students responded by creating new clubs of their own. Reed became president of the newly founded Cosmopolitan Club, where international topics were discussed. He also used the existing clubs to fill the void created by his social exclusion. Reed was active in the Dramatic Club, devoted to the production of original plays written by Harvard students largely the products of Professor George Pierce Baker's course on 'The Technique of the Drama'. He showed an enthusiasm for the stage, becoming assistant manager for Dramatic Club productions, and wrote and staged plays for the Cosmopolitan Club. He also joined the Western Club, which brought together students from the far western states, and presided over its lunchtable as his father had once done at the Arlington Club in Portland. (T. S. Eliot joined the Southern Club.) He went along to meetings of the Socialist Club, founded by Walter Lippmann in May 1908 to consider 'all schemes of social reform which aimed at a radical reconstruction of society'.[13] By Harvard standards, Lippmann's small band of radicals was daring and iconoclastic, and the idea of a radicals' club appealed to a growing number of undergraduates. By 1909 it had fifty members. Lippmann displayed the energy and intelligence which marked him out as a remarkably promising young man. His club affiliated with the Intercollegiate Socialist Society, got involved in municipal elections, badgered the Overseers of the College about underpaid workers and brought daring speakers whose sole brief was to disturb the peace. (Among the visiting speakers was Lincoln Steffens, who renewed his acquaintance with Reed.) Like Reed, Lippmann hoped to join the waiting clubs, and aspired to the social acceptance which led to the aristocratic life on Mt Auburn Street. By chance, in the spring of 1908, Lippmann had volunteered to help victims of a fire in a working-class district of Chelsea, near Boston's docks. There he saw poverty and suffering for the first time, which transformed the abstractions of 'the poor' into human reality. He was soon announcing a conversion to socialism, and read as many Fabian texts as he could find. Reed had had no such experience, and his Harvard years were the poorer for it. He remembered in 'Almost Thirty' the impact of the Socialist Club:

> All over the place radicals sprang up, in music, painting, poetry, the theatre. The more serious college papers took a socialistic, or at least progressive tinge. Of course all this made no ostensible difference in the look of Harvard society, and probably the clubmen and the athletes, who represented us to the world, never even heard of it. But it made me, and many others, realize that there was something going on in the dull outside world more thrilling than college activities...

But it never seemed quite important enough to join, though he and Lippmann became friends. There were too many disturbing contradictions and paradoxes about his life at Harvard for him to dream of taking the side of everything in society which was the opposite of Harvard and its privileges. He could scorn the aristocrats, yet still agree to write lyrics for a Hasty Pudding production. Reed's social conscience was still dormant. Perhaps in reflective moments Reed felt that he was an aristocrat in exile, a shadow ruler who would one day inherit the world and the Gold Coast. Lippmann accepted that he could not be an insider at Harvard, and vowed to become a brilliant outsider.[14] Reed had nothing like Lippmann's clarity of understanding in that grim spring in 1908 in which they were both passed up by the waiting clubs, and had to remake their Harvard careers.

The man who honed Reed's weapons for the battles of the future was 'Copey', the waspish, affected Charles Copeland. Reed took Copeland's expository writing course in his junior year. It met in Hollis 15, the scene also for Copeland's teatime and evening entertaining. His open house at 10 p.m. on Saturdays invariably saw Reed shine, for he soon became one of the elect, one of Copey's boys. Copeland had worked for a decade as a journalist after graduating from Harvard (Owen Wister and Kittredge were also members of the class of 1882) and when he returned as instructor in English in 1893 his sharp, dry wit and gifts as a performer of literary texts made him an influential teacher. Copeland had a theatrical quality, a capacity to project and dramatise the role of being Copeland, which made him an unforgettable teacher. He did not so much analyse sonnets as perform them, and the theatricality of his readings from the great masters of English literature drew vast audiences. Reed remembered Copeland's readings at the Union, attended by two or three hundred students, 'the most representative crowd ever gathered at Harvard, except for a football game'. These 'sports', 'grinds', athletes and dilettanti listened appreciatively as Copeland read his favourite passages from his favourite authors: Kipling, Bret Harte, Shakespeare, Burns, Hardy, the Bible and Boswell.[15] Like Wendell, he was consciously addressing a wider audience, and sought to make even the most casually interested students share his passion for literature. Those select few admitted to English 12 were always in Copeland's eyes individuals. Walter Lippmann recalled being summoned to Copeland's chambers in Hollis:

> You were told how to read what you had written. Soon you began to feel that out of the darkness all around you long fingers were searching through the layers of fat and fluff to find your bones and muscles underneath. You could fight back but eventually he stripped you of your essential self. Then he cuffed the battered remains and challenged them into their own authentic activity.[16]

Reed remembered 'the privileged individuals who stay after hours in his room, who walk across the Yard with him, who sit with him on the bench under the elms on spring afternoons. He treats them as his brothers; some of them would rather tell their troubles to him than to their families.'[17] (At moments of emotional stress in New York, Reed would escape to Harvard to talk to Copeland.) He disliked 'literary' effects, and – at the height of *fin de siècle* mannerism when Harvard aesthetes walked in the Yard with copies of Pater and Wilde in their hands – called for a prose which was terse, forceful and responsive to the world. Reed was excited by such a message: 'Professor Copeland…has stimulated generations of men to find color and strength and beauty in books and in the world, and to express it again.' It seemed to make heroic some of the things which he began to feel after the founding of the Cosmopolitan and Socialist Clubs. Reed dedicated *Insurgent Mexico* to Copeland:

> Dear Copey:
> I remember you thought it strange that my first trip abroad didn't make me want to write about what I saw there. But since then I have visited a country which stimulated me to express it in words. As I wrote these impressions of Mexico I couldn't help but think that I never would have seen what I did see had it not been for your teaching me.

Copeland helped to open Reed's eyes. Amidst the intellectual riches of the university, Reed became a disciple of the teacher who made the lightest demands upon his intellect.

Not every student was as responsive to his message or mannerisms as was Reed. Van Wyck Brooks did not enjoy Copeland, but it was not until after he left Harvard and came under the influence of J.B. Yeats, who was living in New York, that he understood why. Copeland favoured a prose which was vivid, emphatic and adorned by striking phrases. Yeats talked of the virtues of the inner eye and a literary language of nuance which haunted the mind. Copeland's pupils were encouraged to travel, to look at the world around them and to 'see life'. (Critics called Copeland more a teacher of journalism than of writing.) Yeats despised newspaper reporting, and taught Van Wyck Brooks the need to stay at home in the imagination.[18]

It was after taking Copeland's course that Reed began to discuss with his father the possibility of a career in journalism. When he returned to Harvard for his senior year, the paradoxes of his relationship to the institution were every bit as troubling as before. Taking time out from the romantic and mysterious themes of his stories, and his evanescent, late romantic verse, Reed wrote editorials denouncing the new President, A. Lawrence Lowell, for restricting the *laissez-faire* elective system of President Eliot. He was also opposed to the proposal to put all freshmen into the same dormitories. Despite his hostility to the new reforms, he accepted a role in creating 'college spirit' by running for election to the new post of sports cheerleader. It brought out the supreme showman in him. Lippmann recalled that Reed

> would stand up alone before a few thousand undergraduates and demonstrate without a quiver of self-consciousness just how a cheer should be given. If he didn't like the way his instructions were followed he cursed at the crowd, he bullied it, sneered at it. But he always captured it. It was a sensational triumph...[19]

Reed's criticism of changes in college life, and his willingness to embody the new demand for organised enthusiasm, nicely captures the ambivalence of his experience of Harvard. By contrast, his academic work was largely untouched by modern developments in art or literature. Reed chose no course at Harvard with a subject-matter more recent than the eighteenth century (Rosenstone, *Romantic Revolutionary* p.56). One looks similarly in vain for sociology or modern political thought among the courses which Pound and Eliot studied as undergraduates. (Reed's friend Alan Seeger similarly devoted himself to medievalism.)

He was a a mass of inchoate feelings in 1910, yearning romantically for the past, identifying with the aristocrats who spurned him and combatively asserting his egoistic claim to distinction. In campus political life, he was drawn into the campaign which pitted 'the Yard' (the student outsiders) against 'the Street' (the aristocratic clubmen who dominated student activities). It is a sign of Reed's equivocation on such matters that he allowed himself to be nominated on the snobbish ticket of 'the Street' against his friends and against the radicals. The campaign was bitterly conducted, and caused Reed to scribble (on *Harvard Lampoon* stationery) an illiberal parody of Tennyson:

> 'The Charge of the Political Brigade'
> Twenty votes, thirty votes,
> Forty votes onward
> Into the voting booth
> Strode the three hundred.
> 'Forward the Fools' Brigade,
> After their votes!' he said
> So to the ballot box
> Strode the three hundred.
>
> 'Forward, O Democrats!
> Down with black Derby hats!'
> How could the party know
> Someone had blundered?
> Theirs not to make reply,
> Theirs not to reason why
> Theirs but to vote – and lie.
> Into the voting booth
> Strode the three hundred.
>
> Pickets to the right of them,
> Jobs to the left of them
> Soreheads in front of them
> Shouted and thundered.
> Hounded with shot and shell
> 'Let the Street go to Hell
> We'll do the job as well!'

As they collected votes,
Cried the three hundred.

'Charge the Committee then!'
Three hundred stalwart men
Traitors to Nineteen Ten
Broke the class spirit, while
All the world wondered.
Swayed by false argument
Urged to the Polls they went,
Scoundrels and ignorant,
Worthy three hundred![20]

With these rather angry sentiments in mind, it is not surprising that
Reed accepted a request to write the lyrics for the Hasty Pudding's
1910 production, *Diana's Debut*. He was admitted as a late member
of the Society.

Acceptance by the elite had come, at last, but with so many
reservations as to render it all but meaningless. His energy, rather
than maturity, had enabled him to survive at Harvard. The real
prizes went elsewhere. His friend Edward Eyre Hunt was elected
to write the class poem. T. S. Eliot asked the time-honoured
question in the graduation ode of the Class of 1910:

...who knows what time may hold in store,
Or what great deeds the distant time may hold in store...[21]

2 Bohemia 1911-1913

After returning from a merry post-graduation visit to England, France and Spain, Reed settled in New York in March 1911. For the next three years learning to write, exploring the city and understanding the intricacies of personal relationships (with Lincoln Steffens, Max Eastman and Mabel Dodge) were more important to him than formulating political positions. If he had a 'politics' it was a politics of feeling and instinct, of Bohemian rebelliousness, which had not yet begun to address the great social issues of the day. Chapter 3, which begins with Reed's trip to Mexico in 1914, is inevitably more preoccupied with politics and public affairs. From 1914 the tensions between his private life and his career as a correspondent, so visible in his relationship with Mabel Dodge, began to be resolved in favour of a struggle to understand war and revolution, and the United States's place in the world order. In New York, he was trying to understand himself.

The young felt free in New York and responded to its bustling promise. When he came to New York in 1913, Floyd Dell recalled that he 'stopped wearing my high collar and black stocks; I wore a flannel shirt instead. It was a place where one could dress as one pleased.'[1]

With the invaluable help of his friend Steffens, Reed found work with the *American Magazine*, where, among other editorial tasks, he selected from poetry manuscripts those worth arguing for in the editorial committee. The *Monthly* and the *Lampoon* at Harvard had trained him in such disputations, and in *The Day in Bohemia*, a delightful verse parody written during the summer of 1912 during a long stay in Portland after the death of his father, Reed recalled an editorial meeting with Albert Jay Nock, J. S. Phillips and other staff members over a poem ('The Minstrel of Romance') which he wanted to published:

> 'The poets all abhor us!'
> 'Our verse is rotten!' – NOCK and I in chorus;
> REED'S going to cast another pearl before us!'
> 'I am!' I answer with an angry hiss,
> Tapping my poem, 'What is wrong with this?'
> 'THE MINSTREL OF ROMANCE' - 'No harmony-'
> Cries Nock 'Too much cacoethes scribendi-'
> 'Genus irritabile vatum-' 'You should read
> 'Your Matthew Arnold,-' 'Arnold! Huh! Indeed!
> 'A polished, strengthless, sapless, hide-bound bard-'
> 'Walt Whitman? Hardware cataloguing by the yard-'
> 'Foot-rhythm-rhyme-stanza-Sapphics-Lessing-Pope-
> Hellenic-Dionysus-couplet-trope-'
> 'Horace,-' ('Assistance! cried the SID 'Police!')
> 'Poetic Laws-'(NOCK) 'Hold!' says PHILLIPS 'Peace!
> 'Down with the stilted numbers of the Schools!
> For Rules were made for Art, not Art for Rules!
> 'Poetry is – – at least I hold it so'-
> 'Poetry's-' (gesture),(gesture),'-er-,' you know...[2]

And on that Babel-like note Reed escaped to the washroom.

Work on the *American Magazine* occupied only part of his days. What most delighted him in the spring of 1911 was exploring the city. C. J. Reed's wishes for his son were protective: 'Get him a job', he wrote to Steffens; 'let him see everything, but don't let him be anything for a while. Don't let him get a conviction right away or a business or a career. Let him play.'[3] Curious advice: if any Harvard graduate in 1911 needed encouragement to play, it was not Reed. In a sense, he had done little but play, and even his closest friends struggled to find a hint of earnestness or conviction in his manner. But, with Steffens's support, Reed was turned loose upon New York. His mentor watched the result with considerable delight:

> When John Reed came, big and growing, handsome outside and beautiful inside, when that boy came ... to New York, it seemed to me that I had never seen anything so near to pure joy. No ray of sunshine, no drop of foam, no young animal, bird or fish, and no star, was as happy as that boy was.[4]

Reed was soon expressing in verse his sense of wonderment at the city:

> This City, which he scorn
> For her rude sprawling limbs,her strength unshorn,-
> Hands blunt from grasping, Titan-like, at Heav'n,
> Is a world-wonder, vaulting all the Seven!
> Europe? Here's all of Europe in one place;
> Beauty unconscious; yet, and even grace. (*Collected Poems*, p. 76)

For many younger poets at that moment, the discovery of the city was a crucial component of the 'modern'. The editor of *Poetry*, Harriet Monroe, warned that poets had reason to fear the city: 'The danger is that the man of vision may be blasted by immensities – the immensities of sound and silence, of crowds and emptiness, of truth and denial, hope and despair.'[5] But Reed's city was not the threatening metropolis of the naturalistic novelists, or the grimy scene evoked by the Ash Can painters. Reed's city was a place of romance and adventure. He was not alone in seeing in the harsh reality of the city an apotheosis of romance. New York photographers of the Photo-Secession led the way. Alfred Stieglitz captured the unsuspected beauty of the urban scene in a photograph of a train moving through New York on a calm evening ('The Hand of Man', 1902). Alvin Langdon Coburn found something romantic, even exotic, in working men standing before the Williamsburg Bridge, and presented 'The Tunnel Builder' (1910) as an epitome of the heroic. The poets, too, sought beauty in the city. John Gould Fletcher, who left Harvard in 1907 and travelled to Europe to become a poet, wrote of cities awash with unexpected romantic beauty:

> Whirlpools of purple and gold,
> Winds from the mountains of cinnabar,
> Lacquered mandarin moments,palanquins swaying and balancing
> Amid the vermilion pavilions…[6]

In William Carlos Williams's 'The Wanderer' (1914) the poet's quest brought him to look for beauty in the harsh ugliness of the Passaic, 'that filthy river'.[7] Reed's Harvard contemporary T. S. Eliot was alone among his generation to seek in the urban metropolis metaphors of a quite different kind to express the spiritual state of modern man:

> The morning comes to consciousness
> Of faint stale smells of beer
> From the sawdust-trampled street
> With all its muddy feet that press
> To early coffee-stands.[8]

Nothing of Eliot's despair touched Reed. In 'Almost thirty' he described with lyric delight an exploration of New York. It was 'an enchanted city to me', he wrote.

> Everything was to be found there – it satisfied me utterly. I wandered about the streets, from the soaring imperial towers of downtown, along the East River docks, smelling spices and the clipper ships of the past, through the swarming East Side – alien towns within towns – where the smoky flare of miles of clamorous pushcarts made a splendor of shabby streets; coming upon sudden shrill markets, dripping blood and fishscales in the light of torches, the big Jewish women bawling their wares under the roaring great bridges; thrilling to the ebb and flow of human tides sweeping to work and back, west

and east, south and north. I knew Chinatown, and Little Italy, and the quarter of the Syrians; the marionette theatre, Sharkey's and McSorley's saloons, the Bowery lodging houses and the places where the tramps gathered in winter; the Haymarket, the German Village, and all the dives of the Tenderloin. I spent all one summer night on top of a pier of the Williamsburg Bridge; I slept another night in a basket of squid in the Fulton Market, where the red and green and gold sea things glisten in the blue light of the sputtering arcs. The girls that walk the streets were friends of mine, and the drunken sailors off ships newcome from the world's end, and the Spanish longshore-men down on West Street.[9]

In 1918, taking a brief moment from his deepening political involvements, Reed wrote an autobiographical poem in which he looked back at the glories of New York as he first encountered it in 1911:

> By proud New York and its man-piled Matterhorns,
> The hard blue sky overhead and the west wind blowing,
> Steam plumes waving from sun-glittering pinnacles,
> And deep streets shaking to the million-river —
> Manhattan, zoned with ships, the cruel
>   Youngest of all the world's great towns,
> Thy bodice bright with many a jewel,
>   Imperially crowned with crowns...
> Who that has known thee but shall burn
>   In exile till he come again
> To do thy bitter will, O stern
>   Moon of the tides of men! (*Collected Poems*, p.110-11)

New York was a land of magic and enchantment, of diversity, vistas and power; it was above all a terrain through which he moved with freedom. Unlike Fletcher and Eliot, for whom the city had ulterior meanings (aesthetic or moral), all Reed wanted to do was celebrate the city.

This heightened romantic sensitivity of Reed's to the city paradoxically made him seem less modern as a poet. The purity of his delight, and his desire for a poetry which was wholly responsive to a sharp intensity of feelings, made him a vivid singer of the poetic renaissance. But, as Martin Green has argued, it was the affirmative idea of the poet as singer, and his belief in the artistic adequacy of freshly felt experience, which set him apart from the modernism which was to sweep across American literature.[10]

When John Gould Fletcher took the manuscript of his 'Irradiations' to Ezra Pound in London in 1912, Pound's response hints at the new era being born. 'What he chiefly objected to, in my verse, was their not infrequent descent into what he called the "obvious."'[11] What was 'obvious' was unnecessary, cheap and boring. The new spirit rejected sweetness and prettiness; the revolutionary poets give expression to their contempt for the softness and sugariness of the older poetry.[12] Alfred Kreymborg, poet and editor of various little magazines in the Village, wrote a one-sentence manifesto for *Others*: 'The old expressions are with us always, and there are always others.' There were in total 200 subscribers to *Others*.[13] But that scarcely mattered to Kreymborg, or to his contributors, who came to his editorial notice out of an impenetrable isolation. One day, while walking together through the streets of New York, Wallace Stevens gave Kreymborg a packet containing the manuscript of 'Peter Quince at the Clavier' and said: 'I must ask you not to breathe a word about this. Print it if you like it, send it back if you don't.'[14] The new modernist poetry had emerged in obscurity; its practitioners without readers, its journals without subscribers.[15] For the poets, the stark differences between traditional values and the modern spirit emphasised their isolation from the ordinary life around them.

Poets were perhaps hungrier for community than other artists, and were among the first to spot the flickering hints of cultural renewal which beckoned across the continent – in Chicago, with Harriet Monroe's *Poetry* and Margaret Anderson's avant-garde *Little*

Review; in Boston, with the *Poetry Journal*; in St Louis with the circle around William Marion Reedy. Above all, Greenwich Village was the promised land of the new spirit. Reed's poems began to appear in *Poetry*. He lived in Washington Square South, took his meals at Polly Holliday's restaurant, and was soon part of the new bright creative spirit. Even as late as 1913, however, he had not abandoned the idea of finding a meaningful, lively audience for the kind of writing he wanted to do. In part, he hoped the *Masses* would reach readers which the little poetry magazines could not hope for.

Although Reed felt at home in the Village, he kept some distance between himself and the intense, hostile cliques which were characteristic of its artistic and literary life. There were countless groups, crowds and circles, sometimes defined by employment or politics, sometimes by a magazine or journal, a saloon or restaurant. There was a prominent journalism crowd, for example, and a group of artists around John Sloan and Robert Henri; the anarchist group was to be found at the East 13th Street offices of Emma Goldman's *Mother Earth*. There was a university crowd, a social settlement crowd at the University Settlement on Rivington Street and at Lillian Wald's Henry Street Settlement; a feminist group at the apartment of Crystal Eastman, where the suffragists and feminists gathered who were defining the 'New Woman' (Madeleine Doty, Inez Milholland, Ida Rauh); a socialist crowd; a group formed around Kreymborg's little magazines, and Albert and Charles Boni's bookstore on Macdougal Street (where the first plays of the Washington Square Players was performed). There was a group of young writers around Guido Bruno, publisher of the *Chapbooks*. Alfred Stieglitz's circle of artists, photographers and younger writers were to be found at his 291 Gallery on Fifth Avenue. The mid-town New York of newspaper journalists and the theatre crowd would sometimes go slumming to the Village, but it was like visiting a foreign city. Some few individuals in the Village transcended these little crowds and connected the diverse world

33

of Village life. Villagers were united in their passion for Isadora Duncan.[16] Henrietta Rodman's Liberal Club became a symbol of the new spirit of Greenwich Village life. Everyone who was anyone came to the Liberal Club for good meals and even better conversation, where they could argue with her cook and lover, Hippolyte Havel, and admire the strikingly beautiful Rodman.

Reed was introduced to New York by Steffens, whose closest friends were journalists and writers of liberal sympathy. After the breakup of his marriage, Steffens, who felt comfortable around younger men, took a room in 42 Washington Square South, the building where Reed lived. Steffens took Reed to meet the Hapgood brothers, both Harvard graduates, who had worked with Steffens on the New York *Commercial Advertiser* a decade earlier.[17] Norman Hapgood was editor of *Collier's*. Hutchins, who had published a remarkable study of the Jewish lower East Side, *The Spirit of the Ghetto*, in 1902, was on the staff of the *New York Globe*, was a man of unusual generosity of spirit and independence of mind. Hutchins appealed to Reed rather more than his straightlaced brother.

Although the heyday of the muckrakers had passed, everywhere around him in New York Reed encountered the individuals who had led the great crusade against 'the interests' and corruption. These were the men and women who stood shoulder to shoulder with his father in the fight against the Oregon timber frauds. But Reed was not wholly comfortable with their agenda of social reform and hopes for progress. Their response to the city, which often had about it an evangelical fervour, was not his own. New York did not call out to a sense of mission or guilt-ridden social conscience in Reed.

This is what most clearly marked the generational fissure which separated him from those like Robert Hunter (1874–1942), who grew up in a small town in Indiana, trained as a social worker, lived in Hull House in Chicago and then came to New York in 1902 as the head worker at the University Settlement. Hunter's *Poverty* (1904) was a classic of the progressive conscience confronted by urban conditions, and for a decade he was a leading intellectual in the Socialist Party. Ernest Poole (1880-1950), the son of a wealthy grain broker, was raised in prosperity and strict Presbyterianism in Chicago. After graduating from Princeton in 1902 he too settled in the University Settlement in New York. Poole was assigned by Hunter to do a report on newsboys, bootblacks and messenger boys for the New York Child Labor Committee, and was persuaded by the radical lawyer Morris Hillquit to join the Socialist Party. Together with William English Walling, he organised a mass meeting at Carnegie Hall in support of strikers at Lowell and Lawrence, Massachusetts, and wrote a novel which ended with the titanic efforts of a fictional Wobbly organiser on the New York waterfront (*The Harbor*, 1915). Like Hunter, Poole resigned from the Socialist Party over its opposition to the war in 1917. Such men had grown up in families dedicated to the most rigid Calvinist beliefs but found themselves unable to accept a call to the ministry. The city, and in particular the urban poor, offered an outlet for emotions which society and its pervasive materialism and competitive selfishness seemed to have stifled elsewhere. The decision to live in the slums and to affirm the brotherhood of man was an expression of a need to serve, to 'do something'.[18] The way such men saw the city and all its complex problems was essentially simplistic. But the emotions behind their troubled consciences were anything but simple: they sought to arouse the public in its complacent blindness to threatening dangers.

Reed's biographers note that he was baptised in the fashionable Trinity Episcopal Church in Portland in 1887. That is to say that the Green and Reed families were, religiously speaking, at the top of the pecking order. Reed's family were prominent 'old' settlers. Had they stood out against conventional theology, some word of this surely would have reached Granville Hicks, Reed's biographer in the 1930s. His silence on this matter, and that of Robert Rosenstone in the 1970s, suggests that the Green and Reed families were little bothered by the subject. Public observances were probably fulfilled, but whether religion had any internalised meaning for any of them we cannot say. In any event, Reed's religious education seems not to have left him with a guilty conscience, nor did he carry into the city a missionary's need to reform conditions and thereby to save souls. He came to New York free from such feelings. 'I haven't any God', he wrote in 'Almost Thirty', 'and don't want one; faith is only another word for finding oneself.' William James, who wrote with incomparable insight into the American civic religion of healthy-mindedness, could not have put it better. Reed's involvement with radicals in New York worried his mother, but he reassured her: 'I am not a Socialist temperamentally any more than I'm an Episcopalian. I know now that my business is to interpret and live Life, wherever it may be found – whether in the labor movement or out of it. I haven't ever been patient with cliques any more than Paw was, and I won't be roped in, any more than he was, in some petty gang with a platform.'[19]

New York neither excluded him nor enfolded him in self-images of weakness and inadequacy. In New York he could be boldly independent. The real meaning of New York for Reed was freedom – from his mother's love, from his father's (imagined) expectations and from Harvard snobbery. Reed's editorial work on the *American Magazine* left him with time to write sketches, stories and poems which suggest that as a young writer the city was his real subject. But he did not see New York as the modern metropolis of commerce, modern art and soaring architecture. Rather, it was inhabited by lonely, alienated people. Their stories invariably contained some unexpected twist, something which caught his imagination. Like Hutchins Hapgood's *The Autobiography of a Thief* (1903) and *An Anarchist Woman* (1909), Reed saw in their stories human documents for the understanding of the city itself. He wrote about an old woman sitting on a park bench, a hungry bum, a prostitute, a street vendor. The generosity of his response, the leanness of his prose and the clarity of effect he achieves in these sketches marked him off as a writer of promise.

One of his sketches, about a prostitute who had travelled the world but could not wait to come home to New York, was turned down by the *American Magazine*. Reed decided to try the *Masses*. The magazine ('Devoted to the Interests of the Working People') had been founded by Piet Vlag in January 1911. Vlag, a socialist co-operator who ran the restaurant in the basement of the Rand School of Social Science on 19th Street, enlisted financial support from a well-meaning executive of an insurance company. As one of the early contributors recalled: 'The *Masses* promised to be a publication for the release of socially conscious anti-capitalist literary and artistic expressions for which there was hardly any demand by the well printed news-stand variety of magazine. And there were artists and writers who felt the need of such an outlet – pay or no pay.'[20] The contributors in 1911 were familiar to the readers of the *International Socialist Review*, and other publications of the respectable left: W. J. Ghent, May Wood Simons, John Spargo, Gustavus Myers, Henry Slobodin and Inez Haynes Gillmore. The culture of the first *Masses*, like that of the Socialist Party, was profoundly European, and great prominence was given to translations by Tolstoy, Sudermann, Bjornson and Zola. By 1912 the *Masses* had begun to publish American younger writers, such as Mary Heaton Vorse, Randolph Bourne, Louis Untermeyer, George Cram Cook and Walter Lippmann. Vlag was an advocate of 'applied Socialism', and deplored the efforts of radicals to solve problems by 'emotional methods, by tears and cheers'.[21] The *Masses* protested at the attacks on syndicalists like Frank Bohn and Bill Haywood from within the Socialist Party (a campaign which led to Haywood's removal from the party's National Executive Committee in February 1913), but accepted that any association with violence and industrial sabotage, which clung so strongly to the Industrial Workers of the World (IWW), could do nothing but harm to the Socialist Party's reputation.

The *Masses* was worthy but dull and when the chief backer withdrew his financial support in August 1912, Vlag's magazine looked like like it would quietly expire. Vlag went to Chicago in search of a potential sponsor. Not finding the person he sought, he held merger discussions with Josephine Conger-Kaneko, editor of the socialist-feminist *Progressive Women*. Floyd Dell, who had made a strong impact as the editor of the Friday Literary Review of the *Chicago Evening Post*, was present at this meeting, and he was to be one of the editors of the newly merged magazine.[22] When Vlag returned to New York he told the staff writers of the proposed deal, and of his intention to make Max Eastman the new editor.

There were several camps among the staff of the *Masses*: the artists wanted the magazine to become a broadly satirical magazine. The writers, Louis Untermeyer recalled, 'wanted a magazine in which they could print the naked transcripts of reality which the commercial monthlies would not consider'.[23] Instead of agreeing to close the magazine, or to merge it as Vlag wished, they decided to relaunch it – in effect, to hijack it away from Vlag – under Eastman's editorship. Sloan and Untermeyer drafted the letter offering him the job: 'Dear Eastman: we have just elected you editor of the *Masses* at no salary per annum'.[24] Vlag moved to Florida.

Eastman made a striking impression on everyone in the Village. Tall, handsome, eloquent, somehow remarkably favoured, he had graduated from Williams College in 1905, and had studied philosophy under John Dewey at Columbia. He soon abandoned the idea of an academic career, and made a name for himself as a lecturer on female suffrage. Through Ida Rauh, whom he married in 1911, he was introduced to the most advanced radical circles in the Village. He wrote poetry, began to read Marx and joined the

Socialist Party. Eastman was uninterested in Vlag's consumer co-
operatives, and quickly ended the magazine's cumbersome tradition of collective editorial management. The selection of material
to be published continued to be done by ballot, but in most respects
the *Masses* was Eastman, and Eastman was the *Masses*. Funds for the
magazine were raised from 'a henna-haired, pug-nosed and pink-
painted old lady', doyenne of the New York social élite, Mrs O.
H. P. Belmont.[25] He particularly liked the realist drawings which
John Sloan brought to the editorial meeting for the second issue
in December 1912, and had received a ballad from Arturo
Giovannitti, the Wobbly militant. But he saw few signs of prose
of equal strength – until he received a phone call. 'I am a person
named John Reed. I work on the *American Magazine*, and I've got
a story they won't print. I'd like to offer it to the *Masses*.' 'Fine!'
he said. 'Send it along'. 'No, I'm right here on 11th Street, and
I'll bring it over. I want to see you.' Eastman later set down his
impressions of that first meeting:

> He had a knobby and too filled-out face that reminded me, both in
> form and color, of a potato. He was dressed up in a smooth brown
> suit with round pants' legs and a turned-over starched collar, and
> seemed rather small and rather distracted. He stood up or moved
> about the room all through his visit and kept looking in every direction
> except that in which he was addressing his words. It is difficult for me
> to get the sense of togetherness with a stranger, even if he looks at
> me. And when he looks at the walls, or the house fronts on the other
> side of the street, and talks into the air, and walks around in this
> excessively steamed-up manner, I am hopelessly embarrassed and
> want to lie down and rest after it is over.[26]

Eastman inwardly doubted whether things which could not be
sold to magazines would be any good. But Reed's 'Where the Heart
Is', written in a style both 'vivid and restrained', was an example
of 'a man writing about a significant phase of American life that no
other magazine would dare to mention unless sanctimoniously'.[27]

For the first time the idea that the *Masses* might be good struck him. Reed was only a little less important than Eastman in the fortunes of the magazine. Between 1913 and 1917, when it was suppressed by the government, he contributed over fifty articles, reviews and shorter pieces to the *Masses*.[28]

The *Masses* expressed the rebellious soul of Greenwich Village, but never quite considered itself to be part of the Village. In later years Eastman portrayed himself as being anti-bohemian ('Greenwich Villagism' was a particularly scornful term of abuse in Eastman's eyes), but in the heady mix of Freud, Marx, pragmatism and sexual liberation which he imparted to the magazine, it was the Village at its most intellectually vibrant. He resisted the free-floating enthusiasm around him for dogmas and nostrums of all kinds, except those which he found personally interesting. In his first editorial in December 1912 he demanded 'a radical democratization of industry and society', but which would only be achieved 'when and if the spirit of liberty and rebellion is sufficiently awakened in the classes which are now oppressed'. He had a way of allowing his readers a glimpse of momentous things and great changes, and then qualifying hope into the ground. From Dewey he retained a suspicion of metaphysics, a pragmatism and an abiding concern for freedom. He believed in freedom perhaps more than in socialism, and argued that feminism had begun to raise issues of personal freedom which transcended Marxist analyses of class politics. The '*Masses* crowd' shared his basic allegiances, while not always agreeing with his extended discussions of politics and economics in the two pages set aside for editorial comment. There were divergent strands of *Masses* thinking and it was a sisyphean task to construct a coherent policy from the libertarian anarchism of Sloan and Robert Henri, the sexual radicalism of Floyd Dell, the hard-hitting socialist fundamentalism of Art Young, the syndicalism of Giovannitti and Eastman's idiosyncratic Marxist science of revolution.

The bubbling enthusiasms of Reed's instinctive rebelliousness were soon added to the editorial counsels of the magazine. In January 1913 he hesitantly offered Eastman a statement of purpose which might be run below the masthead. In later years Reed's text was the occasion of an ill-tempered argument between Eastman and others who were then writing about the legacy of the 'old' *Masses*. The dispute concerned Reed in 1913. Was he, as Eastman argued, 'a brilliant and audacious art-rebel with no thought of the class struggle', who was thus incapable of formulating the more serious nature of the magazine? Or was Reed, as Hicks saw him, the one who expressed the spirit of the enterprise 'with considerable exactness'?[29] Reed's statement of purpose:

> We refuse to commit ourselves to any course of action except this: to do with the *Masses* exactly what we please. No magazine has ever done that in this country and preserved a wide influence. The *Masses* is neither a closet magazine nor a quarterly philosophic review. But we have perfact faith that there exists in America a wide public, alert, alive, bored with the smug procession of magazine platitudes, to whom What We Please will be as a fresh wind... The broad purpose of the *Masses* is a social one: to everlastingly attack old systems, old morals, old prejudices – the whole weight of outworn thought that dead men have saddled upon us – and to set up new ones in their places... We intend to be arrogant, impertinent, in bad taste, but not vulgar. We will be bound by no one creed or theory of social reform, but will express them all, providing they be radical...[Hicks, *Reed*, p.94]

Little of Reed's rather muddled language survived to appear in the final statement of purpose in the January 1913 issue. Reed was, of course, not a trained 'thinker'. He had absorbed from Steffens, Lippmann and from the Village a restless hunger for change, but his statement reveals how little beyond gestures his radicalism had progressed. One assumption, at least, links him to Harriet Monroe and the modern movement in poetry, for *Poetry*, too, shared his belief in the need for 'a wide public, alert, alive, [which was] bored with the smug procession of magazine platitudes'. Within a year Pound, that weathervane of modernist sensibility, was writing that the 'artist has no longer any belief or suspicion that the mass, the half-educated simpering general, the semi-connoisseur...can in any way share his delights or understand his pleasure'.[30] The decisive abandonment of 'the public' by the 'serious artist' was another way in which Reed became detached from the avant-garde. Eastman argued that the most appropriate description of Reed in 1913 was that he 'represented the Bohemian-anarchist ingredient in that extraordinary amalgam of young rebelliousness'.[31]

The central emotional relationship of Reed's life in New York was with Mabel Dodge. She was eight years older than he, and had a long, plain face, dark hair, a characterless nose, thin lips and wore loose-fitting gowns in floral patterns, fancy turbans and elegant jewellery. He learned more in his torturous relationship with Dodge than he had in any other romantic entanglement. Their romance showed him, paradoxically, that the new sexual freedoms and the cult of self-expression in the Village could render him unfree. Dodge, the Lorelei who brought D. H. Lawrence to Taos in the early 1920s, has been – since Christopher Lasch first discussed her in *The New Radicalism in America* (1966) – a type not so much of the 'new woman' of Greenwich Village bohemia but of the intellectuals' will to power.

She grew up believing that the world into which she had been born was corrupt.[32] The hypocrisies of middle-class Buffalo filled her with loathing. These half-articulated rebellious feelings could find no expression except through one emotional crises after another: neurasthenia, boredom and ill-health combined to make Mabel intensely alive to the power relations submerged within sexuality. She saw in sex a way of domination, and throughout her life, in heterosexual and lesbian relationships, approached her emotional life as others might approach a war.

In 1912 Mabel and Edwin Dodge settled at 23 Fifth Avenue, after living for several years at the Villa Curonia, near Florence. Their son John was five and they wanted to send him to an American school; Edwin planned to open an architectural office. The apartment was redecorated under Mabel's expert guidance: the woodwork was painted white, heavy textured white paper was put on the walls, white curtains were hung from floor to ceiling, embroidered white shawls were placed as decoration on the walls and – at a moment when middle-class opinion had swung decisively from gas to electricity – a decorated Venetian glass chandelier for candles was hung in the living room. The effect was stunning. The apartment made a very large statement about herself, and about her relationship to the city to which she had just returned. The chandelier, she recalled,

> hung from the ceiling in the living room, fresh as morning while the streets outside were dingy gray and sour with fog and gasoline. It overcame the world outside those walls. It made exquisite shadows on the white ceiling and altogether it acted as a charm with which to conquer cities…when the apartment was all put together, it seemed, at first, to do the thing I meant to have it do. It diminished New York, it made New York stay outside in the street.[33]

Expressive interior decoration became a distinctive feature of Greenwich Village. On nearby Tenth Street the painters and sculptors William and Marguerite Zorach covered the walls of their apartment with Gauguinesque murals redolent of Bali or Tahiti. As Orrick Johns recalled:

> every piece of furniture was painted a different crude color, vermilion red, lemon yellow, bright orange or purple. There was a cobalt blue chest of drawers. As one came in the door, one was greeted by a big flat group of Adam and Eve, the Serpent and the Tree of Life, alone in the same flaming hue. The stove was pure white, and the other walls were covered with tropical foliage and flowers, an orange leopard, birds and other creatures.[34]

Fashionable New York domestic interiors in the 1890s were crammed, as Edith Wharton recalled, with 'curtains, lambrequins, jardinierès of artificial plants, wobbly velvet-covered tables littered with silver gew-gaws, and festoons of lace on mantel pieces and dressing-tables'.[35]

Edwin Dodge, a debonair man not much given to introspection, enjoyed the city, taking their son to the Polo Grounds to watch baseball games. Nothing could have displeased Mabel more. She visualised the scene, 'the crowd of dingy, dusty men and boys sitting in huge circles all chewing gum and wearing derby hats', and shook her head in disapproval. It became another source of irritation between them. Edwin's 'hard-shelled, American aplomb' annoyed her, as did his incapacity for self-analysis. When he was driven to examine his motives and inmost drives, and to explore 'the darks of his consciousness', Mabel found him even more tedious. She believed that he was blocking her growth. 'If I wanted to go ahead and live mentally, I had to send Edwin away – that was all there was to it' (*Intimate Memories*, 3, p. 13). Her few friends in New York (Carl Van Vechten, Hutchins Hapgood, Jo Davidson, Lincoln Steffens) brought some animation to her apartment, but most of the time she felt aimless and tired. It was as though she suffered from Oblomovism, the malady of the indolent hero of Goncharov's novel (1859) who became a symbol of the Russian nobility before the emancipation of the serfs: 'I lay listless on the pale French gray couch, dangling a languid arm, eyes closed before the recurrent death of the sweet antiquities about me that lapsed lifeless between-whiles' (*Intimate Memories*, 3, pp. 16-17).

In February 1913 she became involved with the planning for the great show of modern art to be held at the 25th Street Armory. She knew Berenson in Florence and, through Gertrude Stein in Paris, was familiar with the younger experimental artists. Mabel gave modest financial support to the organisers, and helped them select pictures from New York collections:

I felt as though the Exhibition were mine. I really did. It became, overnight, my own little revolution. I would upset America; I would, with fatal, irrevocable disaster to the old order of things. It was tragic — I was able to admit that — but the old ways must go and with them their priests. I felt a large, kindly compassion for the artists and writers who had held the fort heretofore, but I would be firm. My hand would not shake nor could I allow my personal feelings of pity to halt me. I was going to dynamite New York and nothing would stop me. Well, nothing did. I moved forward in my role of Fate's chosen instrument, and the show certainly did gain by my propulsion. The force was there in me — directed now. [*Intimate Memories*, 3, p. 36][36]

In her own eyes, she had emerged from exhaustion and passivity to play a Napoleonic role in the city. Her friends — Carl, Jo, Hutch and Steff — began to brings interesting people to 23 Fifth Avenue in the evening for conversation (and a smart midnight supper). It was the first real 'salon' in the city, the first time in living memory that someone with money showed an interest in ideas, politics and art. The newspapers took up her 'Evenings' and wrote about them as quite important events. When the Wobbly leader Bill Haywood and the anarchists Emma Goldman and Alexander Berkman debated 'direct action' with the socialists Walter Lippmann and William English Walling, the whole city was reading about it the next morning.

I kept meeting more and more people, because in the first place I wanted to know everybody, and in the second place everybody wanted to know me. I wanted, in particular, to know the Heads of things. Heads of Movements, Heads of Newspapers, Heads of all kinds of groups of people. I became a Species of Head Hunter, in fact. It was not dogs or glass I collected now, it was people. Important people. [*Intimate Memories*, 3, pp. 83-4]

She nevertheless remained largely passive and withdrawn, amidst the sparkling talk. 'For the most part', according to Max Eastman, 'she sits like a lump and says nothing.' More graciously, Steffens recalled that Dodge 'sat quietly in a great armchair and rarely said a word; her guests did the talking, and with such a variety of guests, her success was amazing'.[37] On her own account, she did not enter into the discussions and confined herself to a remote greeting and a low good-bye. She had created the salon, but chose to allow others to shine. It was a demonstration of power and modesty.

Mabel's 'Evenings' and her involvement with the Armory Show in February 1913 made her famous and powerful. But the boldness of her success seemed to lack savour; it was living in the head at the expense of the heart. She tried to make love to a young man in her immediate circle, but instead of finding herself melting 'into the joys of the flesh and the lilies and languors of love', as she implausibly recalled the occasion years later, she remained cold and unresponsive, 'my blood and nerves not interested' (*Intimate Memories*, 3, p. 169). She wanted something out of experience which was subtle, occult, secret and feminine, something which she called '*la grande vie intérieure*'. The phrase was given to her by Violet Shillito, the sister of a friend from Miss Graham's School in New York. She met Violet – known universally as 'Veeolette' – in Paris when she was sixteen and stayed for part of the summer with the Shillito family. Violet preached a doctrine of aesthetic bliss, contemplation and introspection: whatever there was to be experienced in life, it was of value principally for its inner effect. The conscious turning inwards, the deliberate search for the exquisite, made Mabel someone who carried the *fin-de-siècle* passion for self-cultivation into the Village. The doctrine of '*la grande vie intérieure*' remained as a powerful loadstone which served as a link between her moments of passivity and of furious activity. Oblomov and Napoleon were metaphors for Mabel's strategies for the enhancement and enjoyment of '*la grande vie*'.

Mabel Dodge met John Reed in the early spring of 1913, when she was taken by Hutchins Hapgood to hear Bill Haywood talk about the silk-workers' strike in Paterson, New Jersey. A suggestion on her part that they 'bring the strike to New York' to break the embargo of newspaper coverage was enthusiastically taken up by Reed. In this early period of their relationship Mabel slipped into a 'feminine' role which, in most circumstances, was far from congenial for her. 'I kept having ideas about what to do and he carried them out', she recalled. One imagines that she saw herself in those hectic weeks as wife and mother, the woman who was the power behind the throne, the woman who enabled her man to achieve things in the world (*Intimate Memories*, 3, pp. 200, 205). Once, when Reed faltered and seemed to despair of ever succeeding with the pageant, she sharply rebuked him and sent him back to the fray. As a performance, her handling of Reed was masterful.

The Paterson Strike Pageant was a great deal more than an important turning point in the relationship betwen Reed and Dodge. The strike of silk-workers in Paterson began in mid-winter, and dragged on through the spring without sign of either concession on the part of the mill owners or collapse of the morale of the largely immigrant workforce. One out of three workers in Paterson dyed and wove the fine silks which made the city's three hundred mills the leading production centre in the nation. The unskilled silk-workers, who tended looms for as little as $6 or $7 a week, rebelled against the introduction of the four loom system. The employers' answer was to hire yet lower paid immigrant women to tend the looms, and to lower piece-rates. When the workers spontaneously walked out of the Doherty Mill, the leaders of Local 152 of the Industrial Workers of the World (IWW) offered their help to widen the strike. By early March 25,000 silk-workers had walked out. Ethnic divisions in the workforce, and traditional antipathy to radical immigrants on the part of American Federation of Labor craft unions, left the IWW with no serious rivals for control of the strike. Victory in the Lawrence, Massachusetts, strike a year before gave the IWW immense prestige with the immigrant workers, and membership of Local 152 grew tenfold in the early days of the strike. The employers played the anti-union and anti-immigrant card to great effect, and hostility to the strike swept across Paterson itself. 'Outside agitators', in the time-honoured American tradition, were blamed for the intransigence of the strikers. The leading IWW organisers – Elizabeth Gurley Flynn and Carlo Tresca – were arrested. Fred Boyd, a friend of Reed's, was arrested by police for a speech during which he read the free-speech clause of the New Jersey constitution.[38] Intemperate language, calls for sabotage and industrial disobedience played into the hands of the enemies of labour and immigrants. Local courts and the police did their best to demoralise the strikers and break the strike. After three months, the strikers seemed to be getting nowhere. Appeals for support to socialists (the nearby town of Haledon had a socialist administration, and allowed mass meeting and processions which were regularly broken up in Paterson) extended to New York. There was little love lost between Socialist Party leaders and the IWW, but criticisms were stifled and support was offered.

Bill Haywood, who arrived to take control of the strike at the end of March, was taken by Hutchins Hapgood to meet poets and painters in the Village. He was lionised by the Village, and adored by women in the throes of a sexual revolution. Hapgood saw Haywood as a magnificent primitive ('This simple, strong, big man, with one piercing eye, was a person as straight as a die. I was struck again with the real marriage there was between Haywood's feeling and his active life. His was not a complex or split-up personality... His nature was that of a straight line.')[39] and delivered him to one of Mabel Dodge's Evenings as though in tribute. He struggled with the alarmingly articulate Villagers and generally failed to live up to his reputation. None the less, Dodge invited him back, for an evening devoted to modern art. At one of Mabel Dodge's Evenings he bitterly complained that radicals in the city had done nothing to help the strikers in Paterson. Several days later Reed and a friend, Eddy Hunt, visited Paterson. His account of that visit, published in the *Masses* in June as 'War in Paterson', was a brilliant, impressionistic, ironic account of tensions between strikers and police, of his arrest, brief hearing before Recorder Carroll and (brief) experiences in prison.[40] There may have been a war in Paterson, but Reed had little to say about the causes of the strike or the tactics of the IWW. The people he met in prison who expressed in broken English the fundamentals of class solidarity appealed directly to him. Reed's article explained how he was won over to the cause of the strikers. The political conclusions he drew from his experiences allied him with the IWW. As Rosenstone put it: '[i]n Paterson, Jack had smelled, tasted and felt the spirit of radicalism and found it good' (p. 131). But he kept a clear-headed grasp of who he actually was. Although widely admired in the Village for his arrest and imprisonment, Reed knew that he was not yet a 'hero nor a martyr – the whole business is a joke. I'm not even a socialist, you know.'[41] The idea that Reed entered the jail a bohemian and emerged a radical wildly over-simplifies both the effects of his arrest at Paterson and the stuttering course of his political evolution.[42]

Reed's visit to Paterson was soon followed by a suggestion, made by Haywood, supported by Mabel Dodge and enthusiastically picked up by Reed, that they bring the strike into New York in the form of a pageant.[43] From Haywood's point of view, the pageant would break the impasse of the strike. In effect, the pageant would turn the strike into theatre, and turn New York radicals, liberals, socialists and trades unionists into a participating audience. Reed's Harvard experiences made the strike pageant a natural way to bring together his undoubted theatrical enthusiasm with his intense sympathy with the Paterson strikers. His Harvard friends, Mabel Dodge's set, the IWW organisers, suffragists, socialists and others launched the idea in a blaze of enthusiasm. Their lack of money and time soon led to a strategy session at the Liberal Club at which Reed, Haywood, Dodge and other members of the Executive Committee proposed to all those who had begun work on the project that the venue selected (Madison Square Garden) was too expensive and too vast for the pageant to be a financial success. The Paterson workers at the meeting pledged to raise the additional money needed, and the project was once again underway.

Robert Edmond Jones, Reed's contemporary at Harvard, drew the deservedly famous poster for the pageant which featured a gigantic worker rising up out of the industrial cityscape, as well as constructing the stage setting, a spare canvas backdrop portraying a mill scene. Reed rehearsed the workers for the crowd scenes and songs. Tresca, Flynn and Haywood gave abbreviated versions of the speeches they had been making at Paterson for months. It was very much an occasion for IWW propaganda, whose initials, in large red light bulbs, were displayed outside the Garden for weeks before the pageant. The participating strikers came across to New York on the morning of 7 June and marched impressively up Fifth Avenue. The pageant was divided into six episodes, with large posters indicating, in the fashion of silent movies, the subject of each scene. The simplicity of the set, which seemed utterly to be without staginess or striving for theatrical effect, impressed the audience. And when in the first episode the workers poured out of the factory on to the stage, and marched the entire length of the main aisle, cheering and singing, the audience of 15,000 cheered and sang with them. It was an electrifying moment of theatre. The second episode ended with arrested strikers being walked down the long aisle again, to 'boos' and hisses from the audience. The third began with a funeral procession beginning at the rear of the Garden carrying the coffin of a dead striker to the stage. The strikers and the audience joined together in the fourth episode to sing the 'Marseillaise', the 'Internationale' and other songs in English, German and Italian. The strikers again proceeded through the audience waving banners and recreating a May Day parade in the fifth episode. The final episode was a strike meeting, which the strikers reached by walking from the rear of the Garden. They stood at the front of the stage, with their backs to the audience, as Haywood addressed them, and the audience, at the same time. These processions through the Garden, and the strike meeting with which the pageant ended, were important symbolic carriers of the pageant's meaning. Reed's first significant political act affirmed the solidarity of strikers and the audience.

The unfolding plot of the pageant concerned the transformation of the strikers' self-understanding. Several reviewers noted that Reed had found a theatrical form which portrayed the complex development of consciousness in archaic and 'simple' structures. The *Independent*, in an enthusiastic notice, pointed out that the pageant had returned to the origins of drama. 'There was no plot – no more than in the crude Elizabethan history-plays. There was no play-acting. The strikers were simply living over, for their fellows to see, their most telling experiences. No stage in this country had ever seen a more real dramatic expression of American life – only a part of it, to be sure, but a genuine and significant part.' The *Survey* saw the pageant as a living 'human document' of 'inarticulate eloquence'. Hutchins Hapgood, noted author of 'human document' books, wrote in the *Globe*: 'The art of it was unconscious, and especially lay in the suggestion for the future. People interested in the possibilities of a vital and popular art, and in constructive pageantry, would learn much from it.'[44]

Reed achieved a simplicity of effect with subtle means. The central innovation lay in the self-presentation of the strikers by themselves. They became in Reed's pageant both strikers and players in a representation of social conflict, both the object of the pageant and the subjects through which the pageant took place.

When the pageant was over, and when Mabel Dodge swept Reed off with her to Europe, their relationship began in earnest.

She would not sleep with him on board the ship: 'something in me adored the high clear excitement of continence, and the tension we had known together that came from our canalized vitality' (*Intimate Memories*, 3, p 213). It was a pre-emptive coup, a seizure of the high ground. If he assumed that he would remain the dominant male, she had a surprise for him. The relationship was consummated in Paris. When she made love, and when she did not, the power relations within sexuality were Mabel's paramount consideration. Not surprisingly, things went wrong almost at once – not in bed, but when they visited old cities, churches and castles. Reed, who had travelled in Europe after graduating from Harvard, was interested in everything. Mabel, custodian of *'la grande vie intérieure'*, was interested in nothing except their relationship:

> I hated to see him interested in Things. I wasn't, and didn't like to have him even look at churches and leave me out of his attention. When we...found the Italians giving 'Aïda' at night in the amphitheater of Verona, I was inclined to force him to go on, drive all night, anything rather than submit to the terror of seeing his eyes dilate with some other magic than my own. Everything seemed to take him away from me, and I had no single thing left in my life to rouse me save his touch. [*Intimate Memories*, 3, p 217]

She was, in crucial ways, an empty person, and possessing Reed alone could 'rouse' her.[45]

While visiting Venice Mabel rather resented Reed's delight at 'the things men have done!' and his wish to be among the doers. She had no interest in those who *did things* or, like Teddy Roosevelt, wrote books about *The Winning of the West* (1889-96) or *The Strenuous Life* (1900). She jumped into her car and returned to Florence, leaving Reed to make his own way back. 'I tried to wrest him away from Things, especially man-made things. He was sturdily loyal to his own wonder' (*Intimate Memories*, 3, p. 218). Inevitably there were reconciliations that summer. One was heralded by Reed's poem, 'Florence', which seemed to placate Mabel's feelings about history and Things. The Florentine air seemed to him to be 'choked with the crowding-up, struggling souls of the dead'. The landscape which once bred 'turbulent armies' now only yields 'olive and wine, wine and oil!' The poem ended with a plea for escape: 'O let us shake off this smothering silky death, let us go away,/My dearest old dear Mabel! What are we living things doing here?' (*Collected Poems*, p. 91) What seemed to reflect a waning of Reed's enthusiasm for Italy hinted still that he remained 'loyal' to energy and life – ominous signs, if she had cared to notice them, as they prepared to return to New York.

For most of the summer Mabel successfully cocooned Reed from political news. As late as 8 September he had heard nothing about the fate of the Paterson strike, and knew nothing of its collapse and acrimonious aftermath.[46] When they returned to 23 Fifth Avenue, the tension between them was scarcely disguised. (We reconstruct their relationship largely through her *Intimate Memories*, written two decades after the events of 1913, and with a very large and very visible axe to grind on Mabel's part. Reed's letters to her were burnt to ease her relationship with Maurice Sterne, Mabel's third husband (*Intimate Memories*, 3, p. 256). That imperious act denies us at least part of his view of their relationship.) Living openly with Reed anywhere except Greenwich Village was an invitation to social condemnation. Mabel wanted to live quietly with him, and do simple things gracefully and slowly. But from the first day of his return to the city, Reed 'was eager to be off and doing'. He became the managing editor of the *Masses* in October, and was never more fully engaged with the rich variety of Manhattan. Mabel placed herself obstructively in his path. One day, when he planned a jaunt to the lower East Side to collect material for the articles he was writing for the *Masses*, Mabel mischievously offered to summon up her chauffer-driven limousine to take them there. Even simple matters were richly productive of conflict. Mabel liked to take her breakfast in bed, where she made calls to her friends to plan the day. Reed put his nose into a newspaper:

> He drank his coffee with the morning newspaper propped up before him, his honey-colored round eyes just popping over 'the news!' Any kind of news as long as it had possibilities for thrill, for action, for excitement. Now newspapers have never meant anything to me. I have never read the news in all my life except when it was about myself or some friend or enemy of mine. But what the morning paper said was happening in Mexico, or in Russia, or at the Poles, seemed to make Reed's heart beat faster than I could, and I didn't like that. I felt doomed. [*Intimate Memories*, 3, p. 233]

Mabel experienced flashes of jealousy. One night when Reed came back and told her of meeting a young prostitute, she threw herself on the floor in a faint. She threatened several times to commit suicide when he seemed to be neglecting her. As he grew busier, Mabel yearned more and more for domesticity. This was, again, a tactic to dominate: 'I tried to hem him in, and I grew more and more domestic except for the Evenings, when I sat tragic and let It do what It wanted' (*Intimate Memories*, 3, p. 235).

It was about this time, in November 1913, that Reed confessed to Hutchins Hapgood: 'Oh, Hutch, Mabel is wonderful, I love her, but she suffocates me, I can't breathe.' Hapgood later used the image of a jail to explain what Reed experienced in his relations with Mabel.[47] A break with Mabel was now inevitable, and he left her a heartfelt note:

> Good-by, my darling. I cannot live with you. You smother me. You crush me. You want to kill my spirit. I love you better than life but I do not want to die in my spirit. I am going away to save myself. Forgive me. I love you – I love you. Reed. [*Intimate Memories*, 3, p. 242]

Mabel fled to the Dobbs Ferry home of Hapgood and his wife Neith Boyce, where she sobbed, chain-smoked cigarettes and talked the evening through, bitterly demanding the return of her lover. That night she took an overdose of veronal.[48] Reed, for his part, retreated to Harvard to see his old teacher, Charles T. Copeland. They were soon reconciled by Steffens and Hapgood, and Reed returned to 23 Fifth Avenue, chastened and repentant. It was, he agreed, '[y]our way, not mine...' (*Intimate Memories*, 3, p. 245). With a clarity which could sometimes be shattering, Mabel wrote to Neith Boyce after their reconciliation:

> To him the sexual gesture has no importance, but infringing on his right to act freely has the first importance. Are we both right & both wrong – and how do such things end? Either way it kills love – it seems to me. This is so fundamental – is it what feminism is all about?...I know all women go thro this – but must they go on going thro it? Are we supposed to 'make' men do things? Are men to change? Is monogamy better than polygamy?[49]

Several weeks later Carl Hovey, managing editor of the *Metropolitan Magazine*, asked Reed to go to Mexico to report the revolution. The *Tribune* was sending Richard Harding Davis. Jack London was going to Veracruz for *Collier's*, at $1,000 per week. It was a challenge Reed could not resist. Mabel tried to persuade him to give up the commission, but he remained loyal once again to his wonder. After his abrupt departure, Mabel felt a 'sudden compulsion' to go with him. She wired ahead that she would join him in Chicago, but when she arrived she was annoyed to find that Reed looked 'rather glad instead of overjoyed. The man in him was already on the job. The woman's place was in the home!' (*Intimate Memories*, 3, p. 247). She travelled with him to El Paso. But with hundreds of *Federales* streaming across the Rio Grande in pell mell retreat, Mexico was no place for a gringa. She tried for a few days to make 'a little life' in a hotel in El Paso, but it did not work, and she returned to New York.

To keep herself occupied, Mabel began an affair with the

handsome young artist Andrew Dasburg. Almost as soon as Reed came back from Mexico he was sent to Ludlow, Colorado, to cover the labour troubles which had culminated in a massacre of striking miners and their families. While there he wrote a letter to Mabel, the only one to her which has survived, in which he describes a relationship with a young woman and her mother. The girl was a violinist from a family deeply respectful of tradition and law. The mother had wanted to get a divorce but in the end decided that the ensuing stain upon the family's reputation was too high a price to pay for her personal happiness. Clearly armed for such a conversation by his years in Greenwich Village, he explained that he doubted whether 'moral standards' should stand in her way. This was William James's 'religion of healthy-mindedness' in action. Values change, and if the family hoped the daughter would fulfil herself and become a great violinist there were no rules to follow: 'There isn't any law you have to obey, nor any moral standard you have to accept, nor in fact anything outside of your own soul that you have to take any account of' (*Intimate Memories*, 3, pp. 259-61).[50] When the significance of his ideas sank in, the girl was transformed; life seemed at last something to be lived and not just something to endure. The conversations thrilled Reed, too, in part because he knew he was saying what Mabel would have said. 'I wish it could have been you that told her, and could show her at the same time what a marvelous thing is the result of a soul. You are so beautiful to me for just that soul of yours, and so alive. You are my life.' He had learned much from her. It is hard to think of the young man who left Harvard four years before writing such a letter. If in the end the cult of '*la grande vie intérieure*' could not hold him, he had at least come to sense some of its richness of cultivation, some of its beauty.[51] It is hard to see Mabel having learned much, if anything, from her relationship with Reed. She asked Neith Boyce 'Are we supposed to "make" men do things?' In truth, the question was rhetorical: she had tried, and for a time succeeded in an attempt to 'hem him in'. But she did not care for his ideas, and had little of his passion for social change. 'I wasn't dying to alter everything', she explained. Reed's imagination was fired by the struggles of ordinary people; hers was repelled by men who sat in the bleachers at baseball games and wore derby hats and chewed gum. She was a heroine looking for a tragedy which she could dominate; Reed was a hero who searched for a community, a cause, to give his life meaning. Mabel craved submission and peace; he wanted freedom and excitement. So fierce was the struggle between them that the struggle itself kept them together. It took them several years to understand this.

3 War and revolution 1914-1916

Reed's first book of prose, *Insurgent Mexico*, was published in 1914 after the European war had begun. His articles on Mexico in the *Metropolitan* and the *Masses* were greeted with enthusiastic praise. Lippmann wrote that in Reed's articles the revolution of Pancho Villa 'began to unfold itself into throngs of moving people in a gorgeous panorama of earth and sky'.[1] John Dos Passos praised the 'startling vividness' of Reed's prose, which gave the sketches 'wonderful color and tangibility. To read them is to feel that you have been in Mexico, that you have felt the hot blast of the Mexican deserts, lived the passionate picturesque life of the country.'[2] Rudyard Kipling was quoted by the *Metropolitan* as saying '[h]is articles...made me see Mexico'.[3] Reed's biographers, however, have pointed out that the Mexican book cannot be taken as a record of biographical fact or historical truth. Granville Hicks, who generally followed Reed's description of his experiences in Mexico, carefully provided a chronology which established that the story which he told in *Insurgent Mexico* diverged in some particulars from his actual travels. Jim Tuck, whose *Pancho Villa and John Reed* (1984) substantially adds to our understanding of *Insurgent Mexico*, calls Reed's book a 'hybrid' work, composed partly of fact and partly of fabrication, whose chronology is 'extremely haphazard'. Tuck argued that Reed 'was not above embellishing incidents, even to the extent of creating fictitious characters and arbitrarily changing their identities when it suited his purpose'.[4] Rosenstone attributes these swerves from fact and accuracy to the 'poet' and the 'dramatist' in Reed, which made him seek ways to heighten the exciting possibilities of an exciting story (p. 168). What makes Reed's book factually somewhat suspect also makes it, in literary and political terms, rather more intriguing.

He was generally sparing with literary references in his writings, but *Insurgent Mexico* contains two allusions which tell his readers that he was concerned to separate himself from the western adventure story and from the jingoistic war reporting of the day. Although his references to Owen Wister and Richard Harding Davis are brief, they are suggestive. Both Wister and Davis were born in the 1860s. While Reed was at Harvard after 1906, they were among the most popular writers in America. (From among their contemporaries, Reed very much preferred the iconoclastic Steffens.) In *Insurgent Mexico* the sheriff of the Texas town of Presidio appears dressed in a comic outfit. It was as though he had just read Owen Wister 'and knew what a Western sheriff ought to look like: two revolvers on the hip, one slung under his arm, a large knife in his left boot, and an enormous shotgun over his saddle'.[5] Wister had been elected to the exclusive Porcellian Club while he was at Harvard – a detail which would certainly have registered with Reed. After studying medicine and establishing a lucrative practice in Philadelphia, to improve his health he travelled widely in the west. His novel *The Virginian* (1902) eventually sold 1.5 million copies. While at Harvard Reed had praised Wister and Roosevelt as 'activity men', whose vigorous lives embodied all that was best in the Harvard tradition (Hicks, *Reed*, p. 47). It was exactly this kind of comment, carefully calculated to enrage his more thoughtful fellow students, which made Reed's later radicalism somewhat hard to believe. After his life in Greenwich Village, and the literary milieu of Mabel Dodge's salon, he had grown impatient with Wister's myth of the gentleman cowboy of the west.

When he first came under fire during the attack by the *colorados* at La Cadena, Reed tried to explain the curious sense of unreality he felt by comparing it with a page of Richard Harding Davis's prose

(*Insurgent Mexico*, p. 98). He subsequently used a phrase, 'soldiers of fortune', made famous by Davis as the title of a novel in 1897 about revolution and romance in a South American setting, in which the hero, a mining engineer, asserted the superiority of the American gentleman against the lower breeds. Reed met five Americans at Jiminez who were in Mexico for adventure and loot, and who had come away empty-handed: they were 'hard, cold misfits in a passionate country, despising the cause for which they were fighting, sneering at the gaiety of the irrepressible Mexicans' (*Insurgent Mexico*, p. 157). These 'soldiers of fortune' were Reed's ironic riposte to Davis's heroic imperialist tales. The greatest American war correspondent of the age, Davis was aware of the public's insatiable appetite for the romantic and the heroic, and, in their different ways, both writers accepted that the reality of war (and the west) was seldom as richly satisfying as the myth. But they connived at the romantic myth, while proclaiming their desire to record things as they really were. No matter how many times Davis told his readers that war was low, chaotic and consisted 'largely of commonplaces and trivial details', when he wrote of Roosevelt's Rough Riders (the western cowboys and East Coast bluebloods recruited by Roosevelt who formed the First Regiment of the U. S. Cavalry Volunteers in the Spanish–American War) a different and more heroic meaning was communicated:

> The men were panting for breath; the sweat ran so readily into their eyes that they could not see the sights of their eyes; their limbs unused to such exertion after seven days of cramped idleness on the troop-ship, trembled with weakness and the sun blinded and dazzled them; but time after time they rose and staggered forward through the high grass, or beat their way with their carbines against the tangle of vines and creepers.[6]

The *Metropolitan Magazine*, which sent Reed to Mexico, enthusiastically compared his dispatches to those which Davis sent home from Cuba during the Spanish–American war. The comparison was a sign of the growing respect with which he was coming to be regarded. There was a part of Reed which responded to the sweep of war, which saw the events in Mexico as an incomparable journalistic opportunity; he was every bit as much of an adventurer as Davis, and indeed became his rival as a self-publicist. On the other hand, he had nothing of Davis's racism or jingoism. The author of *Soldiers of Fortune* had little of Reed's empathy for ordinary Mexicans, nor Reed's enthusiasm for the harshness of the landscape. (Newly arrived in Veracruz in April 1914, Davis wrote sympathetically of the people he met. But by June, frustrated at the absence of battlefield action, Davis complained that Veracruz was 'a town of flies, filth and heat' and remarked that Mexican women were hideous – a cross between apes and squaws.[7]) Reed's *The War in Eastern Europe*, with its message that there was no reason for America to enter the war, could be understood as a riposte to the impassioned pro-war advocacy of Davis's *With the Allies* (1914) and Wister's propagandistic *The Pentecost of Calamity* (1915). When it was revealed that Reed and a friend had fired rifles while in German trenches, Davis stormed into the offices of the *Metropolitan* to denounce Reed's behaviour.[8] He can only have regarded Reed, the 'new' Richard Harding Davis, with some professional jealousy and political distaste.

Reed, Wister and Davis were connected as well through their relations with Teddy Roosevelt. Wister had known Roosevelt at Harvard, and they had travelled together in the west in the 1880s. He dedicated *The Virginian* to the (then) President in 1902, and published a memoir of their relationship some years after Roosevelt's death in 1919. Roosevelt looked upon Davis with particular approval. He pulled strings to ensure that Davis accompanied the Rough Riders to Cuba in 1898 and, in return, Davis's reports did much to foster the Rough Riders' wildly exaggerated reputation. When Davis died in 1916, Roosevelt was among the eulogists: 'His writings form a text-book of Americanism which all our people would do well to read at the present time.'[9] Reed's attitude towards Roosevelt embodied many of the contradictions in his life. Roosevelt was at first connected in Reed's mind with his feelings about his father: Roosevelt was the champion of the cause of progressivism and reform which had transformed C. J. Reed's life. But after the fiasco of the 1912 presidential election, when Roosevelt bolted the Republican Party and ran unsuccessfully for President as a 'Bull Moose', leading progressives across the nation to defeat, Reed came to see Roosevelt as dangerous and unprincipled. His father, appointed United States Marshal by Roosevelt, was sacked by President Taft in 1910. By 1914 he regarded the former President as an aggressive embodiment of militarism and imperialism. When Reed returned to the offices of the *Metropolitan* after his travels in Mexico, he found Roosevelt playing a prominent role in the conduct of the magazine. (The editors were hedging their pronounced liberalism by providing Roosevelt with a platform for his calls for preparedness.) They were soon bitterly arguing about Mexico, the war in Europe and other matters. 'Villa is a murderer and a rapist', Roosevelt said. 'What's wrong with that?' Reed aggressively asked. 'I believe in rape.' 'I'm glad', Roosevelt granted, flashing his awesome teeth, 'to find a young man who believes in something.'[10]

Their conflict was wholly predictable. Greenwich Village disapproved of Roosevelt, not least for his urging that 'duty' meant 'pain, hardship, self-mastery, self-denial' and his alarmist and ethnocentric campaign against what he called 'race suicide'.[11] The *Masses* mocked him. There was a deeper antagonism in his relationship with Roosevelt, as there was in his disagreements with Steffens, an entanglement of aggression and embarrassment at the memory that he had once admired such men. *Insurgent Mexico*, then, was a declaration of independence against the pedlars of mythic western adventures, the celebrators of imperialism and heroic notions of war, and the nexus of American self-deception and self-interest.

What he hoped to show through his own experiences was the possibility of another way of understanding the Mexican people and their revolution. *Insurgent Mexico* traces the texture of Reed's self-understanding as a way of bringing the readers of his articles in the *Metropolitan* and the *Masses* to see the revolution as sympathetically as he had done. To read his sketches, as Dos Passos wrote, 'is to feel that you have been in Mexico...[and] lived the passionate, picturesque life of the country' (review of *Insurgent Mexico*).

Dodge accompanied Reed to the Mexican border, stayed a few days and then returned to the culturally more nourishing life of 23 Fifth Avenue. He was to be left to get on with a man's business of writing about war and revolution. American interest in the Mexican revolution was at fever-pitch in December 1913. The fall of the dictatorship of Porfirio Díaz in 1910, and the spiralling confusion of coup and counter-coup, interrupted by the elections which brought Francisco Madero to power and then which saw him overthrown and murdered by General Victoriano Huerta in February 1913, alarmed the American people. There were 40,000 Americans living and working in Mexico, and a capital investment of \$1,000 million. With the advent of the railroads in northern Mexico, much of the land had come under the control of firms owned by Americans. They were entrenched at the top of the hacienda system. A hue and cry for military intervention was raised by business interests, led William Randolph Hearst who had extensive holdings in Mexican property.[12]

When the followers of Madero raised the banner of rebellion in the name of constitutionalist government in northern Mexico, led by the governor of Coahuila state, Venustiano Carranza, the new administration in Washington hoped for the restoration of a friendly democratic government. The Wilsonian policy of 'watch-ful waiting' and neutrality between *Huertistas* and the Constitutionalists or *Maderistas* satisfied no one. An arms embargo declared by Washington left Huerta free to buy war materiel from 'hungry' powers like the Japanese and Germans, who hoped to strengthen their influence in a country where the British had for long been the only rival to American dominance.[13] Huerta's tyranny and the threat of civil war, persuaded Wilson of the need to intervene and restore constitutional government. Negotiations were opened with Carranza, but the stiff-necked governor was reluctant to commit himself, and the revolution, to policies which would assure the position of foreign nationals and all foreign-owned property. Within the political and military struggle between Huerta's *Federales* and the Constitutionalists a social and agrarian revolution was taking place. Emiliano Zapata in Morelos in central southern Mexico, and Francisco 'Pancho' Villa in Chihuahua in the north, were leading a revolt by land-hungry *peons* whose support Carranza needed. His attitude towards these agrarian rebels was ambiguous. 'Have you any definite plans for land reform?', he was asked by the British journalist H. Hamilton Fyfe in 1913: 'He thought for a moment. Then he replied: "The first necessity is the fair and free election of a President. The election which is proposed now [by Huerta] will be a farce."'[14]

He similarly declined to give an unambiguous guarantee to the Americans about the position of foreign capital or the safety of foreign nationals, and was regarded with considerable suspicion by Wall Street. Because he strongly opposed American intervention, he had the 'right enemies' and retained the support of the American socialist press. The *New York Call* and the *Milwaukee Leader* saw him as a necessary step along the Mexican evolution towards socialism. Steffens was impressed by Carranza's independence, and tried to persuade President Wilson that he had been ill-informed about Carranza's real aims.[15] Reed's doubts about Carranza, which strengthened as the events of 1914 unfolded, put him at odds with Socialist Party opinion.

As Reed described the scene at Presidio, Texas Rangers, customs and immigration officials, the Army Border Patrol, and a swarm of agents and salesmen for American corporations, were watching events unfold on the far bank of the Rio Grande. There was much talk of those 'damned greasers' and of the need for intervention. The military forces of Huerta were in disarray, and the legendary brigand-guerrilla, Pancho Villa, seemed on the verge of a military triumph in northern Mexico. Reed sought an interview with the *Huertista* commander, General Salvador Mercado, but his note fell into the hands of a rival federal commander, General Pascual Orozco, who threatened Reed with death if he dared to enter Mexican territory. (American press coverage of the war displeased the federal leaders.) *Insurgent Mexico* began with an almost light-hearted act of defiance as he crossed over into the war zone. Instead of excitement and danger, he found a city, Ojinaga, which had changed hands five times during the war and was in a state of ruin. The *Federales* were near starvation, dressed in ragged uniforms, and the main street was crowded with 'sick, exhausted people' fleeing the war who were desultorily being stripped of their possessions by the federal soldiers.

Reed's introduction to 'insurgent' Mexico set the anti-heroic tone for much of what was to follow. The Mexicans were not incandescent with revolutionary fervour. They seemed to him an oppressed people, downtrodden but hopeful for a better life. He repeatedly asked those he met about the revolution: what was its cause, what did they hope to get out of it? One old man told him: 'The Revolución is good. When it is done we shall starve never, never, if God is served' (*Insurgent Mexico*, p. 43). A doctor he met at Las Nieves, who behaved with brutality to his patients and who later stole the horse of a friend of Reed's, saw the revolution as 'a fight of the poor against the rich. I was very poor before the Revolución and now I am very rich' (*Insurgent Mexico*, p. 49). Captain Fernando of *La Tropa*, the mounted irregulars with whom

Reed travelled, pointed to the solid gains of the revolution: '[w]e are riding over the lands of the men. They used to belong to the rich, but now they belong to me and to the *compañeros*' (*Insurgent Mexico*, p. 57). Reed found that some were fighting for 'Libertad' and against despotism, exploitation and slavery; one soldier insisted that he was fighting for better whisky (*Insurgent Mexico*, p. 174). Asking one 'sullen-face' Indian woman, who was wearing two cartridge-belts, triggered off a piece of Mexican music hall banter:

> 'Why are you fighting?' I asked her.
> She jerked her head toward the fierce figure of Julian Reyes.
> 'Because he is', she answered. 'He who stands under a good tree is sheltered by a good shade.'
> 'A good rooster will crow in any chicken coop,' capped Isidro.
> 'A parrot is green all over,' chimed in someone else.
> 'Faces we see, but hearts we do not comprehend,' said José, sentimentally. [*Insurgent Mexico*, p. 64]

But the theme which runs through virtually all of their answers is the desire for a better life:

> ... they tell me [an old peasant said to Reed] that there are many rich lands to the north and south and east. But this is my land and I love it. For the years of my father and my grandfather, the rich men have gathered the corn and held it in their clenched fists before our mouths. And only blood will make them open their hands to their brothers" (*Insurgent Mexico*, p. 166-7).

Reed was aware that many *peons*, the *pacificos*, chose to watch the revolution from the sidelines. Some, like the father of his friend Longinos Güereca, regarded the revolution with traditional peasant scepticism: 'Three years ago I had four *riatas* like this. Now I have only one. One the *colorados* took, and the other Urbina's people took, and the last one José Bravo... What difference does it make which side robs you? (*Insurgent Mexico*, p. 76-7). The warm, friendly side of the Mexican people was not all that Reed saw. There was a vein of wild brutality in the revolution, and an element of naïvety in the *peons*. But the instinctive generosity he encountered remained an enduring part of Reed's experience of Mexico. Two *rancheros* who insisted upon offering him their unstinting hospitality became symbols of the people: 'courteous, loving, patient, poor, so long slaves, so full of dreams, so soon to be free' (*Insurgent Mexico*, p. 166). During the siege of Torreón a ragged soldier gave Reed half a 'lopsided brown cigarette'. As they sat smoking, a pearly mist rose in the dusk. A dozen soldiers began to improvise a new ballad of the day's fighting. 'I felt my whole feeling going out to these gentle, simple people – so lovable they were...' (*Insurgent Mexico*, p. 217). The physical landscape itself, barren and hostile, was in the American's eyes almost magical. The dust, mountains and cacti aroused in him a powerful empathetic emotion. 'It was a land to love – this Mexico – a land to fight for' (*Insurgent Mexico*, p. 73).

At the heart of Reed's understanding of Mexico, with all of its paradoxes, was his response to the people. Indeed, Lippmann praised Reed for the absence in his work of 'white man's superiority' or condescension.[16] Reed was not a *peon* and did not pretend otherwise; there were many things about Mexican life which he found exotic. But he felt an instinctive sympathy towards the people which enabled him to identify with their struggle for freedom and economic justice. Rosenstone attributes much of the power of *Insurgent Mexico* to Reed's close identification with his subject (p. 167). This is most vividly present when Reed entered the masculine world of *La Tropa*. The pages describing his adventures with these men are among the most boyish, vivid and attractive in his books. Everything in these pages is alive with a freshness of feeling, and a growing understanding of the people and the landscape, which prepares the way for a symbolic rite of passage (the drinking of a bottle of *sotol*) which admits him to become a *compañero* with *La Tropa*. He was now fit to drink, dance and sing with them. 'We shall be *compadres*, eh?', said Longinos Güereca.

'We shall sleep in the same blankets, and always be together. And when we get to the Cadena I shall take you to my home, and my father shall make you my brother...' (*Insurgent Mexico*, p. 70). Güereca defended Reed and made him one of the boys.

He rode with *La Tropa*, who wore cowhide sandals, sombreros, swords, immense spurs, serapes, automobile goggles and dusty uniforms, the 65 miles from La Zarca to the Hacienda of La Cadena in a single day. His friendships with Güereca and Luis Martinez blossomed swiftly and intensely as they prepared to guard the pass of La Cadena against a force of twelve hundred *colorados*. The outnumbered defenders were soon outflanked and routed. Reed watched the distant movements of men on horseback, not understanding what was happening and thinking that it seemed unreal. The shooting sounded like 'a clicking typewriter' (*Insurgent Mexico*, p. 96). But then riders came away from the battle, screaming, their horses terrified. 'They passed us without stopping, without noticing, all blood and sweat and blackness' (*Insurgent Mexico*, p. 97). Juan Vallejo shouted to Reed to flee, but the desert was flat and he was burdened with a heavy camera, an overcoat and notebooks. One after another were abandoned as Reed followed Vallejo onto a path off the main road. Groups of mounted men rode past, shooting repeatedly, as Reed ran as far as he could before cramps forced him to stop. Horsemen fired at Vallejo, who dived into the bush. Running again, it still seemed unreal to Reed 'like a page out of Richard Harding Davis'. He ducked into an arroyo when *colorados* approached, and then fell asleep. He headed northwest when he awoke, towards the mountains, walking through a burning landscape of sharp-spiked cacti and jagged stones. What a story this was going to make for his friends in Grenwich Village! Reed had nothing to drink, and did not arrive at the Güereca house until the middle of the next day. Güereca had just heard of the battle of La Cadena. The rout of *La Tropa* posed terrible risks for them all and he was determined that Reed could not stay. He feared that they would all be killed by the *colorados*. When Reed arrived at Santo Domingo later that day he learned that his four closest friends had been killed in the disaster at La Cadena.

These matters precede the main business of *Insurgent Mexico*, the presentation of Villa, and the great assault by the Division of the North on Torreón, the battle which opened the way for the constitutionalist advance on Mexico City. The battle of La Cadena precedes the introduction of Villa because it implicitly explains the people and their revolution, and its roots in the demands of ordinary people (for land, justice, freedom, good whisky), and the bonds which held them together. Reed became one of the *compañeros* and so too have we as his readers become one with *La Tropa* and partisans of Villa. When he wrote about Mexico he sought to make his readers share his experiences and to awaken their sympathy. His feelings were passionately engaged and he wrote to Lippmann that if the United States intervened he would fight on Villa's side.[17] Little did he imagine that when the Marines landed at Veracruz, Villa would be the only significant military or political figure in Mexico who did not object. Villa naïvely chose to understand the American move as being directed against the cruel and obstinate Huerta. Carranza saw the intervention as an insult to Mexican sovereignty. This was not the only paradox in Reed's admiration for Villa.

They first met in December 1913 in Chihuahua City. Reed saw Villa two months later at Yermo, at the beginning of the drive south which culminated in the battle of Torreón. Reed learned that Villa, a bandit by profession, had volunteered to support the Constitutionalists in 1910. He was soon in conflict with his military superiors. Huerta, then still a follower of Madero, tried to imprison Villa for insubordination, but he escaped across the border and lived for a time in El Paso. In April 1913 he returned to Mexico, raised an army and defeated Huerta's forces. He seems to have enjoyed the nerve of *chatito*, pug-nose, as he called Reed. The account of their conversations in *Insurgent Mexico* suggests that Reed was given extraordinary freedom of access to Villa. Attempts to question him on matters of economic or political policy largely yielded answers which were comic in their ineptitude. Villa approached monetary problems with a pistol in his hand, and rather chuckled over the idea that women should be invited to play a role in ruling the country. He knew little about socialism. But Reed found much to admire in Villa's cunning. His conduct of the war was brilliantly innovative (Reed particularly admired Villa's use of night attacks and his field hospitals, which were brought close to the battle by train). Villa, who had given some thought to problems of post-war reconstruction, expansively talked of his hope to settle his soldiers on the land, in what would be Imperial Roman military-agricultural colonies. (In 1920 Reed heard a very similar idea from Trotsky.)

Reed was sorely puzzled by Villa's loyalty to Carranza. The contrast between the two was striking. Carranza was a landowner and a bourgeois reformer; Villa, 'the Mexican Robin Hood', had been a butcher and led a *peon* army. Carranza remained deliberately vague on the subject of land reform. When Villa made substantial grants of land to every male inhabitant of the state of Chihuahua, Carranza demanded that he return the land to its former owners (*Insurgent Mexico*, p. 140). Villa's advisers, perhaps including Reed, tried to make him see that Carranza was 'essentially an aristocrat and a reformer, and that the people were fighting for more than reform' (*Insurgent Mexico*, p. 139). Villa refused such advice, and repeatedly sought to conciliate Carranza. In the end their disagreement over the land question, the American occupation of Veracruz and other matters led to open conflict and civil war which destroyed Villa's military power and turned him back into a bandit leader whose men were treated like criminals. In October 1915, in a policy reversal which left Villa stunned, Wilson announced the diplomatic recognition of Carranza. Carranza's northern commander was allowed to use American railroads to transport reinforcements to Agua Prieta in early November, where their unexpected presence broke Villa's power. His surviving forces retreated into banditry in the mountains of Chihuahua and outrages against American citizens. After an unsuccessful attack by *Villistas* at Chihuahua City in 1917, hundreds of his men were hung by Obregón on the main street leading to the centre of the city. His army was finally destroyed by the US Cavalry, which crossed the Rio Grande in 1918 and staged a co-ordinated attack upon Villa's irregulars. In 1914 Villa was at the height of his power. The civil war which followed settled the fate of all of the revolutionary leaders. Huerta died in American exile in January 1916. Carranza laid waste to Morelos in 1919, and arranged for the assassination of Zapata. The triumphant regime of Carranza soon sank into corruption. When Obregón raised the standard of rebellion under the old *Maderista* banner of constitutionality in May 1920 Carranza fled to Veracruz, and then to the state of Puebla, where he was murdered by a local bandit. Villa was assassinated in 1923. For many years his widow insisted that he had been killed at the behest of Obregón, who was himself assassinated by a religious fanatic in 1928.

Reed saw the revolution at its moment of greatest hope, when the cause of the people looked strongest. For all his professed sympathy for Villa, he seems not to have misjudged the likely strength of the leading figures. Hicks, Rosenstone and Tuck have noted the various ways in which Reed altered the chronology of his travels during the writing of *Insurgent Mexico*. It might be possible now to suggest why he placed the profile of Carranza *after* the battle of Torreón, when in fact he interviewed Carranza at Nogales in late February, a month *before* the battle. The victory at Torreón was won by an army of *peons*, led by a bandit. Yet when Reed talked to Carranza he sensed nothing of the charismatic revolutionary leader in the person who 'seemed like nothing so much as a slightly senile old man, tired and irritated' (*Insurgent Mexico*, p. 251). Carranza discussed the Benton case (the murder of a British national and prominent landowner by one of Villa's gunslingers) exclusively in terms of diplomatic protocol. Everything Reed admired in the passionate and instinctive Mexicans was reversed in Carranza. Even in talks with Carranza's advisers Reed 'never detected one gleam of sympathy for, or understanding of, the peons' (*Insurgent Mexico*, p. 252). Placing this profile after the long account of the battle invites his readers to conclude that the revolution was going to be taken over and betrayed by the 'organisation men' like Carranza and Obregón.[18] The chilling portrait of the governor of Coahuila says, in effect, that men like *this* are going to decide the fate of the revolution.

Reed may not have been prepared to state boldly such a pessimistic conclusion in April or May 1914. After all, the civil war which destroyed Villa's Division of the North was still in the future. He did not publish his profile of Carranza for six months after his return to New York. (It appeared in the September 1914 issue of the *Metropolitan*.) His silence was an act of self-censorship, a gesture of hope and solidarity with a revolution which was on the verge of tearing itself apart; his caution over Carranza also served to keep open the lines between himself and the administration, whose reservations about Carranza were approximately balanced by its disapproval of Huerta and Villa. The shifts in the chronology of *Insurgent Mexico* imply perspectives upon the meaning of the book which, for reasons political and literary, were best left unstated. While working on the manuscript he was firmly aware that he had 'present[ed] pictures of the struggle down there as I saw it, keeping as far as possible my own opinions in the background'.[19] When he returned to New York he wrote that the revolution had been caused largely by the land hunger of the *peons*, but that Carranza, either by calculation or principle, 'avoided the question entirely'.[20] This was a silence whose significance in the rush of events took months to emerge. It was as though time itself began to speed up for Reed in 1914. Events elsewhere, in Colorado and in Europe, claimed his attention.

On 20 April 1914 the attitude of the American government towards the Huerta regime stiffened. The pretext for this change of policy occured several weeks earlier, when the crew of a US Navy boat was placed under arrest when they came ashore near Tampico to purchase fuel. The apology offered by the local *Huertista* commander was profuse, but no apology could have satisfied the Americans. When Huerta rejected a demand that the American flag be raised over Tampico and given a twenty-one gun salute, the administration decided that the psychological moment was right in the aftermath of the Constitutionalists' victory at Torreón to humiliate Huerta and drive him from power. On 20 April the administration quickly pushed through Congress a joint resolution supporting the use of naval power to enforce the demands made of the Mexican ruler.[21] One day later, 1,000 Marines were landed, unopposed, at Veracruz, and on the following day 3,000 additional troops joined them. Contrary to American expectations, the Mexicans fought back. Before they were routed they suffered 126 dead; the Americans nineteen. The American press was filled with the sensational story of battles and heroic deaths, which largely displaced the news that, on 20 April, state militiamen had fired on a tent colony of striking coalminers, mainly immigrants, near Ludlow, Colorado, killing twenty-one people, mainly women and children. More Americans died at Ludlow than at Veracruz.

Reed, who had returned earlier in the month from Mexico, watched the signs of American intervention with foreboding. And on 26 April he sent an article to the *New York Times* in which he tried to explain the causes of the revolution, and the likely consequences if the administration decided to extend its military presence in Mexico. He correctly expected that the Mexican people would not welcome the arrival of Marines ('They will take up their guns with reckless bravery and resist us, desperately in the streets and at the doors of their houses') and wrote that though the United States would prevail, the consequences would be disastrous: 'The revolution will be done for ever.'[22] Reed's article was highly regarded, and was published as a pamphlet by the American Association for International Conciliation. It was also admired in unexpected places: President Wilson sent a clipping of it to the United States Ambassador in Britain as something 'which sums up as well as they could be summed up my own conclusions with regard to the issues and personnel of the pending contest in Mexico.'[23]

Reed wrote thirteen articles on Mexico in 1914. But for many American radicals the epic and violent struggle of the Colorado coalminers was a portent closer to home of the impending class war. They believed that the forces behind American intervention in Mexico were the same 'iron heel' which crushed trades unions in America. As he had felt while visiting the scene of the strike at Paterson the year before, Reed wanted to throw himself into the conflict, to tell its story, to rouse the nation's dozing conscience.

He travelled to Colorado in the company of Max Eastman, arriving on 30 April.[24] Eastman was as angry as Reed about the Ludlow massacre, and as determined to break through the distortions and anti-union bias of the national press coverage of the events in Colorado. They travelled to Trinidad and then on to Ludlow, where they found the ruins of the tent colony still smoking. They interviewed survivors of the massacre, striking miners and local residents. A physician who worked for one of the mining companies spoke bitterly against 'outside agitators'. A leading figure in the local Salvation Army referred to the strikers as 'nothing but cattle'.[25] One of the survivors of the massacre, Pearl Jolley, told Eastman that the 'respectable people' of Ludlow were bloodthirsty in their hatred of the strikers. Somewhat doubtful of her account of public opinion, Eastman arranged for a dozen representative ladies to be invited to tea, among whom was the governor's sister. What they said over tea deeply shocked him. The afternoon had been 'a conversational debauch of murder-wishing class-hatred'.[26] Such sentiments made all too credible the idea that the Colorado National Guard had repeatedly provoked the strikers, and that on 20 April they had assaulted the tent colony with lethal intent. Eastman remained in the mining district to investigate the ethnic and class hatreds behind the strike, while Reed travelled to Denver to observe the response of Governor Ammons and the state legislature to the massacre. He was outraged at the governor's pusillanimity, and spoke passionately at mass meetings on behalf of the strikers. Along with Judge Ben Lindsey and the journalist George Creel, who represented the best tradition of crusading Colorado progressivism, Reed joined a committee to express support for the striking miners.

Eastman and Reed learned something of the reality of class conflict in Colorado. They found a community in which the middle ground had virtually ceased to exist. The political choices were clear enough: you were either on the side of the miners; or on the side of the mineowners, who were suported by the police, state and local government, National Guard, judiciary and the press. They found in Colorado a mining community which was isolated geographically (the mines were in remote, unpopulated areas south of Denver), ethnically divided, and composed largely of immigrants who were feared and hated by the middle class. The mine managers, gauleiters of a rough, aggressive frontier capitalism, had fought and defeated successive attempts to unionise the Colorado minefields since the 1880s. The United Mine Workers (UMW) had lost the massive strike in 1903-04 to a combination of intimidation and strike-breakers. The message in September 1913 when the dispute broke out again, as delivered by Mary 'Mother' Jones, the peppery octogenarian UMW organiser, was to stress the need for absolute solidarity.[27] The strikers of 1913 had been brought to

southern Colorado as strike breakers in 1904. It had taken them nearly a decade of harsh, exploiting company towns, company guards equipped with rifles, and an aggressive and hostile management, to reach the breaking point. Reed saw in the miners the same simple courage which held the silk-workers together during the strike in Paterson in 1913. But there were crucial differences. In Colorado the strikers were tough miners, not female silk loom tenders and weavers; there was a tradition of reckless violence in Colorado labour disputes; the miners were more isolated physically; and the managers were men of incomparably greater political influence than the mill-owners in northern New Jersey. John D. Rockefeller, Jr, the dominant owner of mining interests in Colorado, pursued an implacable anti-union policy everywhere. Since the waning of the muck raking movement in 1906, the influence of the mine-owners upon the local and national press had strengthened. The *Masses* had long campaigned against the anti-union bias of the Associated Press; and Eastman and Reed were determined to break the blockade which had prevented Americans from reading the truth about what had happened in Colorado. Eastman's three articles about Colorado are among the most brilliant he ever wrote.[28]

Reed was in Colorado for little more than a week. The narrative which he produced on his return to New York, published as 'The Colorado War' in the *Metropolitan* in July, was one of his finest pieces of journalism. In it he created out of a complex sequence of events a comprehensible narrative which gave meaning to the miners' struggle. Reed tried to show the sequence of events which led to the Ludlow massacre as they would have been seen by the striking miners and their families. He suggested that there was a rhythm in the events of the strike, an alternation between moments of frantic struggle and joyous celebration, and the most gripping moments in 'The Colorado War' came when he showed the sudden swings of mood occasioned by events. He gave a wonderful sense of the gigantic banquet which celebrated the turning back of an armoured train, and how that mood suddenly changed to fear when rumours swept the throng that armed guards were coming down the canyon. Reed lovingly described the gaiety of the national costumes (many were immigrants from Greece) worn when the strikers celebrated Easter with festive dancing, a baseball game and lunch. But when parades were broken up, and when the National Guard made aggressive armed searches of the tent colonies, the mood sharply changed. At first welcomed by the strikers, the militiamen – fed, housed and paid by the mine- owners – soon came to be feared and hated. The logic of the pattern Reed described revealed itself on 20 April at Ludlow.

'The Colorado War' was an impassioned piece of prose. What makes it so striking an achievement is only in part due to the sympathy he felt for the strikers, and to his outrage at the oppressive nature of the system created by the mine-owners. *Insurgent Mexico* was largely impressionistic and autobiographical, but in Colorado he had a complex sequence of events to unravel, and an analysis to make of motivation and ideas, which did not hang upon his personal presence or involvement. The clarity and coherence of Reed's management of the narrative is wholly praiseworthy.

After Ludlow, as Granville Hicks forcefully put it, class war was a reality for Reed 'and his sympathy for the workers was secure' (p. 144). He worked on *Insurgent Mexico* at Provincetown that summer, living with Mabel Dodge, her son and her retinue of servants. Reed's articles on Mexico gave him a national reputation, and the heartfelt admiration of his contemporaries.

> Your first two articles [in the *Metropolitan Magazine*, wrote Walter Lippmann] are undoubtedly the finest reporting that's ever been done. Its kind of embarrassing to tell a fellow you know that he's a genius... I can't begin to tell you how good the articles are. If you keep it up we'll all be able to sit comfortably at home and know all that we

wanted to know. That's the only immoral thing about your work. You make it unnecessary for the rest of us to stir. You have perfect eyes, and your power of telling leaves nothing to be desired.... Incidentally, of course, the stories are literature, but I didn't realize that till afterwards, they were so much alive with Mexico and with you.[29]

Edgcumb Pinchon, who was in Mexico during the revolution, enthusiastically praised the 'emotionalism' of Reed's articles: '[w]here, as in your own work, it is superbly artistic and sane, I cannot get too much of it...'.[30]

His ambition to affect events kept pace with his growing reputation. He applied on 4 June through an intermediary to be given an interview with the President, who was surprised at the unanimous opposition in Mexico to the occupation at Veracruz, and who was shocked by the vehemence of the worldwide denunciation of American policy. 'I do not think the various moves of the Administration with regard to Mexico are at all understood, even in the United States', he wrote, and proposed to give the President an opportunity to explain American policy, his thoughts about the desirability of peace, the inside story of the non-recognition of Huerta and other issues. 'I have an idea that it [the President's policy] is a pretty careful, well-thought-out plan.' He proposed to publish an account of the interview in a magazine, and wanted to devote an introductory chapter to *Insurgent Mexico* 'to put over the Administration's point of view'.[31] He may have had other thoughts about the administration policy, best kept out of such a letter. Indeed, Reed thought he could show President Wilson that the official sources of information about Villa were inadequate, and hoped that the President could be persuaded to change the course of intervention or stop it altogether. Steffens wrote encouragingly to Reed about the proposed interview with the President:

'[t]he idea back of his Mexico policy isn't yet doing its best work among the people, and you could put it to work, if you could have your talk with him and put out his idea in a wrapping of your observations and experiences. But the only way to do that; to get him to see it, is to have a conversation with him yourself and not show him, but let him see it'.[32]

Reed listened, perhaps with some inward scepticism, as Wilson explained on 16 June that the landing at Veracruz was designed to check Huerta's provocations and to strengthen the Mexican will to resist the dictator. But he was happier to hear Wilson reject in forthright terms any interference in Mexican internal affairs. Reed was impressed by the President's evident goodwill towards the Mexican people, but was a little shocked at what seemed to him the President's simplistic view of the problems raised by the Mexican revolution. The White House was alarmed at the text of Reed's article, and Wilson wrote to him requesting that the final text be based solely upon Reed's thinking. Reed wrote and rewrote an article to convey the gist of the American leader's thoughts. But the President did not wish to be quoted.[33] He sent a copy of the revised text to the President on 27 June, and a further revision on 30 June, but by this time the White House was having second thoughts about the article altogether, and the editors of the *Metropolitan* were growing increasingly restless. The final draft of the interview was flat from over-writing and seemed to lack newsworthiness.[34] The failure of his interview with the President somewhat tempered his enjoyment of the summer, but his articles on Mexico and on the Ludlow massacre, and the prospect of the publication in September of *Insurgent Mexico* kept Reed buoyant and optimistic.

His summer was interrupted in late July by a cable from Carl Hovey, managing editor of the *Metropolitan*, telling him to hold himself in readiness for a trip to France. Hovey offered Reed $500 a month, plus expenses. The assassination of the Austrian Archduke Franz Ferdinand on 28 June in the Bosnian capital of Sarajevo led to a diplomatic crisis which was resolved only when the Germans declared war on France in early August and sent their army marching into Belgium. In Provincetown, the outbreak of war stunned the regulars. Floyd Dell recalled that '[n]obody knew what to think, what to hope for, or what to fear. Minds, trying hard to think, were dazed.'[35] 'It was personal and impersonal', wrote Hutchins Hapgood of the week when war broke out, 'a turmoil from within as well as from without. Where was our propaganda now? What part had our ideas held with reality? Where were we? What were we?'[36] Fred Boyd, a 'shy, dry, colourless, narrow-faced, brilliantly rational little Britisher', as Eastman recalled him, and who gave Reed his first touch of 'hard Marxian *mentalness*',[37] proposed an immediate conference of intellectuals at Provincetown for the purpose of drawing up a statement to the working class which would reveal the economic cause of the war and thus nip it in the bud. The IWW poet Joe O'Carroll, the anarchist Hippolyte Havel, Max Eastman, Hapgood, Mary Heaton Vorse and others met and argued the fate of the world. 'Immersed in whisky and wisdom', as Hapgood recalled, the evening ended in black comedy and mayhem: O'Carroll tried to commit suicide, Havel had to be restrained from attacking his mistress, Polly Holliday, and Boyd got hold of a revolver and threatened to impose universal peace.[38]

Reed's friends and Harvard contemporaries suggest something of the diversity of responses to the war. Reed's relations with Edward Eyre Hunt and Alan Seeger reflected different sides of his personality. Seeger was a bohemian and a poet; Hunt was a high achiever, a radical, President of the *Harvard Monthly* and a writer of considerable talent. When war broke out Hunt immediately sailed to Rotterdam, and then went on to Berlin where he interviewed two leading German Marxists, Karl Liebknecht and Karl Kautsky. He then went to Belgium, and was present in Antwerp during the German bombardment and occupation. He crossed the border into Holland , and returned to Belgium again in late November 1914. Shocked by the collapse of the Belgian economy, and by the extent of hardship, Hunt joined the staff of the Committee for the Relief of Belgium (CRB), under the leadership of the American ambassador, Brand Whitlock. He was appointed American Delegate in charge of the Province of Antwerp, where he was legal owner for all supplies which entered the province. Hunt conducted surveys of need for some 1 million noncombatants, and, despite increasing tension with the German authorities, sustained them throughout the first grim winter of military occupation. In the late spring of 1915 he returned to America to strengthen charitable support for the CRB. Hunt represented the finest expression of the practical idealism of Harvard men, which reached its fullest flowering in the Norton-Harjes volunteer ambulance corps which later included John Dos Passos and E. E. Cummings. Seeger had lived in Paris after leaving Harvard. While Reed had been in Paterson, created the Strike Pageant, travelled with *La Tropa,* met Pancho Villa and visited Ludlow, Seeger had written romantic poetry and enjoyed the gay irresponsibility of *la vie bohème.* The prospect of a general European war appealed to Seeger. Since Harvard his imagination had been fired by dreams of chivalry and knighthood, and by a dream of warfare in the service of Right as the ultimate experience life had to offer. Without hesitation he joined his friends, Americans in Paris who were not yet ready to chase the Almighty Dollar, when they volunteered for military service in France. At the end of August, when the first contingent of American volunteers marched from the Place du Palais Royal to the Gare St-Lazare, to board a train which would take them to training camp, Seeger was at the head of the column, proudly carrying a large American flag. Onlookers applauded and cried out *'Vive les américains! Vive les brave gens'*.[39] 'I am happy', he wrote to his mother in October, when his unit of the French Foreign Legion was ordered to the Front, 'and full of excitement over the wonderful days ahead.'[40] Even in the midst of active service in the trenches Seeger dreamed of heroic triumphs, and of leading glorious advances through enemy lines, and wrote poems which celebrated his feeling that life had at last given him a glorious purpose. (He died on 4 July 1916, in a French attack supporting the British offensive on the Somme.)

Reed saw the war in somewhat different terms. In early August he wrote an unsigned article for the September issue of the *Masses* ('The Traders' War'). He, or Eastman, already sensed that such views were going to be deeply unpopular. The commission for the *Metropolitan*, which was perceptibly moving to the right in its politics, made it unwise for Reed to say publicly what he so strongly felt, that the war was not a struggle between 'the White Knight of Modern Democracy' and 'the Unspeakably Vile Monster of Medieval Militarism'. He felt that the American press, which largely took its news from reports coming out of France and Britain, was distorting the true nature of the conflict. The behaviour of the press during the strike at Paterson in 1913, and the lies printed about the Ludlow massacre in the preceding spring, left him with few illusions. Once the British cut the cables which carried German communications to the United States, Britain effectively controlled the way the war was reported in the American press – through censorship, and through the aid offered to American correspondents in Britain by the Neutral Press Committee, the News Department of the Foreign Office and Wellington House, the body given responsibility for British propaganda in 1914.[41] Reed saw the war emerging from imperialist commercial rivalries among the European powers, and freely described in 'The Traders' War' the blocking of German economic expansion by the British and the French. 'German Capitalists want more profits. English and French Capitalists want it all.' He accepted the view that the Germans were being smothered by their rivals, and that they became militaristic because they felt they were being menaced.

Reed voiced some of the commonplace arguments within the American socialist movement, which had little political or cultural sympathy for Britain. But he tried to counter-balance his greater instinctive sympathy for the German predicament by a powerful denunciation of Hohenzollern tyranny, reactionary policies and 'brutalizing ideals'. The British seemed to him hypocrites, mouthing pacific sentiments while acting in an aggressive manner towards their rival. Reed found their sanctimoniousness hard to swallow. The war, as he saw it in the first weeks of August 1914, was 'a falling out among commercial rivals'. All the talk about high ideals was so much 'editorial buncombe'. He ended the article with what was probably the most frequently quoted sentence he ever wrote: 'This is not Our War.'

Mabel Dodge set off for Italy while Reed travelled to Portland to visit his mother. He was fêted as a local boy made good. But Portland was boring, and he deliberately chose to annoy his hosts when asked to give a talk. He spoke of the war in terms of economic manipulation and rivalry, a message more likely to receive a sympathetic hearing at the IWW Hall, where Reed had gone to hear a lecture by Emma Goldman. He found his mother as loving as ever, but unable to understand the position he was taking on the war. Reed travelled from Portland to Washington, where he prevailed upon Secretary Bryan to provide him with letters of introduction to United States consular and diplomatic officers in Europe. The Germans declared war on France on 3 August. Eleven days later Reed sailed for Italy. It was widely expected in America that Italy would quickly join the war on the side of Germany and Austria-Hungary, but when Reed arrived in late August the political situation was deeply confused. (It was only when the Austrian Army attacked Serbia on 7 October that the Italians declared their neutrality.) Mabel Dodge met Reed at Naples, from where they travelled to Geneva, and then on to Paris. They had travelled from France down to Italy in 1913. Retracing their route, in the other direction, the change in their relationship was striking. They felt uneasy with each other. Dodge was depressed and withdrawn. His worldly success in Mexico convinced her that Reed's need for excitement and the challenge of external events could not be restrained. She understood now that she could never wholly possess him. The tension between them, which had once made her feel alive and joyous, now left her feeling hostile and distant.[42] Reed's health was poor, and what he saw in Europe, combined with the deterioration of his relationship with Dodge, plunged him into a personal and professional crisis. The brilliant successes of the first half of 1914 left him unprepared for the swiftness of the demoralisation which followed his arrival in Europe.

In part the problem was simply that France was not Mexico. The easy and informal contact he made with Villa, the experiences he had while travelling with *La Tropa*, and the instinctive feeling he had that the Mexican revolution emerged out of what was good in the people, had no parallel in France. Even Richard Harding Davis, *persona grata* on so many military campaigns, was maddened by the official attitude towards war correspondents. With every army they seemed 'as popular as a floating mine':

> The hand of every one is against him. 'Keep out! This means you!' is the way they greet him.... You knew you had no wish to pry into military secrets: you knew that toward the allied armies you felt only admiration – that you only wanted to help. But no one else knew that; or cared. Every hundred yards you were halted, cross-examined, searched, put through a third-degree. It was senseless, silly and humiliating.[43]

The Allied armies' tight control of news, radical restrictions upon the movement of journalists and their exclusion from the war zone, left Reed, and every other reporter, continually obstructed and harassed by military police. He achieved his greatest successes in Mexico when he could talk easily and informally with soldiers and *pacificos*. It was as though France in September 1914 was designed to prevent people like John Reed from working at all.

He was determined not to be one of those 'war correspondents' to be found mainly at the bar of the Ritz. Reed tried, on 9 September, at the height of the first battle of the Marne, to break out of the bureaucratic prison and see the battlefield. Along with Robert Dunn, representing the *New York Evening Post*, he obtained a medical pass to travel to Nice, and left Paris in a rented car. They soon turned east and then north, before sending the car back to Paris. They saw destruction, and something of the confusion of warfare on a scale which was new to Europe, but the practical difficulties of travelling in the war zone caused Reed and Dunn to appeal for help from a British field headquarters. They were turned over to the French gendarmerie on 10 September and taken in a train carrying German prisoners of war to Tours, where they were interrogated and made to sign an oath promising never to enter the military zone again without permission. In October he tried once again to see the war at first hand. He went on a walking tour of the Marne battlefields between Esternay and Sezanne with Fred Boyd and Andrew Dasburg. But they were repeatedly interrogated by police and military authorities and had their passports stamped with a warning that if they were found in a military zone again they would receive two years' imprisonment.

Such experiences were not uncommon for energetic young war correspondents in France in August and September.[44] The restrictions upon the movements of journalists were so tight that they threatened to dampen support for the Allies. 'I realize perfectly that it would be criminal to permit correspondents to act as they acted as late as our own Spanish War', wrote Theodore Roosevelt to Sir Edward Gray, British Foreign Secretary,

> but as a layman, I feel sure that there has been a good deal of work of this kind of which I have spoken in the way of censorship and

refusing the correspondents permission to go to the front, which has not been of the slightest military service to you, and which has had a very real effect in preventing any rallying of public opinion to you.[45]

Reed travelled with Mabel Dodge to London. In 'The Traders' War' his hostility to England was already evident, and nothing he saw in London changed his mind. He wrote a sharply argued thirty page article for the *Metropolitan* about England in wartime. He was trying to show American readers that the passionate pro-war enthusiasm of the British was confined mainly to the upper class. The people seemed to him largely without interest in the war, but the intense social pressures to enlist did much to foster the impression of a united country. The President of the *Metropolitan*, H. J. Whigham, was British and was deeply offended by Reed's article. Hovey, who thought it slightly less than Reed's best work, agreed to reject it. This was one of the first signs that the brilliant journalistic successes of his visit to Mexico were not going to be repeated.[46]

Reed angrily noted the docility of even the politically conscious working class. Socialists and pacifists in England were leading recruitment campaigns and bond sales. Everywhere it seemed to him that patriotism had swamped socialist internationalism. Cannier observers of the socialist movement than Reed were stunned by the rapidity with which the German socialists in the Reichstag voted for war credits on 4 August, and were followed by the British and the French, fellow signatories of the anti-war resolution of the Second International at Stuttgart in 1907. The extravagance of the language of the Stuttgart resolution, which endorsed the *possible* use of a general strike against war, was toned down at the Copenhagen Congress in 1910, but the threat of a general strike was widely regarded as the most potent weapon the working class had against war and militarism. There was a huge gap between the language of high-minded resolutions at international congresses and the behaviour of socialist leaders and their party rank and file in wartime. The war posed a moral challenge to the socialist movement in Europe from which it reeled into confusion and disarray. The Second International was dead. What Reed saw in France and England was a proletariat silenced and docile before the rampant forces of militarism, and intellectuals gone over to nationalism. It left him frustrated, angry and, in a surprising way, homeless.

As he saw things in Europe in 1914, there was no drama or heroism in the war. Soldiers were dying without glory or romance. The fighting on the Western Front was merely a form of mechanised annihilation. The war seemed to him to be ultimately meaningless, and he found himself unable to take sides, to make that investment of sympathy which had made his articles about Mexico and Ludlow so memorable. He found it hard to write the promised articles for the *Metropolitan*, and the struggle to write was intertwined with a deterioration of his relations with Mabel Dodge. They both wanted, at times, to believe in their love for each other. Despite renewed professions of their mutual devotion, when Dodge returned to New York directly from England he seemed relieved – and went off on an alcoholic and sexual binge which lasted for several months. Whores in France, and an affair with Freddie Lee, the wife of Arthur Lee, Andrew Dasburg's best friend and a sculptor Reed had known in the Village, failed to distract him from the breakdown of his world. Carl Hovey wrote reassuringly: the *Metropolitan* would be understanding, they were sure that he would produce the goods. Mabel Dodge summoned their mutual friends to a meeting at 23 Fifth Avenue to discuss Reed's new romance, which she regarded as an unmitigated disaster. She cabled Reed reassuringly that no matter what she would remain his friend, and would make no claims upon him. Steffens, after talking to Dodge and Carl Hovey, wrote to Reed a letter which mixed sympathy, reassurance and some good professional advice:

> I think you should tell us what you see and hear, just as you did in
> Mexico.... Your views on Mexico were not nearly so good as your
> descriptions and narrative. And that will be so for some years yet.
> You're not wise, Jack; not yet. But you certainly can see and you
> certainly can write.[47]

After returning to France with Fred Boyd, Reed decided to look
at the war from other side of the hill. In early December he
travelled through Switzerland to Berlin with Freddie Lee. He was
thinking of marrying her, and Lee, who was German, wanted to
introduce Reed to her family. But once they arrived in Berlin it was
broken off.[48] Once again Reed began to drink heavily and launched
himself into another affair. On 16 January he wrote to Hutchins
Hapgood: 'I'm still all smashed up, but have recovered the faculty
for getting drunk. Liberty's a damn sobering state' (Rosenstone,
Romantic Revolutionary, p. 198). While in Berlin he interviewed Karl
Liebknecht, whose vote against the second war loan in the
Reichstag on 2 December caused a worldwide sensation. Reed
admired Liebknecht, but, after seeing how the French, English and
German workers had responded to the war, he could not accept
Liebknecht's optimism about the European working class.[49] The
collapse of the Socialist International, Reed's professional frustrations, the roller-coaster of his relations with Mabel Dodge, and a
drunken procession of romances and sexual liaisons had somehow
become intertwined. The depression he felt about what had gone
wrong with his emotional life, and the tragedy of the European
proletariat, seemed all part of the same problem, the same smash-
up.

He repeatedly sought permission from the German authorities
for a visit to the front. In the second week in January a party of
Americans (including former Senator Albert Beveridge, Ernest
Poole and Robert Dunn) was taken to Lille to observe the German
occupation. Robert Dunn, correspondent for the *New York Evening
Post* had been with the Allies on the retreat from Mons in August

1914, and had travelled extensively in the Eastern Front before joining Reed on 12 January 1915 to get a closer look at trench warfare. They visited a quiet section of the Front. Reed was still dissatisfied, and requested to be allowed to see a more active sector. Accompanied by Dunn, he was taken to the Front south of Ypres, a very active sector indeed, where the full horrors of trench warfare were abundantly on display. He saw the corpses of French soldiers slowly sinking into the ooze, and came under heavy artillery fire. Their guide in the trenches, Lieutenant Riegel, asked if Dunn would like to 'do something'?

> 'Yes', we answered baldly. 'What?'
> For reply he took the Mauser from the fellow in the scooped place by us. The next moment it was in my hands, with the muzzle pointing through the eyehole atop the bank across that short and hellish space. Be it on my head, I did it, fired twice.

Dunn's first version of this incident implied that Reed, too, had fired, but the widespread condemnation of their behaviour produced a more contrite version in Dunn's memoir, *Five Fronts:On the Firing-Lines with the English, French, Austrian, German and Russian Troops* (1915), which exempted Reed from this act. Dunn's first indiscreet account later plagued Reed, and caused him great trouble later in the year.[50] By the time he sailed for New York in mid-January 1915, he knew that the high hopes of the previous August had been disappointed.

Hoping to reconstruct his relationship with Mabel Dodge, Reed found her living in a small cottage in Croton-on-Hudson, almost completely withdrawn from the artistic and political issues which had made her salon so exciting. He hoped to sweep her off her feet, but he found Dodge 'friendly but untouchable' (Rosenstone, *Romantic Revolutionary*, p. 203). Reed was apologetic about his love affairs in Europe, and then angrily complained at the way she remained coldly distant. Back in New York, he seemed to friends to be moody, sometimes aggressive; he began to write poetry again, for the first time since he had been so unhappy with Dodge in the summer of 1913. Steffens was worried at Reed's state of mind and begged Dodge to take him back. He was sure that she was good for him. Out of kindness, perhaps, she and Reed exchanged rings. But the hopes he had pinned upon a genuine reconciliation were illusory.

Other than for a brief visit to Philadelphia in mid-February, to cover the Billy Sunday revival for the *Metropolitan*, he settled down in New York to write. 'German France' and 'In the German Trenches' appeared in the *Metropolitan* in March and April 1915. Based upon his visit to Lille and to the Front at Ypres in January, they gave Hovey something to show for the magazine's commitment to Reed. Hovey was particularly enthusiastic about the latter article, which was one of the first detailed accounts of the experience of the trenches to appear in the American press. Hovey wrote that this article had a great impact upon reader:

> For the first time the actual ordeal of the soldier – the endurance of mud, monotony, desperate fatigue, the nerve strain of apocalyptic lighting and earth-shaking guns...all they had never known and scarcely guessed of the peculiar awfulness of the new kind of war – was flashed before them indelibly clear. The crushing indictment was the first of its kind. No longer was it possible for the stay-at-home who read it to dream of war as something clean and glorious, uplifting the sluggish spirit of man.[51]

Reed's articles in the *Masses*, especially 'Daughter of the Revolution' (February 1915), were among his best pieces about the moral quandries of the rebellious spirit. The daughter of the revolution is 'Marcelle', a Parisian whore with whom he and Fred Boyd spent an evening drinking and talking in a café. Marcelle accidentally mentioned that her grandfather, a stone mason, had been one of the Communards executed in 1871 at Père Lachaise cemetary. Boyd's interest was sharply aroused, and he egged her on to tell the story of her family. The more Marcelle denounced the idleness and trouble-making boisterousness of her grandfather and father (who continually got involved in strikes), the more delighted Boyd and Reed seemed to be. Her own yearning for joy and happiness, and desire for 'jewels, fine dresses, automobiles', brought Marcelle repeatedly into conflict with her father. To realise her own dream of freedom she left home, found a boyfriend and eventually became a whore. Marcelle remained in close contact with her brother – who was also a militant – but she was denounced by her father, and then one terrible morning, not recognising his daughter, he tried to proposition her. Boyd saw in her story the same revolutionary spirit, broadening out from generation to generation, and caught the irony that *her* search for liberty was unacceptable to her revolutionary father. But Marcelle declined his interpretation, agreeing with her father that what she had done was bad, and that women should not achieve liberty as she had done. 'Women must be – *respectable*', she said. Boyd sighed. The struggle for women's liberation would take at least another generation.

'Daughter of the Revolution' was an ironic sketch of the fate of the revolutionary spirit. Reed's next article, 'The Worst Thing in Europe', in the March issue of the *Masses*, revealed a duality in his feelings in early 1915. He felt a heavily qualified optimism about the long-term fate of the revolutionary spirit and a short-term pessimism and disillusionment about the events which followed the outbreak of war in 1914. The article attempts to assess the effects of militarism upon the people of Europe. Reed understood little of the 'veritable ecstasy of community' which the war brought, and unlike Alan Seeger, he was quite immune to the promised cure war offered to anomie and the overweening bourgeois spirit of materialism and mundane calculation.[52] The working classes throughout Europe, he wrote, had been seduced or coerced into supporting the war. Their leaders, with the exception of Liebknecht, justified their decision to trample upon every ideal of internationalism. He saw little reason to hope that the workers could act against war. The revolutionary scenario of the Second International, the great romance of proletarian revolution, seemed further and further away. Reed saw the German workers as being 'corrupted and coerced'. The English did not need coercion for, knowing their place, 'they obey of their own free will'. The spirit of militarism itself, its glorification of force and obedience, filled him with disgust:

> I hate soldiers [he wrote]. I hate to see a man with a bayonet fixed on his rifle, who can order me off the street. I hate to belong to an organization that is proud of obeying a caste of superior beings, that is proud of killing free ideas, so that it may the more efficiently kill human beings in cold blood. They will tell you that a conscript army is Democratic, because everybody has to serve; but they won't tell you that military service plants in your blood the germ of blind obedience, of blind irresponsibility, that it produces one class of Commanders in your state and your industries, and accustoms you to do what they tell you even in times of peace. ['The Worst Thing in Europe']

Everywhere the seeds were being planted for blind obedience and blood-lust. There was no meaningful answer to this world-historical disaster, except refraining from joining in. 'The Worst Thing in Europe' reinforces his message: this is not our war. 'Our' here refers, of course, to the American people. Reed's slogan directly addressed the aim of British pro-war propaganda in the United States, which was 'to establish the conviction in the minds of Americans that their interests and aspirations were directly involved in the Allies' cause'.[53] Reed's 'our' refers more specifically to those liberals, progressives, trade unionists and socialists who thought that their social and economic objectives could be harnessed to the turmoil and social change produced by the war. (Arthur M. Schlesinger wrote to John Spargo warmly supporting the latter's resignation from the Socialist Party in 1917: 'The times call imperiously for the marshalling of the liberals of the country for the purpose of making the war an instrument for the promotion of social justice and public ownership.'[54])

After he returned from Eastern Europe Reed published 'The World Well Lost' in the *Masses* (February 1916), a description of a Serbian socialist whose experience of war had shattered his hopes for reform. This bleak warning was directly aimed at the opportunists on the left who supported the war, and at those who saw the war bringing 'a very large installment' of socialism.

Barred from returning to France, Hovey sent Reed and Boardman Robinson to the Balkans. Nine years older than Reed, Robinson was born in Canada, had studied art in Paris and had worked as a social investigator in New York with the Association for Improving the Condition of the Poor. He became a political cartoonist for *Harper's Weekly* and the *New York Tribune*, and made frequent contributions to the *Masses*. He represented Uncle Sam in his *Cartoons on the War* (1915) either as an innocent bystander, bombarded by cannon balls (inflation) or else as being drawn from the path of neutrality by German—Americans towards a cloaked, haughty figure of Kaiser Wilhelm. Robinson, universally known as 'Mike', and his wife Sally, lived in Croton-on-Hudson, where Mabel Dodge had a cottage, and where Eastman, Dell and Reed were to buy houses. Hovey could not have picked a more congenial companion for Reed's second trip to Europe as a war correspondent. Mabel Dodge saw him off on the boat which was to carry them to Brindisi and then on to Salonika, their starting-off point for a planned three-month visit. Writing on board ship to his mother, he sounded enthusiastic. 'The Caucasus is something like Mexico, they say, and I'm sure I'll like the people. It will be great to get on a horse and ride over mountain passes where Genghis Khan invaded Europe.'[55]

The War in Eastern Europe was based upon what Reed saw while in the Balkans and Russia in 1915. It was largely written in

Bucharest, at the end of Reed's and Robinson's travels, and almost wholly without the benefit of his notes. Their hurried departure from Russia had resulted in the seizure of all of Reed's papers, and all of Robinson's drawings. They holed up in Bucharest and tried to reconstruct what had been taken from them, to fill in the missing the details, which would give the narrative some shape. Reed seems not to have worked very intensively on the manuscript. Tell-tale slips and repetitions survived into the final text, as well as references to the obviously journalistic origin of the enterprise. He allowed asides like 'I could write another article...' to remain.[56]

The story he has to tell is interesting, and some of the writing is remarkable. If taken simply as an autobiographical narrative, as a striking piece of war reporting, as superior travel literature, there is much to recommend *The War in Eastern Europe*. But to measure his achievement against the highest seriousness is to acknowledge that Reed did not possess an inwardness and psychological depth, a *need*, which would have transformed this book into a *Heart of Darkness* of the First World War. The elements for such a piece of writing are present. Reed's travels up country from Salonika, the Greek port, took him to Nish, the Serbian wartime capital, and then on to the Serbian Army headquarters at Kraguijevatz, the ruined, primitive Belgrade, the destroyed market town of Shabatz, the typhus hospital at Losnitza, and then culminated in the long horseback journey in the mountains to the summit of Goutchevo, where he saw the site of a vicious fifty-four day battle between the Austrians and Serbs. This was a journey into the darkest heart of darkness of the European continent, through a diseased land. Serbia was virtually in ruins. Everywhere he travelled Reed saw graves, cenotaphs, black flags, death notices and white crosses indicating deaths from typhus. 'It seemed as if this buoyant fertile land held nothing but death or the memorials of death' (*War*, p. 77). (Since this was the disease which killed Reed, some discrimination is appropriate: typhus, often confused with typhoid fever, shared some of the same symptoms. Typhus, which Reed contracted in the Caucasus in 1920, an infectious disease caused by bites of infected lice, has an incubation period of eight to fourteen days, followed by chills, fever, pains, a purplish rash and, sometimes, pneumonia. Typhoid fever is caused by bacteria taken into the body in food or water contaminated with faeces from a case of the disease or by a carrier. From five to fourteen days after infection there is fever, aching, a rash and haemorrhage of the intestine often causing fatal peritonitis.)

The country near Losnitza bore the signs of war and something more than war:

> We went slowly along a vast fertile plain, white with fruit orchards and green with tall grass and new foliage, between uncultivated fields rank with weeds, and past white houses blackened with fire. All this country had been burned, looted, and its people murdered. Not an ox was seen, and for miles not a man. We passed through little towns where grass grew in the streets and not a single human being lived. (*War*, p. 87)

This is the real wasteland – diseased, ruined, despoiled. Austrian shelling had reduced Belgrade to a shell, and Austrian atrocities were well documented and attested to everywhere he went. (While giving a lecture in Boston on 5 March, Reed had argued that the reports of atrocities were exaggerated and untrustworthy. He learned otherwise on the Eastern Front.) What artillery had not destroyed, the occupying Austrian soldiers wrecked.

In this stricken land, Reed was overwhelmed by the generosity of his hosts. In Shabatz, the postmaster, Matitch, and his wife, fed Reed and Robinson, toasted their health, and initiated them into the old Serbian ceremony of drinking with linked elbows, followed by an embrace, which made them *pobratim*, blood-brothers. It was a reduced version of the same rite of passage which admitted him as *compañero* to *La Tropa*.

When they reached the summit at Goutchevo, Reed came upon a vast killing field, a devastation which no American had seen since the Civil War battles at Antietam and Chancellorsville. 'Here and there', he wrote,

> both trenches merged into immense pits, forty feet around and fifty feet deep, where the enemy had undermined and dynamited them. The ground between was humped into irregular piles of earth. Looking closer, we saw a ghastly thing: from these little mounts protruded pieces of uniform, skulls with draggled hair, upon which shreds of flesh still hung; white bones with rotting hands at the end, bloody bones sticking from boots such as the soldiers wear. (*War*, p. 97)

As they walked across the battlefield, yet more horrors awaited them:

> We walked on the dead, so thick were they – sometimes our feet sank through into pits of rotting flesh, crunching bones. Little holes opened, leading deep down and swarming with gray maggots. [*War*, p. 98]

He ends the description of the visit to Goutchevo with a reflection that the streams which flowed down from the mountain carried the 'poison' of the 'rotting dead' to the Drina, Save, Danube and ultimately into the Black Sea. There is a powerful symbolism throughout his description of the journey, and a symbolic structure to give it meaning, yet one suspects that nothing within Reed was *deeply* touched by this scene. (He had written to Mabel Dodge, after his first visit to the European war, that he now felt 'immune from sin, sickness and death' [Rosenstone, *Romantic Revolutionary*, p. 214]). The description has not engaged certain depths of dread, or understanding, which the journey up from Salonika might have revealed. Even in 1915 readers of the *Metropolitan* would certainly have been shocked by such writing. Interpretations of the war in terms of heroism and fellowship required a softening of outline and harsh detail. Those who favoured American entry into the war understood that the 'hideous aspects' of war could be screened from public gaze. As Harold D. Lasswell ironically noted of the thinking of wartime propagandists: '[p]eople may be permitted to deplore war in the abstract, but they must not be encouraged to paint its horrors too vividly'.[57] Writers who were against the war searched for ways to emphasise its horrors; those who favoured it talked of patriotism, bravery and the comradeship of military life.

In the late spring of 1915 things looked quiet on the Serbian front. German and Austrian attentions were turned eastward, and on 2 May launched an offensive in Galicia, south of Cracow, which proved to be one of the greatest military victories of the war. Within six weeks the Germans had taken the great Russian fortress at Przemysl, and threatened to occupy Lemberg (Lwów). The Russian Army experienced something approaching wholesale collapse; there were unreplaced losses of 400,000 men.[58] Reed concluded that the Russian Front was likely to yield better opportunities for his reporting, and applied to the Russian Ambassador at Bucharest for permission to visit the front. He was told that such permissions were only to be had from Petrograd. Other correspondents told him that no passes were being issued. A little private enterprise seemed appropriate. The United States legation had provided him with a list of its nationals in Bucovina and Galicia, and with this as a pretext he negotiated to have himself and Robinson smuggled across the border into Russian Bessarabia.

This was the Pale of Settlement, the westernmost territory of the Russian Empire, from Lithuania and eastern Poland south to the Ukraine and the Black Sea coast, where Jews were legally allowed to reside. Images of the *Ostjuden* which the photographer Roman Vishniac took in the 1930s inevitably have about them what Roland Barthes called a 'punctum', our knowledge that awaiting those Jews was the Final Solution.[59] Reed, with no such foreknowledge, wrote plainly that he found the Jews he met in a degraded, horrible state. He wrote with a lack of sentimentality which could easily be mistaken for anti-Semitism:

> And always Jews, Jews, Jews: bowed, thin men in rusty derbies and greasy long coats, with stringy beards and crafty, desperate eyes, cringing from police, soldiers and priests, and snarling at the peasants – a hunted people, made hateful by extortion and abuse, by murderous competition in the foul, overcrowded cities of the Pale. Excitable, whining Jewesses in filthy wrappers and coarse wigs; venerable *ravs* and great scholars bent under the weight of virtuous years, with leather-bound tomes under their arms; sensitive-faced boys who passed repeating their lessons, on the way to the *heder* – a race inbred and poisoned with its narrow learning, because it has been 'persecuted for righteousness' sake', and butchered in the streets by men whose banner was the Cross. Jews impregnated the mass – the air smelled of Jews [*War*, pp. 123-4]

Reed knew the lower East Side in New York, whose teeming numbers and squalid environment stunned even well-meaning observers of the city, but nothing had prepared him for the degradation he saw in the Pale. Visiting the ghetto at Rovno, he saw 'people who smiled deprecatingly and hatefully when you looked at them, who stepped into the street to let Gentiles past'. There were many indications of Russian hatred for the Jews, and of the deportations, persecution and pogroms. Reed found it easy to understand why Jews felt no loyalty to the Tsarist regime.

He spent the entire time of his stay in Russia looking for an authority which would give him permission to visit the front. At every stage he was passed on from one level of army bureaucracy to another: he was sent from Novo Sielitza to Zelezchik, on the Dniester river, where the local army commander put him on a train for Tarnopol. The speed of the German advance had caught these rear-echelon garrisons by surprise, and the commanding officers were anxious to get unwanted visitors out of the way. From Tarnopol they were sent to Lwów to request the permission of the

Governor-General of Galicia. The approaching German Army had clearly unsettled the garrison, which Reed found in a state of utter disorganisation. He was advised either to go to Petrograd, and seek through his Ambassador the Grand Duke's permission to visit the Front, or to go to Cholm, to the headquarters of the Commander-in-Chief of the South-West Front. They chose the latter, stopping at Rovno along the way. The location of the HQ was a military secret, and the unannounced arrival of a foreign correspondent was viewed with the utmost suspicion. Jews in the military zone had been accused of treason and deported. The nerves of senior staff were at breaking point in June as the full, inexorable nature of the military collapse unfolded.

Arthur Ransome, correspondent for the *Daily News*, recalled that as Russian military fortunes declined on the Eastern Front, war correspondents 'were hampered in every way and had to make shift as best they could'. It was not until March 1916 when he received his first, limited permission to visit the Russian Front.[60] There was another reason behind the Russian response to Reed's and Robinson's presence. In March 1915 Colonel S. N. Miasoedov, a Jew serving in counter-intelligence on the North-western Front, was convicted and hanged for espionage. His judicial murder (for there was no evidence to sustain the charge of treason) directly led to the fall in July of the Minister of War, V. A. Sukhomlinov, who was Miasoedov's patron. The suspicion that traitors and spies were to blame for the military disasters of the first year of the war led to Sukhomlinov's subsequent arrest. Reed and Robinson came under immediate suspicion in such an atmosphere.

When they arrived at Cholm and asked permission to go to the Front, they were settled in a hotel, told to cable the Grand Duke – a mere matter of several hours, they were assured – and soon found themselves under close house arrest. They were held under suspicion of espionage, and probably would have been shot had not the American Embassy in Petrograd expressed some interest in their fate. After several weeks' incarceration Reed and Robinson were allowed to proceed to Petrograd, where they found that Ambassador George T. Marye had been convinced by the Russian accusations against them both. Reed was astonished and outraged. Although he found the staff at the Embassy 'frigidly unhelpful', they were comfortably established at a hotel where their rough corduroy breeches, Stetson hats and high boots attracted considerable attention. Reed was frustrated and ready to pick a fight with someone. The Ambassador seemed the best prospect, and his outrage grew ever more eloquent at the gentleman's repeated insistence that he could do nothing in the matter. They tried to escape across the border to Romania, but were returned under guard to Petrograd. Their every move was watched by plain-clothed spies. 'You can always tell a Russian detective', he told Negley Farson, 'because he wears a bowler hat like Charlie Chaplin, carries a little Charlie Chaplin cane, and wears patent leather shoes...'[61] Reed's dealings with Russian officialdom were profoundly unsuccessful. The Russians kept demanding that he leave the country by way of Vladivostok. It was only when Robinson appealed to the British Ambassador, Sir George Buchanan, that they were allowed to depart westwards into Romania. (Though he had lived in New York for many years, Robinson was still technically a British subject.) All of their papers were seized at Kiev.

Reed's Russian venture came close to total disaster. His high spirits, and the presence in Petrograd of Negley Farson, a businessman whom he had known in Greenwich Village before the war (and who was to be Reed's main informant on Russian political and military corruption), could not mask his hatred of the Tsarist regime and its stifling and petty bureaucratic character. The war was going badly ('One had an impression of vast forces hurled carelessly here and there, of indifference on a grand scale, of gigantic waste' [*War*, p. 159]), but despite the suffocating Tsarist oppression he sensed that 'mighty currents' were on the move. He was no prophet, and did not foresee the 1917 revolutions. The more Reed thought about what he had seen, the more intriguing the Russian problem became. His travels, as he readily admitted to friends back in America, had not given him more than a glimpse of such a vast country. And the disorganisation and corruption were such that he was sure no revolutionary spirit was to be expected. In part this was blamed on conscription (a theme Reed had developed in his article 'The Worst Thing in Europe'), but the phlegmatic nature of the Russian masses, their affection for the Tsar and the rotten bureaucracy each contributed significantly to draining away revolutionary energy. He suspected that if a revolution came from the war, it would emerge from seeds as yet invisible.[62] If anything, he thought that the corrupt, materialistic Romania was ripe for overthrow (*War*, p. 302). But there was something in the Russian crisis, a 'powerful, quiet menace, as yet vaguely defined' (*War*, p. 232), to which he responded. The pervasive corruption, the disorganisation and the repeated disasters of the first year of the war had produced a political crisis. The workers at the great Putilov factories in Petrograd went on strike in September. The Duma had been dissolved. But something in him reached out with sympathy and fellow feeling towards the Russian people. The Russian way of life unexpectedly appealed to him:

> it takes hold of the minds of men because it is the most comfortable, the most liberal way of life. Russian ideas are the most exhilarating, Russian thought the freest, Russian art the most exuberant; Russian food and drink are to me the best, and Russians themselves are, perhaps, the most interesting human beings that exist. (*War*, p. 210)

There were many things Reed admired in Serbia, Bulgaria and Romania, but he had never written so unqualifiedly of his admirations.

While Robinson worked on his drawings in Bucharest, Reed

travelled to the Turkish capital, Constantinople, in hopes that he might be allowed to visit the Front at Gallipoli, where the Allies had landed a strong force in late April. He found the Turks every bit as unhelpful as the Russians and soon rejoined Robinson in Bucarest. They returned to New York in October 1915.

4 New York 1916-1917

When he landed in New York in late 1915, Reed found a city whose emotional geography had subtly changed. He did not return to Mabel Dodge's comfortable home on Fifth Avenue, but went instead to his rooms in Washington Square. Since their final exchange of letters, Dodge had largely abandoned her interest in contemporary affairs. There were no more evenings spent arguing culture and politics at her salon. Dodge devoted more time to her life at Croton-on-Hudson, where aesthetic interests, '*la grande vie intérieure*' and a relationship with Maurice Sterne, a painter whom she subsequently married, were cultivated.

Reed worked on the manuscript of his book about the Balkans, and then went by train to spend Christmas with his mother in Portland. Since the death of C.J. the family had experienced severe financial problems. Reed sent his mother money as often and as generously as he could, but there was no obvious solution to Margaret Reed's problems. They did not get along well enough for Reed to bring her to the east coast to live with him. Visits, as often as he could manage, would be a help. His previous stays in Portland since leaving Harvard in 1910 had left Reed with a settled dislike of the city. 'It is awful beyond words', he wrote to Sally Robinson. The prospect of an extended visit, sorting out family finances, seemed akin to a living death, a 'suspended animation'.[1]

But he was soon writing to friends in Greenwich Village about a girl, a 'wild and brave and straight' creature who was 'graceful and lovely to look at'. Reed had met Louise Bryant Trullinger, the wife of a local dentist, and they had fallen head-over-heels in love.

Born Anna Louisa Mohan in 1885, her parents divorced when she was three, and she grew up with a step father, Sheridan Bryant, who was a railway conductor. She lived for some years in the Nevada desert with her grandparents, and was at various times a student at the University of Nevada and the University of Oregon, where she had a reputation for strong-willed independence and rebelliousness. In 1909 she secretly married a Portland dentist, Paul Trullinger, and tried to carve out a career for herself as a writer. She contributed poems to Alexander Berkman's anarchist journal, *Blast*, and to Emma Goldman's *Mother Earth*, and she sold subscriptions to the *Masses*. Bryant became something of a protégé of Colonel C. E. S. Wood (Indian-fighter, explorer, lawyer and poet) and Sara Bard Field, who later became Wood's second wife, thirty years his junior, and who was a crusading activist for equal suffrage and a poet in her own right. Wood's literary reputation encouraged a small liberal artistic crowd in Portland.

While he was growing up Reed had known the children of Wood's first marriage. His striking reputation as a journalist made the young artists and writers who had been encouraged by Wood anxious to meet him. Bryant had read his articles in the *Masses* and was perhaps half in love with Reed before they met. They shared an enthusiasm for the outdoor life, admired Emma Goldman (Bryant had written an article about Goldman's visit to Portland in the September 1915 issue of *Mother Earth*), were radically impatient with convention; and they shared a powerful sexual attraction. One note stands out in the enthusiastic descriptions of Bryant which he sent to friends: she was someone who '[r]efuses to be bound, or to bound...'[2] Those who knew the struggle he had waged against Mabel Dodge's possessiveness would have appreciated the significance of these words. In theory Greenwich Village believed in open relationships, in desires freely explored. But inevitably the Villagers' memoirs are filled with anecdotes which reveal the destructive effects of jealousy and sexual infidelity. Reed seldom felt the need to articulate the case for sexual liberation, but he acted upon it, and felt confident enough in his self-identity to want a woman who could share his need for sexual and emotional freedom. Dodge had sought to possess him while claiming for herself the sexual opportunities which came her way. Bryant agreed that what mattered between men and women was spontaneity and affection, not the legal contract of bourgeois marriage. She and Reed took sexual freedom literally to mean what it implied, and it was after his relationship with Bryant began that he spoke out in public on the subject of birth control.[3] Before Reed returned to New York, they arranged for Bryant to follow several weeks later.

She arrived in New York on 4 January, and went to live with Reed at 43 Washington Square South. He was intensely proud of his dark-haired, slender girl and took her to meet his friends – Steffens, Eastman, the Hapgoods and Robinsons; they drank at the Liberal Club and ate together at the Brevoort Hotel and at Polly Holliday's restaurant. Not everyone shared Reed's enthusiasm for Bryant, but she was a vivid, talkative, striking woman who made a strong impression on the Villagers.

With the arrival of Bryant the shape of Reed's life seemed to change. He had spent much of 1914 and 1915 away from New York, travelling and working; as his relations with Mabel Dodge flickered and then died altogether, he looked to the places he visited, the people he met, for community and sustenance. His experience of the European war had proved so disturbing, so disorienting, that Reed began to express in public some of the accumulated pessimism that he had begun to feel. 'The World Well Lost', his article about the Serbian artillery officer who lamented that 'I have lost my arguments, and I have lost my faith' (*Masses*, February 1916), was a warning about the war, which also contained hints of a deep tiredness on Reed's part. The pain and discomfort caused by his infected kidney during his rough travels in the Balkans persisted after his return. He came back to America worn-down and depressed. Falling in love with Bryant helped Reed to restore his emotional resilience. Although throughout 1916 he was as busy as ever, his journalistic activities came to be seen as something of a distraction from the relationship which was rapidly becoming the core of his emotional and creative life. He was twenty-eight, and had achieved a remarkable national reputation for his book on Mexico and his articles in the *Metropolitan* and *Masses*, but he wanted something more than the challenges offered to the war correspondent. Later in the year he bought two houses, a gesture which his relationship with Bryant made possible.

He had largely been out of touch with America during his travels in the Balkans. Reed returned to find a country being pushed into the European war. The sinking of the British liner *Lusitania* on 7 May 1915, with the loss of 785 passengers and 413 crew, including 128 American citizens, stunned the nation. President Wilson's desire for neutrality struggled against a public opinion, largely influenced by the pro-Allied slant of the press, in which influential groups – especially on the east coast – had become increasingly partisan in their denunciation of German atrocities, and regarded the unrestricted submarine campaign as final proof that the Germans threatened world civilisation. 'After May 7, 1915', wrote H. C. Peterson, 'German–American relations could be conducted only through the portholes of the *Lusitania*.'[4]

Those who had seen the war at first hand felt with particular force the strangeness of the situation. There was widespread agreement that the public did not want to go to war, yet advocates of preparedness, led by Theodore Roosevelt, campaigned up and down the country and seemed to be dominating the national debate. Those determined to preserve American neutrality struggled to be heard. On her return to New York in 1915, Mary Heaton Vorse wrote that '[a]ll that summer I was cut off from other people. I had a sense of a transparent barrier between me and them. I had had an awful experience which I was unable to communicate to anyone. It was as though I were living in a world of deaf people.'[5]

Reed shared her sense of alienation from the direction which propaganda seemed to be pushing public opinion. He was particularly incensed when Walter Lippmann criticised pacifists and defenders of American isolationism in the *New Republic* with the same effective scorn he had recently directed against Bill Haywood and the Wobblies in *Drift and Mastery*.[6] Here at least was someone who should know better. He wrote angrily denouncing Lippmann for selling out to the capitalists, financiers and the warmongers of Wall Street. Lippmann's reply challenged Reed's radical credentials:

> You may be able to create a reputation for yourself along that line with some people, but I have known you too long and I know too much about you. I watched you at college when a few of us were taking our chances. I saw you trying to climb into clubs and hang on to a position by your eyelids, and to tell you the truth, I have never taken your radicalism the least bit seriously. You are no more dangerous to the capitalist class in this country than a romantic guer[r]illa fighter.[7]

Lippmann declined to answer Reed's specific point, which was unfair (by the spring of 1916 Lippmann was assiduously pushing his colleagues on the *New Republic* away from their previous allegiance to Teddy Roosevelt and towards advocating the re-election of the President). But there was a prophetic element in Reed's attack, for within a year Lippmann had completely gone over to the side of intervention. Reed, who tended to forget his own support for Wilson in 1916, was delighted to have stung the austere Lippmann into such an outburst, and had the letter framed and put on display at 43 Washington Square South. Their sometimes uneasy friendship was patched up, but the European war was beginning to strain relations between American liberals and radicals.

In February Reed was sent by *Collier's* to accompany William

Jenning Bryan on a lecture tour in the south. He had some sympathy for Bryan, and gratitude for his help while still Secretary of State. (Bryan had resigned from Wilson's cabinet in June 1915 in the aftermath of the *Lusitania* crisis.) Reed wrote generously of Bryan's democratic instincts and the farseeing political positions he had advocated:

> whatever is said, Bryan has always been on the side of democracy. Remember that he was talking popular government twenty years ago and getting called 'anarchist' for it; remember that he advocated such things as the income tax, the popular election of senators, railroad regulation, low tariff, the destruction of private monopoly, and the initiative and referendum when such things were considered the dreams of an idiot.

The enormous cultural gap between the brightest spark of Greenwich Village and the 'great Commoner' precluded any but the most ironic response.[8] The article on Bryan, and an another piece he wrote in the early summer about the supporters of the Progressive Party, manipulated and betrayed by their great paladin Teddy Roosevelt, interestingly suggest the trend of Reed's politics. The old populist tradition, which since 1896 had been led in successive presidential campaigns by Bryan, and the progressive hopes for reform, embodied by Teddy Roosevelt in 1904 and again in 1912, seemed now, in the year of another presidential election, to have been finally eclipsed. The European war totally dominated American politics in 1916, and everything Reed had written since the war broke out in August 1914 drew him closer and closer to Woodrow Wilson.[9]

He had opposed the President's Mexican policy in the past, and was reminded again in March 1916 that the pressures for military intervention were still a powerful factor in the evolution of American policy. In January a gang of *Villistas* massacred seventeen American engineers in Chihuahua State, and on 9 March armed bandits crossed the border and raided Columbus, New Mexico. The response in Washington, taken against the context of a preparedness campaign led by Theodore Roosevelt, was to send General Pershing and a force of 6,000 men riding into Chihuahua to deal once and for all with Villa. Reed argued against intervention in the *New York American*, but the public demanded action and got it. Pershing's men rode up and down northern Mexico chasing Villa's shadow until late January 1917, and accomplished little except making more likely an armed conflict with the forces of Carranza. It was, as one historian remarked, 'a prolonged and famous fumble' which Reed anticipated and cautioned against.[10]

The War in Eastern Europe appeared in April 1916, but the public was rivetted by the titanic struggle on the Western Front around Verdun, and barely a thousand copies were sold. Reed, who hoped the book would improve his financial position, was disappointed, and was driven to hackwork to earn additional money. His friends in the Village, however much they argued about the war, and published impassioned anti-militarist cartoons in the *Masses*, were still in 1916 less interested in the distant noise of the conflict than with things which immediately concerned them – like the dire state of Broadway theatre. George Cram Cook, known as 'Jig', and his wife, the novelist and playwright Susan Glaspell, had written a play, *Suppressed Desires* which satirised Greenwich Village enthusiasm for Freudian psychoanalysis. When *Suppressed Desires*, and a play by Reed entitled *Freedom*, were turned down by the Washington Square Players, there was much discussion among their friends of the need for absolute freedom of artistic expression on the stage. The Washington Square Players were primarily interested in new developments in European theatre. For all his passionate classicism, Cook was anxious to encourage an indigenous and organic theatre in America. The Cooks staged a play reading in their living room and participated in the excited talk about new theatrical forms which would break away from the commercial demands of

Broadway and the 'European' preferences of the Washington Square Players.

In April Reed was invited to serve on the organising committee of the Labor Drama Association, which hoped to raise funds to put a professional theatre company into a slum high school in Brooklyn where they would perform plays for labour audiences. Since his schooldays at the Portland Academy Reed had been fascinated by the stage. He had written plays at Morristown and Harvard, and had worked on several plays since coming to New York. His response to the Labor Drama Association was bold and imaginative. He suggested that labour groups should be encouraged to create dramatised human documents of their struggles which, like the Paterson Strike Pageant, could be staged in New York each year on May Day. He was voted $600 to launch the idea, but he was out on his own with it and the plan collapsed. (Twenty years later, he would have been inundated by volunteers keen to work on such a project.)[11]

In early 1916 he met Eugene O'Neill, who had spent the previous year studying drama under Professor George Pierce Baker at Harvard. He was a hard-drinking, morose, handsome and rather romantic figure, who had sailed on a cattle ship to South America, been in a tuberculosis sanitorium, and whose closest friend, Terry Carlin, was a picturesque hobo and philosophic anarchist. O'Neill and Carlin drank at the Golden Swan, an Irish saloon – universally called the Hell Hole – at Fourth Street and Sixth Avenue. Reed encouraged O'Neill's literary work, and introduced him to Louise Bryant; they spent a lot of time together.

In search of an escape from the unbearable New York summer weather, the Villagers discovered Provincetown, a charming fishing village at the end of Cape Cod, as early as 1911.[12] By 1915, while Reed was travelling through the Balkans, the first great Village 'season' at Provincetown had taken place. When they went to Provincetown in May 1916 Reed and Bryant rented a cottage near the Cooks, Eastmans, Mary Vorse and the Hapgoods. They employed the argumentative Hippolyte Havel, the Swiss-born anarchist, editor of *The Revolutionary Almanac for the Year 1914*, and lover of Polly Holliday, as their cook. Reed could hardly resist inviting everyone they met to dinner, or to stay at their cottage, and he soon found it necessary to rent a room nearby to have the peace and quiet to work. (He had begun to write poems again, and thought of putting together a book of his best work; he also had given some thought to writing a novel; but the Villagers were passionate about drama, and Reed believed that was where his creative talents would flourish.) The arguments with Havel provided anecdotes for everyone. One evening, an exasperated Havel denounced Reed as a 'parlor socialist', to which he wittily replied by describing Havel as a 'kitchen anarchist'.[13] O'Neill and Carlin joined them.

In June Reed was sent to cover the political conventions in Chicago and St Louis. Wilson had no serious challenger at the Democratic convention, and Reed and Art Young, on assignment for the *Metropolitan*, spent much of their time in St. Louis staying with Orrick Johns and clowning around. 'Art would declaim in the manner of a Southern Senator, and Reed, a big, curly-haired kid wearing dark blue workman's shirts and the best tweeds, would comment on the wild appearance of the delegates, or tear into the fallacies of the windy monologues.'[14] The real political story of the summer was unfolding in Chicago, where the Republican Old Guard demanded the nomination of Charles Evans Hughes. The progressive Republicans, the Bull Moose Progressives who had supported Roosevelt in 1912, were determined to keep faith with their vision of domestic reform and wanted once more to run Roosevelt as their own candidate. If they could not force him on to the Republican ticket, they were determined to nominate him as an independent. Reed watched the convention managers delay the moment of formal nomination, as they waited to see who the

Republicans would select. At the last minute, in a famous betrayal, Roosevelt declined their nomination. The progressive Republicans were people like his father, respectable, well-meaning men and women

> from great cities and little towns, from villages and farms, from the deserts and the mountains and the cattle ranches, wherever the wind had carried to the ears of the poor and the oppressed that a leader and a mighty warrior had risen up to champion the Square Deal. The love of Teddy filled those people. Blind and exalted, they sang 'Onward Christian Soldiers!' and 'We Will Follow, Follow Teddy!' There was virility, enthusiasm, youth in that assembly; there were great fighters there, men who all their lives had given battle alone against frightful odds to right the wrongs of the sixty per cent. of the people who own five per cent of its wealth. These were not Revolutionists; for the most part they were people of little vision and no plan – merely ordinary men who were raw from the horrible injustice and oppression they saw on every side. Without a leader to express them, they were no good. We, Socialists and Revolutionists, laughed and sneered at the Progressives; we ridiculed their worship of a Personality; we derided their hysterical singing of Revival Hymns; but when I saw the Progressive Convention, I realized that among those delegates lay the hope of this country's peaceful evolution, and the material for heroes of the people.[15]

Lippmann had similar feelings about the Chicago conventions. 'To go from the Republican to the Progressive Convention was to find again the open generosity of a better America', he wrote in the *New Republic*. But he was harsher than Reed in his judgement about the Progressives. 'They have no creed, none whatever.'[16] Their blind worship of Roosevelt, and his cynical abandonment of their cause, made the Progressives objects of Reed's and Lippmann's pity, and also scorn. Reform needed something deeper, and more serious, as the 1916 presidential election was to demonstrate.

Reed was happy for O'Neill and Bryant to spend time together.

Ignoring the Provincetowners' tittle-tattle when the two spent hours sitting apart on the beach engrossed in conversation, he was supremely self-confident (and perhaps a little naive) in his love for Bryant. O'Neill, caught between his respect for Reed and a growing fascination with Bryant, looked at her, and spent hours in quiet talk, but he did nothing; something was clearly happening between them.

The big story of the summer was about the theatre. One evening, while 'Jig' Cook was moaning about the refusal of the Washington Square Players to perform his play, *Suppressed Desires*, Bobby Jones (designer of the Paterson strike pageant and other plays) suggested that they do the play themselves. There was a tumbled-down fish house at the end of a pier owned by Mary Heaton Vorse which Cook commandeered for a playhouse. He installed seating and a stage, and persuaded everyone to write brief plays which they could perform in the little playhouse. Reed's *Freedom* was an obvious choice. Bryant and Susan Glaspell were busy at work on plays of their own. O'Neill, who had a trunkfull of unperformed plays, was asked to submit something to make up the first bill. At an evening gathering he read them the text of *Bound East for Cardiff*, and the idea of a playhouse rooted in their own talents began to take on an exciting actuality.[17] Reed, Cook and O'Neill himself were in the cast of the first production of O'Neill's play on 15 July.

Life had grown very complicated for them all. Bryant was fascinated by the moody O'Neill, and told him that though she loved Reed, he was seriously ill, was going to have a serious operation, and that they were living together as brother and sister.[18] She implied that Reed knew of their involvement but would say nothing about it. O'Neill – uneasy at betraying a friend – was happy to believe what Bryant told him. It was convenient to do so. Did Reed in fact know? One night a drunken Fred Boyd appeared in Reed's and Bryant's bedroom with a pistol in his hand, vowing to kill O'Neill for what he had done to Reed. Boyd was calmed down, and the next day Reed went to O'Neill and told him to ignore any stories which he might hear about what had happened.[19] Perhaps sensing that Reed was in trouble, Mabel Dodge turned up at Provincetown but was firmly told by Reed that he was not interested in resuming their relationship.

While Reed was preoccupied with the Provincetown Players, the presidential campaign got underway. His friends were heavily involved in the effort to re-elect Wilson. In July Max Eastman joined a delegation from the American Union Against Militarism to call upon the President at the White House. They wished to express their unease at the drift in American policy towards preparedness and the increase in public expenditure on the armed forces. Eastman thought that the President handled their visit with consummate skill ('throughout the interview [Wilson] always referred to the Union Against Militarism as though he were a member of it'[20]), and though he deplored the way Wilson seemed to follow Roosevelt in emphasising the necessity for 'intense Americanism', he alone was the candidate who believed in the desirability of international enforcement of peace. It was a decisive edge, and Eastman became a leading left-wing supporter of the president. Norman Hapgood organised the Woodrow Wilson Independent League, a body specifically aimed at capturing independent and Bull Moose Republicans. Walter Lippmann took time out from his work for the *New Republic* to write speeches for Wilson. He also delivered campaign talks from the back of a truck in upstate New York.[21] George Creel, Reed's ally in the campaign to help the Colorado miners, wrote a campaign book, *Wilson and the Issues* (1916), and was busily organising a committee of publicists and authors who would do articles and pamphlets for the Democrats. Among his recruits were the stalwart muckrakers Ray Stannard Baker, Samuel Hopkins Adams, Lincoln Steffens, Ida Tarbell as well as Hapgood, Cook, Glaspell and Frederic Howe.[22]

Frank P. Walsh, who, as Chairman of the Presidential Commission on Industrial Relations in 1915, had made himself 'the tribune for the oppressed American worker' and who throughout the spring and summer of 1916 had collaborated with the American Union Against Militarism to rally public opposition to preparedness and the drift toward war, appealed for support for Wilson among the radicals.[23] Many socialists were more than ready to abandon their party's lacklustre candidate, Allan Benson, and support Wilson. Walsh even asked Emma Goldman to overcome on this one occasion her deep-seated objections to participation in politics. Goldman was not to be swayed. ('I left Walsh', she wrote, 'with a feeling of impatience at the credulity of this radically minded man.... It was additional proof to me of the political blindness and social muddle-headedness of American liberals.'[24])

The election posed many difficult paradoxes for radicals less extreme than Goldman. It was socialist understanding that power was based upon economic interests in capitalist society and not on individual personalities. But American labour and socialists saw Wilson as their best bet to keep the country out of the war. Radicals gagged at the fact that supporting the President involved supporting his party, with its corrupt urban machines and southern racist base. But many, swept up by the campaign, faced such a choice. While still a student at Columbia University, and too young to vote, Joseph Freeman became a 'boy orator' for Wilson. The future editor of the *New Masses* and member of the Communist Party was sent to speak for the President into working-class slums in Brooklyn, where he was heckled by radicals. He was willing to compromise with his socialism on behalf of 'the man who kept us out of the war', but when the Democratic Party district boss asked him to speak on behalf of regular Tammany Democrats – the sworn enemies of New York socialists – he was outraged and ashamed, and campaigned no more in that election.[25] Feminists were equally perplexed by the politics of the 1916 campaign. The

Republican candidate, Charles Evans Hughes, had been an enlightened Republican Governor of New York and seemed of the two candidates the most likely to support suffrage. But the Republicans were notoriously more bellicose. Feminists were faced with a choice between Hughes, who promised suffrage with war, or Wilson, who promised peace without suffrage.[26]

Reed accepted the torturous logic of the campaign: it was necessary to support Wilson to keep the country out of war. (Despite the presence of American troops under the command of Pershing on a punitive expedition against Villa in northern Mexico, Reed still saw the President as someone who would restrain intervention.[27]) He joined Creel's 'free gathering of volunteer writers' and his article 'Why I Am for Wilson' was widely syndicated in September. And with his very public adhesion to Wilson came an ill-tempered attack on the leadership of the Socialist Party as 'smug fakers'.[28]

Before leaving Provincetown the players discussed the idea, enthusiastically proposed by 'Jig' Cook, to do a season in New York. Reed liked the idea of keeping their ramshackle organisation intact, with a permanent group built around a core of two and a half dozen 'active members'. They decided to put Cook on a salary, to appoint a secretary-treasurer, and to create a formal structure of membership, dues and subscriptions. The anarchists were unhappy at the attempt to impose a structure upon a casual and improvisational enterprise. The Villagers had perhaps seen too many interesting ventures squandered by their enthusiasm for spontaneity. After the success of O'Neill's *Bound East for Cardiff* they were ready to make a more sustained statement of their collective values. Cook was sent to New York to find a theatre, and as the Villagers dispersed Reed and Louise Bryant bought a summer cottage in Truro, and then went to Croton-on-Hudson to stay with Sally and Mike Robinson. They decided to buy a cottage in Croton as well and found a tiny place, four rooms and an attic, at the foot of Mt Airy. The purchase was made in Bryant's name. Despite a summer regimen of swimming and long walks, Reed's health had continued to deteriorate throughout the summer; the prospect of a dangerous operation to remove a kidney made him anxious to put his affairs in order. Paul Trullinger obtained a divorce in the summer. When they came back to New York in early October, 'Jig' Cook had rented an old brownstone house at 139 MacDougall Street, one block south from Reed's apartment on Washington Square. The wall between the front and rear sitting rooms was removed. With careful planning they could squeeze in an audience of 140. With characteristic energy, Reed threw himself into the arrangements for the season. He made a deal with the Stage Society which guaranteed the Provincetown Players a sum of $1,600. The 400 members of the Society would have their choice of Sunday or Tuesday evening programmes, which left 450 seats to sell.[29] Requirements of the city laws prevented the seats being sold to the general public. They would have to be sold on a membership basis, for the whole season of eight bills, consisting of three plays, each of which would run for a week, and so buoyant was the mood in the Village about the enterprise that all seats were soon sold out. The first bill on 3 November consisted of Bryant's *The Game* (with Reed playing the figure of Death), O'Neill's *Bound East for Cardiff* and a play by Floyd Dell. A week later Reed and Bryant went to Peekskill and were quietly married. He had been ordered to Johns Hopkins Hospital in Baltimore on the 12 November for the operation, and he wanted Bryant to be his beneficiary. Bryant gave her age as twenty-six on the marriage certificate. She was thirty-one.

They could not afford for Bryant to remain in Baltimore while Reed had the operation, so she returned to New York. The day after, O'Neill moved into the apartment she shared with Reed. While writing letters proclaiming her ardent love for Reed, she was exploring a relationship with O'Neill. She seems not to have intended to leave Reed, and though she occasionally mentioned seeing O'Neill in New York she said nothing to upset Reed or to reveal her relationship with O'Neill. Her behaviour in November suggests that Reed did not know about the affair. He preferred to disbelieve the Villagers who sought to tell him otherwise. Bryant travelled down to Baltimore to be with Reed when the surgery took place on 22 November, and remained several days until he was out of danger. His recuperation proved to be a slower process than had been expected. The talk of nurses and doctors (who included Carl Binger, but nothing was said of Reed's snub at Harvard) led him to write a handful of short verse sketches on pain and the alienating technologies of medicine, and poems which showed that even in hospital he was sensitive to social snobbery and a lack of true human sympathy for the poor on the part of the staff.[30]

Reed was kept in hospital until mid-December. We get an interesting glimpse of Reed's reading from letters he sent to New York at this time: Fred Boyd commented that Reed's interests, as reflected in his library in Washington Square South, were 'almost entirely literary, with incursions into current matters of mines and militarism'. He ordered books from Brentanos by Benét (Stephen Vincent or William Rose: both had published volumes of verse in the preceding two years), Kreymborg, Wilde and John Addington Symonds.[31] His articles on political questions constituted only a part of the reality of Reed's life in 1916. His relationship with Bryant, involvement with the Provincetown Players, and his literary enthusiasms, were every bit as important.

Bryant packed up their possessions from the Washington Square apartment. They planned to live at their cottage at Croton-on-Hudson during his convalescence. Unexpectedly, Bryant's health began to deteriorate in December. She was examined by Dr 'Harry' Lorber, a doctor whose interest in the arts made him popular in the Village. Some of her friends suspected that she had had an abortion which had gone wrong. Bryant's biographers have argued that the symptoms of her illness in December were consonant with an infection in the uterus.[32] At Croton they slowly recuperated, and talked of making a trip to China for the *Metropolitan*.

President Wilson's 'peace without victory' address to the Senate on 22 January inevitably concentrated the public's attention on the prospects for peace in Europe. China was remote from the concerns of the hour, and Hovey and Whigham began to have second thoughts about Reed's proposed trip. He was banned from returning to France, and was obviously *persona non grata* in Russia; there was little he could do for the *Metropolitan* at that moment. Reed drafted an article on Samuel Gompers, crusty leader of the American Federation of Labor, but the criticisms he raucously voiced at Polly's or the Hell Hole had to be put in a coded form for the *Metropolitan*; the editors turned it down. 'Reed had become what he wished to be, the embodiment of rebellion against the course his country had chosen to follow', recalled Hovey.

> The vision that hovered before his eyes – the poet's instinctive dream of a world entirely better – could not be shared…by a publication widely read and with its feet on the ground of native soil. It was fine for Reed to hate war and say so. But the magazine could no longer be his platform; even if its editors saw with his eyes, which was not the case, it would merely mean the end, The *Metropolitan* would have been instantly, cheerfully, squelched.[33]

Reed had been paid $500 per article, but with the ending of his relations with the *Metropolitan* he now faced serious financial problems.

On 31 January the Germans announced that they were resuming the unrestricted use of submarines. Three days later Wilson broke off diplomatic relations. The country was boiling with alarm, and not a little enthusiasm, at the immediate prospect of war. Even the liberal press, which had extravagantly praised Wilson's peace-making efforts, now applauded his decisive response to the Germans.[34] Reed was out of sympathy with the major national magazines, and the radical press could not sustain a highly paid journalist. He found it increasingly hard to find topics to write about. A similar blockage like this in Europe in 1914 had plunged him into drunken despair. Now, in 1917, there were no more warmly encouraging letters from editors. He had been marginalised, and knew it. He pawned the watch which C. J. Reed had left him. Their cottage on the Cape was sold to Margaret Sanger.

Trotsky was in New York from mid-January to the end of April 1917 and at once joined the editorial board of *Novy Mir*, the Russian-language paper edited by Bukharin, Kollontai and Volodarsky, and which briefly included Alex Gumberg as business manager. Reed came to know them all in Petrograd, but like so many other native-born socialists he had little contact with the foreign-language federations (Russians, Germans, Finns, Letts, Jews) of the Socialist Party where Trotsky and the other Russian Bolsheviks campaigned.

Trotsky was agonised by the confused news in early March of an uprising in Petrograd. When reports began to appear in the American press from 16 March which confirmed the abdication of the Tsar, there was a widespread inclination in America to believe that the Revolution had been directed against traitorous pro-German elements in the Tsarist Court. The revolution, at first look, seemed to show strengthened Russian determination to pursue the war against Germany. Bombarded by requests from the *Call* and other socialist papers to explain the significance of the new government, Trotsky's confident assumption that the Bolsheviks would come to power was, he recalled, greeted with incredulity.[35] Reed, who had firm opinions about the nature of the Tsarist government, suggested in the *New York Tribune* that the radical trajectory of the revolution was likely to go further than 'the solid, respectable and conservative elements' who made up the provisional government of Prince Lvov anticipated.[36] But he said nothing about a possible role for the Bolsheviks in government. That astounding idea awaited him in Petrograd.

Opinion against the war strengthened on the American left, precisely when the drift of popular sentiment moved decisively in favour of intervention. Once again in the April *Masses* Reed rehearsed the arguments against war, but rarely had impassioned rhetoric been so emphatically swept aside. The war, he argued, would inevitably mean a curtailment of social and political freedom. An America at war would be 'less tolerant, less hospitable...':

> war means an ugly mob-madness, crucifying the truth-tellers, choking the artists, sidetracking reforms, revolutions, and the working of social forces. Already in America those citizens who oppose the entrance of their country into the European melée are called 'traitors'.[37]

Scarcely had these foreboding words been written than the *Los Angeles Times* published a cartoon in which the Kaiser was portrayed pinning a medal 'For Services Rendered' on the chest of Senator La Follette, who had led the Senate campaign against 'preparedness'. Charles Edward Russell, a war socialist, blamed La Follette and other anti-war senators for the fall of Riga to the Germans in early September.[38] Opposition to preparedness was tantamount to treason – and this was before America entered the war.

No President had struggled more doggedly against war, and none seemed to have had a sharper insight into its domestic consequences than Woodrow Wilson. On 1 April, the day before he was to make a declaration of war, he asked Frank Cobb, editor of the *World*, to come to the White House for a talk. Cobb arrived after midnight, finding the President in a deeply thoughtful mood:

> 'I think I know what war means...It would mean that we should lose our heads along with the rest and stop weighing right and wrong. It would mean that a majority of people in this hemisphere would go war-mad, quit thinking and devote their energies to destruction...'

He said when a war got going it was just war and there weren't two kinds of it. It required illiberalism at home to reinforce the men at the front. We couldn't fight Germany and maintain the ideals of Government that all thinking men shared. He said we would try it but it would be too much for us...

'Once lead this people into war and they'll forget there ever was such a thing as tolerance. To fight you must be brutal and ruthless, and the spirit of ruthless brutality will enter into the very fibre of our national life, infecting Congress, the courts, the policeman on the beat, the man in the street.' Conformity would be the only virtue, said the President, and every man who refused to conform would have to pay the penalty.

He thought the Constitution would not survive it; that free speech and the right of assembly would go. He said a nation couldn't put its strength into a war and keep its head level; it had never been done.[39]

Wilson understood every bit as clearly as Reed that the war would be a disaster for liberalism and progressive social ideals. But on the next day Wilson sent the United States into the war, and Reed, attending a People's Council meeting hastily called in Washington to express opposition to the President's declaration, shouted out: 'This is not my war, and I will not support it. This is not my war, and I will have nothing to do with it' (Hicks, *Reed*, p. 233).

The Emergency Convention of the Socialist Party met at Planters Hotel, St Louis, from 7 to 14 April. Feeling ran high against the war among the delegates, and a majority report of the War and Militarism Committee, drafted by Morris Hillquit and Charles E. Ruthenberg, leader of the left wing in the Ohio Socialist Party, proclaimed the party's 'unalterable opposition' to the war and outlined seven courses of action which socialists could take.[40] A minority report by John Spargo, whose sympathies had been with the Allies from the outbreak of war, supported the war and argued for collectivist measures by which it could be prosecuted. The minority report, supported by seven delegates in addition to

Spargo, began the great schism which nearly tore the party apart. Within weeks many of the most prominent intellectuals resigned from the party in opposition to the St Louis Proclamation. Simons joined the virulently patriotic Wisconsin Loyalty League. Charles Edward Russell, author of *Why I Am A Socialist* (1910), claimed that '... the Socialists who are opposed to the war are dirty traitors [who] should be driven out of the country...'[41] Allan Benson, the Socialist Party candidate for president in 1916, resigned from the party in 1917; as did W. J. Ghent, Upton Sinclair,[42] J. G. Phelps Stokes and Gustavus Myers. It was a larger gesture of protest and ultimately a more damaging one than the resignation of left-wing intellectuals in protest at the recall of Bill Haywood in 1912.[43] The bitterness engendered by these defections, and the damaging charges of pro-Germanism which they launched against those who remained in the party, soured relations on the American left and did horrendous damage to the party's credibility. Reed had never actually joined the Socialist Party, but since the Paterson strike he had been sharply critical of its right-wing leadership. Victor Berger and Morris Hillquit, whatever their failings in the eyes of their left-wing critics like Reed, at least did not succumb to the violent patriotism of the likes of Walling, Stokes and Simons.

It was a moment in the life of each American radical when despair seemed the only appropriate response. The unions, led by Gompers, were competing with each other to demonstrate their loyal support for the war. It seemed as though there was vocal enthusiasm for the war in every working-class district; miners in West Virginia outdid their neighbours in purchasing Liberty Bonds. But, as David Montgomery has pointed out, the ferocious suppression of dissent makes it hard to judge the true nature of the attitudes of the working class towards the war. Pacifists across the country were labelled pro-German, their offices and membership were raided by 'patriots'; and groups which had fought since 1914 to keep the country out of the war were denounced. They would soon be silenced altogether by the Post Office using powers granted to it by the Espionage Act which became law on 15 June. At the discretion of the Postmaster-General, pacifist, socialist and radical periodicals across the country were denied mailing privileges. Despite the barrage of publicity for the war, as the spring progressed it became clear that support for the war was somewhat less fervent in practice than the press suggested. It became necessary to bring in conscription, as much a way to foil Theodore Roosevelt's glory-hunting plan to organise a volunteer division as to provide the basis of a coherent manpower policy. Registration day was 5 June, made a festive occasion by local and state agencies. Afterwards, men attending lectures and meetings sponsored by radicals were required to show their Selective Service registration card or face criminal prosecution.

Reed was invited by George Creel to work for the Committee on Public Information, the body charged by the President with mobilising public opinion behind the administration's war policy, but it was inconceivable that he would accept. Out of financial necessity in late May he joined the staff of the *New York Mail*, a paper which had received secret subventions from the German government. The paper was not pro-German, and Reed found its editor, Dr Rumely, willing to send him on a wide range of assignments as a feature writer. He divided his time between Washington and New York.

His relations with Louise Bryant had become increasingly tense. As ever, Reed was casually unfaithful to her and thought little about it. Bryant, who had affairs with O'Neill and Andrew Dasburg, stormed out of their New York apartment on hearing from a third party about Reed's sexual involvement with another woman. She went to New London to stay with O'Neill. (Bryant had kept in touch with him during the winter, and had recommended his work to the editors of *Seven Arts* in the spring.[45]) O'Neill made little attempt to hide the fact that he still loved her. But Bryant sensed, again, that O'Neill's love was possessive, and the comparison with Reed's confident generosity made her even more unsettled. Reed felt guilty. It was *his* unfaithfulness, he wrote, which had caused them both such deep unhappiness. Bryant returned to New York only long enough to arrange credentials for a trip to Europe as a correspondent for the Bell Syndicate. Reed helped plan the trip, and used his contacts to the full on her behalf; he no longer could obtain such credentials for himself. While she was away Reed was busy with *Mail* features, and tended to stay away from his friends. He promised Bryant that he would remain sexually faithful. New York seemed a lonelier and more depressing place without Bryant, and a note of despair repeatedly surfaced in the letters he wrote to her in Europe in June and July. 'I realize how disappointed and cruelly disillusioned you have been. You thought you were getting a hero – and you only got a vicious little person who is fast losing any spark he may have had'.[46] The tone of self-abasement spilled over in a letter to Bryant on 5 July, which, as Rosenstone says, were 'the most self-revealing words he ever wrote':

> I think perhaps there's something terribly wrong about me – that I may be a little crazy, for I had a desire, once, just the other day, I can't tell you how awful, how wretched that made me feel – how I have looked into myself and tried to know why these things happen. I told you once, my darling, that this had all done something to me. It has, O it has. I am awfully tired a good deal of the time, lonely, and without much ambition or much incentive. I feel pretty dull and old. I don't know why all this is.
>
> But I know why it is that people run to vice when they feel loss – I know that – I can imagine it – I should do it.
>
> You see, my dearest lover, I was once a free person. I didn't depend on anything. I was as humanly independent as it is possible to be. Then along came women, and they set out deliberately, as they always instinctively do, to break that armor down, to make the artist a human being and dependent upon human beings. Well, they did it, and so

now without a mate I am half a man, and sterile. (Now, honey, there is no use denying this. It is true I'm not regretful for it – I'd rather be human than an artist.)

I am under repression a good deal of the time late years. I dare not let myself go. I feel that I am always on the verge of something monstrous. This is not as bad as it seems, dear – it is just that no one I love has ever been able to let me express myself fully, freely, and trust that expression.

I suppose you're right. I suppose it would wreck things to let nature take its course. I am perfectly convinced that this is so. And I am perfectly ready to admit that my nature is not to be trusted. You will remember that among other things I told you in Portland, I said that I had reached the limit of my fighting strength, and that one more combat would bust me. Well, it has. I've had four or five of these things that have worn you down. Still my darling, you've got to make up your mind to trust me to certain extent, or our life together will be a farce.

In other words, you've got to recognize the fact that I'm defective (if that is it) or at any rate different, and though I won't do anything you ask me not to, you must accept a difference in my feelings and thoughts.

It would be intolerable for both of us if you felt you had to direct and censor my thoughts, my actions, as you have in the past – as you did even in your letter telling me not to drink.[47]

This extraordinary letter sums up a relationship with Bryant which was in July 1917 a year and a half old. Its full meaning looks back to Reed's relationship with Mabel Dodge which began in 1913. Linking both relationships was a 'fall' from invulnerability they caused. Both women taught him to care – about themselves, and untimately about himself, in ways which he had not previously understood. Dodge and Bryant were repeatedly unfaithful to Reed, as he was to them, and both were unable to remain content with the freedom which they exercised. They had felt the need to 'direct and censor my thoughts, my actions'. They had made him 'human' but vulnerable, trapped in demands for sexual fidelity which denied his 'difference'. The letter to Bryant affirmed that he *had* remained faithful during her absence, but that it reduced him to deep depression. The price of repression was – as Greenwich Villagers had always proclaimed – frustration and unhappiness. How warmly Reed would have agreed with Freud, who wrote in 1908 that '[e]xperience shows that the majority of the people who make up our society are constitutionally unfit to face the task of abstinence'.[48]

The causes of his unhappiness during the summer of 1917 were as much political and professional as emotional. The depression he felt in Europe in 1914, caused by the war, the frustrations of wartime journalism, and his strained relations with Mabel Dodge, had come back. The woman in his life was new; the war seemed even closer and more threatening.

Mobs of soldiers and sailors broke up meetings called by Emma Goldman's and Alexander Berkman's No-Conscription League. Reed heard that a meeting planned by the League at Hunt's Point Palace in the Bronx was going to be broken up by soldiers. He tried to persuade the police to protect the meeting, but found them aggressively unwilling to do so. He rescued a young speaker from the mob that night.[49] Subsequently Goldman and Berkman were arrested and tried for conspiracy to obstruct the draft. Reed testified as a character witness at their trial, but the mood in court was vengeful. He felt 'despair' at the way the judge charged the jury: first amendment freedom of speech meant no more in his court than 'the right to do what nobody in power can possibly object to'.[50] They received maximum sentences of two years in prison and fines of $10,000. On another occasion, Reed attended an anti-conscription meeting with Waldo Frank (he had submitted an article on the war to Frank's magazine, *Seven Arts*) and was furious at the passivity and timidity of the masses. If only they fought back, if they really stood up to the mobs of soldiers, they

127

would have won.

The August issue of the *Masses* was one of the first victims of the Espionage Act. Acting upon advice from the Solicitor of the Post Office Department, the New York Postmaster declared the August issue unmailable. Legal manoeuvres kept up the editors' spirits throughout July, as did sympathetic replies from President Wilson to letters from Amos Pinchot and others; but it was soon obvious that in wartime the courts were not going to restrict the Postmaster-General's discretion to exclude from the mails anything which could interfere with the successful conduct of the war. Copies were sold by newsagents in New York, but to all intents and purposes the *Masses* had been suppressed by the government. Reed had remained a contributor to the magazine, but played only a minor role in the great editorial struggles of 1916 when the artists led by John Sloan rebelled against Eastman's control. Reed used the *Masses* to say the things, ill-advised in some respects, which could not be said in the mass-circulation magazines; it mattered to him as no other magazine was to do.

In July and August 1917 Reed wrote some of his strongest articles; it was as though he were settling accounts with the situation created by American entrance into the war. In 'Militarism at Play' in the August *Masses*, he gave an unforgettable impression of the 'ugly mob-madness' of wartime (which he predicted in April); in 'One Solid Month of Liberty' in the September issue, but which described the events of July, he made a survey of events nationwide. He drew conclusions from that terrible month, 'the blackest month for freemen our generation has known', which showed how sharply he had been radicalised by the entry of the United States into the war: 'in America law is merely the instrument for good or evil of the most powerful interest, and there are no Constitutional safeguards worth the powder to blow them to hell'.[51] In 'This Unpopular War' in the August *Seven Arts* Reed looked back to his visits to Europe in 1914 and in 1915, and the terrible things he had seen. Despite the many disasters of the war, he was not without hope. An instinctive internationalism had survived, as did the hope occasioned by the deep reservations the 'common man' in America had shown about the war. An 'endless chorus' of the press, churches, universities, banks and businesses swept these doubts aside. And yet, even if there was personal jeopardy in saying so, he insisted that the war to make the world safe for democracy was not popular, and was not being prosecuted in a democratic spirit. As a result of the publication of Reed's article, and a similar piece by Randolph Bourne earlier in the summer, *Seven Arts* lost its financial backing and ceased publication. Another door was closed to him in New York.

5 Petrograd 1917

Randolph Bourne wrote to Esther Cornell in September 1917:

> I seem to disagree on the war with every rational and benevolent person I meet.... I feel very much secluded from the world, very much out of touch with my times, except perhaps with the Bolsheviki. The magazines I write for die violent deaths, and all my thoughts seem unprintable.[1]

Reed, too was stunned, and nearly silenced, by the storm which swept the United States into the war. His career was in ruins, and he had become one of those 'irreconcilable radicals', as Bourne described them, 'wringing their hands among the debris, [who have] become the most despicable and impotent of men'.[2] The nightmare of domestic repression and imperialist war was, with the sole exception of Russia, everywhere triumphant. The Foreign Minister of the Provisional Government, Miliukov, announced in April that the Russians intended to persist in the war with Austria-Hungary and Germany, honour their alliances with the Western powers, and claim their share of the post-war settlement (Constantinople and the Straits). 'Occupying Constantinople as mere parasites', he proclaimed, 'and ruling by the sole force of conquest the Turks cannot, in opposition to the Russian aims, allege their national rights.'[3] In America pro-war sentiments were commonplace, although imperialist motives were seldom as frankly admitted; in Russia Miliukov was repudiated by the Petrograd Soviet of Workers' and Soldiers' Deputies, abandoned by his party (the Constitutional Democrats or Cadets) and bundled out of office.

The Russian revolution, which began with the backing of 'the solid, respectable conservative elements of the community', Reed wrote in March, now seemed to him to contain unexpected possibilities.[4] The successive coalition governments of Prince Lvov and Alexander Kerensky, the radical lawyer of the *Trudovik* group who succeeded Lvov as Prime Minister in July, remained wholeheartedly in favour of the war, but in Russia, alone among the combatants in 1917, public opinion seemed to be shifting. Reed apologised to the readers of the *Masses* in July for his sceptical description of the fall of the Tsar in March as effectively a 'middle-class revolution'.[5] With the departure of Miliukov he sensed that the revolution was picking up pace, and promised to be 'something grand, and simple, and human'.

The Russian revolution, of course, irrevocably changed Reed's life, but it was the United States in 1917 which we must keep firmly in mind as the events in Petrograd unfold. Every source of hope he detected in the Bolshevik Revolution was mentally accompanied by a counterweight of anger and disillusionment at events at home. (In this he led the way, as Stuart Rochester has suggested, in a journey from nullity and rage towards a radical political commitment typical of an influential fragment of his generation.[6]) On the American intervention in Mexico and the European war, President Wilson had been a paradoxical and frustrating source of hope. But in 1917 the tradition of Progressive reform was no more than a memory. For half a dozen years Reed had argued, with varying degrees of conviction, that America needed radical solutions to its problems. The betrayal, as he saw it, of President Wilson when he declared war; the use of espionage laws to suppress the civil liberties of those who opposed the war and the administration's conduct of affairs; the closing of radical papers across the country at the whim of the Postmaster-General; the violence of patriotic mobs against pacifist and radical meetings; attacks on editorial offices and union meeting halls; police harrassment of radicals; the illegal deportation of Wobblies in Bisbee, Arizona, and hundreds of other events left him profoundly pessimistic about American society, political institutions and parties.[7] On 5 September the FBI simultaneously raided IWW headquarters, local offices and the residences of known activists across the country. At the same time Frank Walsh, who had been Reed's ally in the fight against Rockefeller after the Ludlow massacre in 1914, and the left-wing socialist William English Walling, joined forces with Samuel Gompers and the 'war socialist' Charles Edward Russell to create an American Alliance for Labor and Democracy, which was endorsed and financed by Creel's Committee on Public Information. The main purpose of the Alliance was to prevent anti-war and anti-imperialist sentiment from infecting the labour movement. Everywhere Reed looked across the broad spectrum of progressive, liberal and radical opinion, he saw brave men corrupted, the struggle of radicalism betrayed.

By the time Bryant returned to New York from Europe in August 1917, Reed was convinced that the story of a lifetime was unfolding in Russia. He could obtain credentials from the *Call* but no money from the impoverished socialist daily paper. Eastman and Eugen Boissevain helped raise $2,000 for Reed's trip from a wealthy American radical. They sailed on the *United States* from New York to Halifax where the ship was searched for contraband and the passengers questioned by British officials. His letters of introduction from the American Socialist Party were carefully hidden beneath a carpet in his cabin. The fun-and-games of deceiving the police and security forces was becoming second nature for him. After disembarking at Christiania, they travelled by train across Norway and Sweden to Stockholm where they awaited the granting of visas by the Russian Consulate. Reed interviewed leaders of the abortive conference of socialists from all of the combatant nations scheduled for 25 June but which had been repeatedly postponed and then abandoned altogether. He sent several stories off to the *Masses*. On 10 September, the same day the news reached Stockholm of the fall of Riga to the Germans, Reed and Bryant received their visas and boarded the train which would carry them northward to Finland and on to Petrograd. At each successive stop the atmosphere in the train, and the behaviour of troops guarding the track, brought him closer to the drama of revolutionary social change. No one knew the fate of General Kornilov's march on Petrograd, or whether they would find the Russian capital in the grip of a military dictatorship. They heard rumours that Petrograd was in flames; that Kerensky had been murdered. But when they arrived, Petrograd was silent and dark, there were no Cossacks patrolling the streets and Kerensky was still in power.

He had been in Petrograd in the summer of 1915, and could see at once that material conditions in the city had deteriorated. There were fuel shortages, electricity cut-offs and even bread was rationed. Prices seemed frightfully high. Reed and Bryant found expensive rooms at the Hotel Angleterre, the 'old dump' where he and Robinson had stayed while they were under detention in 1915, and hurriedly began to write articles on everything they had seen. After a few days they found an apartment in a private house at 23 Troitskaya Ulitza. The conditions of wartime mail were such that Reed doubted whether all his dispatches would arrive (and he knew that long delays were inevitable), but he wrote to the Robinsons that they were busy. 'Have more stuff than I can write... We are in the middle of things, and believe me it's thrilling. There is so much dramatic to write that I don't know where to begin – but I'll have a tale to unfold if ever.... For color and terror and grandeur this makes Mexico look pale.'[8]

Reed and Bryant looked up old friends and acquaintances, Russian emigrants to America like Volodarsky, Shatov, Voskov and Reinstein who had returned to Petrograd after the March revolution. They brought Reed quickly into contact with the Bolsheviks and other radical groups within the Soviet; he could soon see for himself that real power lay with the Soviets, and not with the Provisional government. Steffens had talked to Reed about the Soviets when he had returned to America in July, after a visit to Russia, but it was not until he arrived in Petrograd that their significance became clear. In September the Central Executive Committee of the Soviets was still dominated by moderate socialists, active supporters of Kerensky and the Provisional government; but the far left-wing parties in the Soviets had regained much ground after the débacle in July – street riots which caused the Bolshevik Party to be banned and Lenin to go into hiding – and their violent hostility to the war and defence of the government against Kornilov had gained them increasing support in the nation. Reed wrote to Sally Robinson on 3 September that 'the Bolsheviki star steadily rises' and that the Soviets were 'the real government of Russia'.[9] Despite the military disaster of the Russian Army's July offensive in Galicia, American opinion was still hopeful that a democratic government, committed to the war, would be efficient and successful. And if Kerensky made too many concessions to the radicals and lacked the necessary leadership qualities, influential segments of American opinion had begun to speculate that a 'strong man' might be needed to keep Russia in the war.[10] The American Ambassador, David Francis, argued at conferences between the Allied Ambassadors that they should remain neutral in the conflict between Kerensky and Kornilov. And if the latter should succeed in overthrowing the Provisional government, Francis believed that 'it would not mean a restoration of the Monarchy, but merely a more vigorous prosecution of the war'.[11] Reed sensed in early September that initiative had passed from the hands of the Provisional government.

They soon met some of the English and American journalists in Petrograd (Arthur Ransome of the London *Daily News*, M. Philips

Price of the *Manchester Guardian*, Albert Rhys Williams of the *New York Evening Post*, Arno Dosch-Fleurot of the *New York World*, Gregory Yarros of the Associated Press and Bessie Beatty from the *San Francisco Bulletin)*, who were more than helpful to Reed and Bryant. Reed felt particularly comfortable with Williams. They had not known each other very well in New York; Williams's religious background (he had graduated from the Hartford Theological Seminary and was an ordained Congregational minister), and active work in urban social settlements, rather put him in a circle remote from Reed's friends on the *Masses*. But he soon found Williams someone who shared his enthusiasm for the Revolution in Russia, and who was every bit as hostile towards bureaucrats and conservatives as Reed. Williams had been in Paris when the war broke out. Like Reed in France, he was arrested as a spy by the German troops in Belgium; and his efforts to report the war were frustrated by the military authorities. He had one story (recounted in his memoir of the early days of the war, *In the Claws of the German Eagle* [1917]) which would certainly have delighted Reed. While in Ghent he met up with several war photographers. They found Belgian soldiers who willingly posed for hoax photographs of 'battle scenes' and then posed Williams as a German spy being executed by firing squad. The photograph appeared in the *Daily Mirror* in London. They drew the line at fake atrocity shots, despite intense pressure from editors for proof of the 'Boche' horrors. Williams had been in Russia since June 1917 and was able to tell Reed about the Root Mission (13 June–8 August 1917), sent by President Wilson to bolster the Russian war effort. Williams had seen the 'July Days', the violent street demonstrations which followed the failed offensive at the beginning of the month. He also spoke of the vast Russian countryside. A journey with Yanishev, one of the Russian-Americans, to Vladimir province; a steamer journey to Nizhni Novgorod; and then a journey through the Ukraine with Alex Gumberg, former business manager of *Novy Mir* in New York, gave Williams an authority on all things Russian which Reed gratefully accepted. Williams had attended the first All-Russian Congress of Soviet Deputies in June, and heard his message of fraternal greetings transformed into a clarion call for revolution by his translator. Reed soon found that he, too, was as sceptical as Williams of the flow of optimistic statements emerging from the American Embassy on the course of events. Williams was regarded with suspicion by the American authorities due to his overt sympathy for the Bolsheviks.

> I liked Reed [he later wrote]... for the very qualities that his pettifogging critics considered his faults, as well as for his accepted virtues. They were very engaging faults, if faults they were, and I responded to the very things in him that the humorless Walter Lippmann failed to understand. To the ham actor in him, to his ebullient pranks and antics and humor, I responded wholeheartedly; to Mr. Lippmann, the future authoritative apologist for the Republican party, they made him a playboy. Like him I did. Which is not to suggest that I had the remotest idea that John Reed would return home to help form a Communist party or would die within a few years, in Russia, as a Revolutionary martyr, and be buried beside the Kremlin wall.[12]

Reed and Bryant called at the American Embassy not long after arriving. The fact that he was a notorious radical (and had engaged in deeply improper activities in the German trenches in 1915) alerted the Ambassador. In a day or two Reed lost his wallet, and had it returned, minus the cash, by officials at the American Embassy who claimed it had been turned in to them. Reed believed it had been deliberately pick-pocketed. (Negley Farson strongly suspected that the Russian Secret Police, in conjunction with the American Embassy, had arranged for the lifting of Reed's wallet to get copies of letters he might have been carrying for prominent Bolsheviks.[13]) Reed's wallet contained a letter from Camille Huysmans, secretary of the Stockholm Conference, to the Hellano

Scandinavian Socialist Committee, and an injudicious letter to Sally Robinson in which Reed talked of the many opportunities there were to make money in Petrograd. 'After these disclosures', wrote Ambassador Francis, 'I naturally regarded Mr. Reed as a suspicious character and had him watched and his record and acts investigated.' He asked in a cable to Secretary of State Lansing for copies of Reed's and Shatov's records. Thus began the sustained government surveillance of Reed.

He soon casually confirmed the Ambassador's suspicions. Williams took him to a meeting on 30 September at the Cirque Moderne, where he shared a platform with Shatov, who had been an anarchist in New York and who in Petrograd was a Bolshevik militant. Before an audience of 6,000 Russian workers Reed protested at the imprisonment of Berkman and Goldman in New York. It was no more than he had done at home. When the Ambassador got wind of the meeting he sent an agent as his observer. Francis believed that Shatov and Reed were the source of a damaging story to appear in the Russian press that Berkman was likely to be extradicted to California to stand trial with Tom Mooney on a capital charge. One of his agents submitted a report of Reed's talk:

'the Bolsheviks are the only Party with a program. The other factions of the Socialistic Party are at sea in regards to a policy and program. Though the Russian workman has not reached the same high standard of efficiency of the American – he is farther advanced in politics and in political thought.' Says – 'That if the workmen were paid in proportion to their labor they would get all the profits. Instead of shutting down, the works should be compelled to furnish the material, or to turn the factories over to the workmen.' Was at the all-night session of the Democratic [Conference] meeting held in the Alexander Theater. Seemed to know all about what took place there.[14]

Reed visited the Vyborg slums with Williams. Sniffing the air, he remarked: 'I thought this was "feudal Russia". Smells more like

Pittsburgh to me. You talk to these Mensheviks and Social Revolutionaries and you get the idea that capitalism hasn't touched
Russia. How come?'[15]

At the Democratic Conference at the Alexandrinsky Theatre
Reed and Bryant heard the leading political figures of Petrograd.
They also attended sessions of the Duma, and the Council of the
Republic (or Pre-Parliament) which met in the hall of the Petrograd
City Duma and then at the Marinsky Palace. There was so much
to see, so many meetings to arrange, that they soon agreed to divide
their work. Bryant went faithfully to the Council of the Republic
at the Marinsky Palace, while Reed (whose boredom threshold for
the blather of bourgeois politicians was quite low) tried to look at
events outside Petrograd, and to do interviews.

He realised that American readers would want to know the state
of the Army. After the fall of Riga, Americans were asking if the
Russian Army was on the verge of disintegration and defeat. On
10 October he travelled with Williams and Reinstein to visit the
Estonian and Latvian Front. They found that the changes ushered
in by the revolution had transformed relations between soldiers
and their officers in the Twelfth Army. The soldiers had elected
a council, a Soviet, of their own not long after the March
Revolution which published a paper, arranged for their own
supplies and it was through the Soviet that the soldiers took part
in the political life of the country. They sent delegates to the Army
staff and to the All-Russian Soviet of Soldiers in Petrograd. In the
aftermath of the fall of Riga, the Soldiers' Soviet took operational
command of the troops. It alone was able to command their loyalty.
The officers, and the Soviet in Petrograd (which was still dominated
by moderate socialists like Chkheidze, who remained loyal to the
Coalition government) demanded that the war be prosecuted.
Reed was told that at first there was little Bolshevik sentiment
among the troops. The soldiers wanted peace and denounced
imperialism, but it was only after the attempted coup of Kornilov

in August that sentiment seemed to turn decisively against the war. Reed believed that the soldiers were now largely Bolshevik.

The brief visit to the Front taught Reed a great deal about what had happened in Russia. It showed him that ordinary soldiers were capable of autonomous self-organisation – an understanding which strengthened his sympathy for syndicalist solutions to American labour problems. The visit to the Front confirmed what Reed had heard in Petrograd that the Bolsheviks were gaining ground. He saw signs that the social revolution, the overturning of the monarchy, had begun to change social relations in the Army. The age-old Russian deference seemed to have vanished.

Not long after his return to Petrograd, Reed succeeded in arranging an interview with Kerensky. David Soskice, a Russian Social Democrat who had lived for years in English exile, and who had translated Miliukov's *Essais sur l'histoire de la civilisation Russe* into French in 1901, had been sent back to Russia to provide the *Manchester Guardian* with alternative perspectives upon the course of the Provisional government. The paper's principal correspondent, M. Philips Price, seemed to the *Guardian's* editor, C. P. Scott, to be too close to the Bolsheviks; he wanted someone in the Winter Palace with Kerensky. Soskice succeeded beyond Scott's wildest dreams when he became Kerensky's press secretary not long after he arrived in Petrograd in early August 1917. Reed had harsh things to say about Soskice, and resented his role in censoring cables to New York.[16] But, on 20 October, Soskice allowed Reed a brief interview with the beleaguered Prime Minister. He was immediately followed by a correspondent from the Associated Press, and to Reed's chagrin (he had long detested the anti-labour bias of the news agency) the AP man, Gregory Yarros, succeeded in provoking an undiplomatic explosion of resentment at what Kerensky saw as unfair criticism of the Russian war effort on the part of the Allies.

His command of Russian was slight, and he worked intensively on mastering written texts. Understanding the spoken language, especially in large public meetings where oratory was violent, was more difficult, and he needed help. Other journalists, especially Williams, provided him with running translations. Before long Reed could, more or less, get the hang of what was being said. This is particularly clear when Reed's first weeks in Petrograd are compared to Bessie Beatty's, the American journalist who arrived by way of the Trans-Siberian Express in early June 1917. Beatty knew virtually no Russian, and was unable to summon a taxi, or even to get food, until aided by a gallant army officer. In consequence, Beatty was far more dependent upon the official American community than Reed – an independence which his radicalism deepened into outright hostility. Beatty made no such enemies. Reed's languge skills, or more specifically, his lack of Russian, puzzled everyone. Williams, who heard Reed make his first address to roughly clad factory workers, said that he 'had picked up a bit of the language when he was in Russia with the artist Boardman Robinson in 1915... His pronunciation was, if anything, more atrocious than mine.' Bertram Wolfe, who knew Reed after his return to New York in 1918, recalled that Reed's knowledge of Russian was even sketchier than his Spanish. Hicks said that he had 'little difficulty' in finding out what was going on (p. 259). Theodore Draper wrote that in 1917 Reed knew no Russian at all. Sidney Hook said that Reed possessed a 'scanty' knowledge of the language. His lack of knowledge of the people and the Russian language puzzled even Krupskaya, Lenin's widow, who wrote a Foreword to a translation of *Ten Days That Shook the World* in 1925. In the eyes of sympathetic critics, Reed's lack of Russian was compensated for by his resourcefulness and persistence as a journalist. Hostile critics have used this as a means to discredit Reed by suggesting that he was fed information by his Bolshevik friends to be used for propaganda purposes in the United States.[17] The question is, in truth, unimportant. Reed mastered the Russian he needed; those who knew the language far better (like Philips Price and Williams) do not seem to have produced better books. He soon began to collect copies of Russian newspapers, and every poster, handbill, and pamphlet which appeared in a city awash with political posters, correctly recognising their documentary interest. And he assiduously collected a daily summary of press comment issued by the French Embassy. He had little time in Petrograd to have translated more than a fraction of this material. Since every correspondent was busy with the same attempt to document the rapidly shifting political climate, and Embassy personnel and bodies such as the Red Cross Mission were equally as concerned to keep abreast of developments, there was a lively trade in translations, and much cross-briefing between sympathetic journalists. Reed, Bryant, Williams and Beatty pooled resources, and sometimes informants.

Reed hurried across Petrograd with tremendous enthusiasm. As Williams recalled: 'Reed and I were going about in a state of intoxication mixed with bewilderment.'[18] He went to Sestroretzk to see a factory which was being run by its workers' Soviet. At a munitions factory in Petrograd he and Williams were invited to give fraternal greetings from the American proletariat to 10,000 workers. He interviewed Lianozov, a Russian oil magnate, and Burtsev, whose journal advocated a 'strong-man' dictatorship. There were many hints of counter-revolution and foreign intervention in their talk. He heard Kerensky's frantic denunciation of the Bolsheviks in the Council of the Republic. The rage of the bourgeoisie – which ostentatiously scorned Kerensky – and the bitter polarization of parties which reduced the Council of the Republic to impotence, left him convinced that the revolution was picking up pace.

The contrast between the Council of the Republic, ringing with the sterile manoeuvres of bourgeois parliamentarians, and the muddy, confused, ill-lit corridors and meeting rooms of the Smolny, several miles away from the centre of Petrograd, began to shape Reed's understanding of the revolution. He noted with a sharp journalist's eye the empty imperial grandeur of the Winter Palace, where Kerensky and the Ministers of the Provisional government were to be found; the Marinsky Palace, where the Council of the Republic met, fiercely divided between Cadet and socialist parties; and the Smolny, a beehive of activity where delegates from soldiers' and workers' Soviets met, and where the caucuses of the left-wing parties were in nearly continuous session. In the crowded corridors and restaurants in the Smolny, where Reed and Bryant regularly ate, they heard political talk, wild rumours and laughter. In the Smolny alone they felt the reality of the forces which were pushing Russia into revolution. And beyond, in Petrograd, they walked the long, elegant streets, ventured into the proletarian districts like the Vyborg, and noted how ordinary life continued in the cafés and private dining rooms in restaurants; they attended ballet (Reed and Bryant saw Karsavina dance). Theatre and opera flourished despite shortages and the war.

It became increasingly clear to Reed that this was *his* revolution. The old order which Kerensky desperately tried to reform was dying. Beyond the control of any party, a new force in the affairs of the world was being born. This was a change occuring in the dark masses of the people, who wanted an end to the war, and who wanted land and bread. Reed did not believe that the revolution was inevitable, or that events were being directed by the Bolsheviks. Better students of Marxian socialism than he believed that a bourgeois and capitalist revolution would have to occur in Russia before a proletarian revolution was possible. (Sukhanov, the editor of Maxim Gorky's newspaper *Novaya Zhizn,* whose diaries of 1917 are incomparably detailed and sharply observed, wrote that the Bolshevik seizure of power was made '*against* Marx, *against* scientific Socialism, *against* common sense, *against* the working class...'[19]) In a letter to Boardman Robinson at the end of October, which was published in the *New York Call* on 26 December, Reed wrote that no one single person 'understands and expresses the will of the Russian people'. It seemed no less possible to him that the generals would re-stage the Kornilov coup than the workers would seize power themselves. The belief he had expressed in the increasing popularity of the Bolsheviks, and the key role played by the Soviets, did not lead him to conclude that a revolution was consciously being planned. From what he saw, there was no single group capable of such an act. The whole tendency of such powerful defences of the Bolsheviks as Trotsky's *History of the Russian Revolution* was to show that the revolution was inevitable, and that it was planned and directed at crucial points by the far-sighted leadership of the Bolsheviks. Reed had no such knowledge on 29 October 1917.

Reed spent as much time as he could at Smolny, where he attended all-night sessions of the Petrograd Soviet and talked to leading Bolsheviks. Kamenev, pessimistic about the immediate prospects, told Reed he thought a Soviet government could only follow the forthcoming meeting of the All-Russian Congress of Soldiers' and Workers' Deputies on 7 November; they would have to await events until then. Karakhan, a prominent Armenian Bolshevik, once described by Radek as 'a donkey of classical beauty', was already thinking about the structure of the post-revolutionary government.[20] In an interview on 30 October, Trotsky dramatically told Reed that '[t]he Army is with us... It is the *lutte finale*'.[21] He was informed by Zalkind that there was to be a closed meeting of Bolsheviks on 3 November at Smolny. Volodarsky, 'a tall, pale youth with glasses and a bad complexion' (p. 36) who had been a militant within the International Ladies' Garment Workers' Union in Philadelphia before returning to Petrograd after the March 1917 revolution, gave Reed a detailed account of Lenin's call for the seizure of power no later than the 7 November (p. 56). But Reed must have got his dates muddled, for there was no meeting on the 3rd, and Lenin did not make a personal appearance at Smolny until late on 6 November.

On 6 November, the newspapers in Petrograd carried reports that the government had ordered the arrest of the leaders of the Military Revolutionary Committee (MRC) and the Soviet. Reed observed military preparations for the approaching conflict. Junker troops wheeled artillery into place before the General Staff building. Squads of armed soldiers and sailors were stopping private motor traffic in the street. It was wet and blustery, and Reed's shoes were soaked as he passed from group to group listening to their angry arguments in the street. He took a streetcar out to Smolny. The MRC was in continuous session. Messengers poured in and out. Trotsky was speaking at the Petrograd Soviet. Shatov told Reed that Kerensky had moved against two newspapers published by the Soviet, and that the MRC had ordered the Litovsky Regiment to re-take the offices and presses. It was a test of wills, a game of move and counter-move. Reed rushed back to the Marinsky Palace where he heard Kerensky's last address to the Council of the Republic, 'full of self-justification and bitter denunciation of his enemies'(pp. 63-5), and the coldly hostile replies from Gotz and Martov. At Smolny, he met M. Philips Price, who was covering the revolution for the *Manchester Guardian*. Reed attended the meeting of the Bolshevik caucus in room 18, and saw the meeting of the Central Executive Committee (CEC), the *Tsay-ee-kah* as he phonetically transcribed its initials, or TsIK in current usage of the Soviet. Things were going badly wrong for the Menshevik and Socialist Revolutionary Party leaders. Philips Price found them depressed at reports from the provinces which indicated that the Bolshevik call for the summoning of a second Congress of Soviets had met with a great response.[22] He heard Dan's bitter denunciation of the Bolsheviks, and a malicious, ironic reply by Trotsky. The Bolsheviks were in a decided minority on the old CEC and after listening to speeches against them by Liber and Martov they walked out. At 4 a.m. Reed saw Alex Gumberg's brother Zorin in the corridor at Smolny who told him. "'We're moving!'" (p. 73) Red Guards had taken control of the Telegraph Exchange and the State Bank. When he left Smolny early on 7 November, Reed looked back. The whole building was bright with lights. It seemed to hum 'like a gigantic hive' (p. 73).

By noon on 7 November Reed, Bryant and Williams were out again on the Nevsky Prospekt. It promised to be the best day of his life. (For Kerensky it was the worst: he discovered that he had been misled about the level of support for the government in the Army, and left the Winter Palace for Pskov at 11.30, determined to rally support among loyal troops.) The morning papers were uncertain whether or not a revolution was actually taking place. He heard rifle fire, and in front of the Marinsky Palace, where the Council of the Republic sat, soldiers were erecting a barricade. No one was sure from what direction trouble might come. Reed talked to sailors who told him that the Council had been dissolved that morning. A sailor had closed the session with a fatherly admonition: "'No more Council. Run along home now.'" (p. 77). The Winter Palace was heavily guarded, but there was no way to tell whether the troops were supporting the government or the Soviet. Reed bluffed his way in, learned that Kerensky had left and felt a cold silence in the vast spaces of the Palace. Out in the street, the crowds on the Nevsky frantically grabbed copies of newspapers. No one knew what was happening. Soldiers stood around, receiving contradictory orders.

They made the long journey out to Smolny at dusk. The second All-Russian Congress of Soviets was due to meet later in the evening, and would have a Bolshevik majority for the first time. They had missed Lenin's first public appearance at the Soviet, but learned something of what was said from M. Philips Price, who was present.[23] Lenin was clean-shaven, wore a wig and large glasses and passed without being noticed in the ill-lit corridors of Smolny. Workers in blouses and black fur hats came flying down the stairs.

The mood among the Americans became more anxious and even frantic as the meeting of the Congress was repeatedly delayed. Reed became irritated and defensive about the delays, unwilling to allow the other correspondents to speculate whether Lenin's tactics were going wrong.[24] Reed saw Kamenev looking harried and anxious, and asked him what had happened. Speaking in French, Kamenev read the text of a proclamation which announced the seizure of power in the name of the Soviet. But Kamenev was far from convinced that they had actually won. Riazanov was even more outspoken in his doubts about the seizure of power. Reed, Bryant and Williams ran into Bessie Beatty and Gumberg, who told them that they had spoken to the Bolshevik Jake Peters, who had lived in London before the March revolution, and had heard about Trotsky's speech and Lenin's introduction at the Petrograd Soviet that evening.[25] They entered the great meeting hall at 10.40 p.m. to see still in place on the platform the old CEC, the leaders of the SRs and Mensheviks who had kept the Soviet loyal to the government. After the election of a new presidium, Tsereteli, Chkheidze, Dan, Liber and Gots stepped down, and in their places appeared Trotsky, Kamenev, Lunacharsky, Kollontai and Nogin. 'How far they had soared, these Bolsheviki, from a despised and hunted sect less than four months ago, to this supreme place, the helm of great Russia in full tide of insurrection!' (p. 88). As the business of the Congress began, the sound of cannons being fired in the city was heard in the hall. (The *Aurora* had begun to fire blank shells at the Winter Palace.) One speaker after another demanded the bloodshed be stopped. Mensheviks denounced the Bolshevik coup against a government in which their own leaders were represented. In protest, the SRs, Mensheviks and the Bund staged a walkout from the Congress, hoping to discredit its authority. Reed heard Trotsky's scathing speech delivered at their departing figures: '"They are just so much refuse which will be swept into the garbage-heap of history!"' (p. 94).

Reed, Bryant, Beatty, Williams and Alex Gumberg went to the rooms of the MRC, where they collected passes, and then grabbed a lift on a truck carrying propaganda leaflets which was heading in the general direction of the Winter Palace. As they sped through the darkened streets they tossed handfuls of leaflets into the air, leaflets which prematurely announced the fall of the Provisional government. On the Nevsky Prospekt at 1 a.m. on 8 November they watched a procession of notables, members of the City Duma, the Mayor of Petrograd and leaders of the Jewish Bund – some 400–500 people in total. Reed noticed among them Avksentiev (founder member of the SRs, member of the CEC of the Petrograd Soviet, until September Interior Minister in the Provisional government, and Chairman of the Council of the Republic); they were all refused permission to enter the Winter Palace by a cordon of armed soldiers. Like the events he had just seen at Smolny, when Trotsky and the other Bolsheviks went to the platform, the obstruction of the procession of notables was a highly symbolic occasion, a vivid moment in the great theatre of revolution. In the confusion, Reed and the others slipped past the soldiers and entered the cordoned-off area near the Winter Palace, precisely at the moment when the Red Guards made their first rush at one of the entrances. Carried in their wake, Reed saw the looting and the frantic attempts to establish some kind of order. Given permission to enter the Malachite Hall, where the Provisional government met, he found a sheet covered with the draft of an appeal for support for the Provisional government, and doodles, drawn while the remaining Ministers waited for the crisis to be resolved finally. It was a little symbol of the completeness with which power had drained away from the government.

Reed's presentation of the revolution is composed of such scenes as the notables being turned away from the palace, and of the discovery of the Ministers' doodles. They are not the stuff of heroic drama (or Eisensteinian film-making), but they convey on a human scale something of the meaning of the Revolution. When Trotsky wrote of the events of 7 November in his *History of the Russian Revolution* (1932-33), he noted the lack of correspondence between the historical significance of the seizure of power, and the nature of the events themselves:

> The reader experiences a kind of disappointment. He is like a mountain climber, who, thinking the main difficulties are still ahead, suddenly discovers that he is already on the summit or almost there. Where is the insurrection? There is no picture of the insurrection. The events do not form themselves into a picture. A series of small operations, calculated and prepared in advance, remain separated from one another both in space and time. A unity of thought and aim unites them, but they do not fuse in the struggle itself. There is no action of great masses. There are no dramatic encounters with the troops. There is nothing of all that which imaginations brought up upon the facts of history associate with the idea of insurrection.[26]

Reed was mightily annoyed when Gumberg described the storming of the Winter Palace as 'the great anticlimax'.[27] But the truth was that he had seen little to suggest otherwise. He did not *feel* that it had all been an anticlimax. That was the difference. Trotsky believed that the revolution had been planned and carefully executed. '[W]ithout any chaos', (he wrote in *From October to Brest-Litovsk* [1919]), 'without street fights, without firing or bloodshed, the government institutions were occupied one after another by severe and disciplined detachments of soldiers, sailors and Red Guards, in accordance with the exact telephone orders given from the small room on the third floor of the Smolny Institute' (pp. 56–7). The confusing events of the revolution as Reed saw them had no inner direction. Much of the tactics of the Bolshevik Party, which had to operate through the Soviet and the MRC, were not known to Reed or to anyone outside the highest party leadership. But the Bolshevik tradition of interpreting the seizure of power had too great an investment in the notion that it was planned and controlled.

The 'revolutionary story' they constructed after Lenin's death in 1924 legitimised the regime itself.[28] Despite his extremely good contacts among the Bolsheviks, Reed saw events which were chaotic and confusing; there was no plan, no master scheme which delivered power to Lenin on 7 November. And if there had been a plan, the arrival in Petrograd some twenty-four hours late of the Kronstadt sailors meant that the revolution succeeded despite the best designs of the MRC. Robert Daniels suggests that the events on that day were, in truth, 'a wild gamble'.[29] Reed, Bryant and the others returned to Smolny where they found the Congress still in session. They heard Kamenev announce the fall of the Winter Palace and the arrest of the Ministers. The crowded delegates roared 'like the sea' (p. 107).

The next morning, 8 November, Reed visited Nikolai Hall, where the City Duma was in session. Mayor Schreider denounced the illegality of the Bolshevik actions. In the nearby Alexander Hall, where the Committee for Salvation was meeting, opponents of the Bolsheviks, including railway workers, post and telegraph unions, the moderate socialists, SRs, Cadets, former Ministers, business-men and journalists crowded together, launched volley after volley of reproach at the Bolsheviks. They all seemed to Reed to be 'well-fed': there were no hungry proletarians among the enemies of the Bolsheviks (p. 120). At Smolny, time itself seemed to move faster:

> The same running men in the dark corridors, squads of workers with rifles, leaders with bulging portfolios arguing, explaining, giving orders as they hurried anxiously along, surrounded by friends and lieutenants. Men literally out of themselves, living prodigies of sleeplessness and work – men unshaven, filthy, with burning eyes, who drove upon their fixed purpose full speed on engines of exaltation.(p. 122)

No reader of *Ten Days* can fail to notice the presence of a system of metaphors in Reed's prose. They fall into two distinct kinds: comparisons of the revolution with natural processes (tides, earthquakes), which reaffirmed the legitimacy of the revolution by suggesting that it was *natural*, not the creation of a German–Bolshevik conspiracy; and metaphors which invite us to see the central institution of the insurrection, the MRC, in terms of machines – comparisons which suggested the wild extremity of human transformations produced by the revolution.[30] Reed was not alone in this way of seeing the events in Petrograd. Williams, for example, wrote in *Through the Russian Revolution*:

> Smolny is now one big forum, roaring like a gigantic smithy with orators calling to arms, audiences whistling or stamping, the gavel pounding for order, the sentries grounding arms, machine-guns rumbling across the cement floors, crashing choruses of revolutionary hymns, thundering ovations for Lenin and Zinoviev as they emerge from underground.
>
> Everything at high speed, tense and growing tenser every minute. The leading workers are dynamos of energy; sleepless, tireless, nerveless miracles of men, facing momentous questions of Revolution.[31]

Reed described the MRC in such terms: in 'Kerensky is Coming!', which appeared in the *Liberator* in July 1918, he wrote: 'the Military Revolutionary Committee roared like a fly-wheel day and night, throwing off spark-like showers of orders'. In *Ten Days* this appeared as: '[w]ith brakes released the Military Revolutionary Committee whirled, throwing off orders, appeals, decrees, like sparks' (p. 113); elsewhere it appears as flashing 'baleful fire, pounding like an over-loaded dynamo'(p. 171). Reed called at Smolny on 11 November:

> On the top floor the Military Revolutionary Committee was in full blast, striking and slacking not. Men went in, fresh and vigorous; night and day and night and day they threw themselves into the terrible machine; and came out limp, blind with fatigue, hoarse and filthy, to fall on the floor and sleep...[p. 201]

The system of metaphor, which works on a pattern of oppositions between energy and paralysis, tidal movement of masses of people and the cold emptiness of deserted palaces, the 'flood' of publications in Petrograd and the 'ripples' which brought news of the revolution to the vast countryside, is elaborate and perhaps somewhat wearying overall. There were things which Reed wished to say which fit uncomfortably within the traditionally spare and direct language of American journalism, and for which 'literature' or at least a kind of literary language, overwrought and metaphoric, could be used.

The session of Congress which opened at 8.40 p.m. on 8 November, did not end until 7 a.m. the next day. Reed was alone among those present to recall Lenin's momentous words, '"We shall now proceed to construct the Socialist order."' Decree after decree were announced: '[t]he Government proposes to all the governments and to the peoples of all the belligerent countries to conclude an immediate armistice... All private ownership of land is abolished...' (pp. 129, 133). Reed's portrait of Lenin was brief and extraordinarily insightful:

> A short, stocky figure, with a big head set down in his shoulders, bald and bulging. Little eyes, a snubbish nose, wide, generous mouth, and heavy chin; clean-shaven now, but already beginning to bristle with the well-known beard of his past and future. Dressed in shabby clothes, his trousers much too long for him. Unimpressive, to be the idol of a mob, loved and revered as perhaps few leaders in history have been. A strange popular leader – a leader purely by virtue of intellect; colourless, humourless, uncompromising and detached, without picturesque idiosyncrasies – but with the power of explaining profound ideas in simple terms, of analysing a concrete situation. And combined with shrewdness, the greatest intellectual audacity. [p. 125]

It is worth remembering that Lenin in particular was the object of a worldwide campaign of vituperation. Catherine Breshkovskaya, deeply admired by Americans as the symbol of Russian courage in the face of Tsarist autocracy, wrote of Lenin in a Russian Information Bureau pamphlet, *Russia and the World* (1919), that '[h]is policy is not that of a sane brain, and girding himself in these policies of incessant terror and violence, it cannot be that he enjoys a normal state of mind and spirit'. Of course Reed was far from being 'neutral' on the subject of Lenin, but it is only against the context of the wild denunciations of Lenin and the Bolsheviks in America that Reed's praise takes its full meaning. He was trying to break down a widespread willingness to remove the Bolsheviks from the realm of human discourse itself. Reed saw Lenin for the first time on 8 November, but they were not introduced until the afternoon of 18 January 1918, during a break during the first session of the ill-fated Constituent Assembly (Rosenstone, *Romantic Revolutionary*, p. 312).

Reed was out on the streets by midday on 9 November. The mood of the crowds seemed angry. Ordinary citizens screamed at the Red Guards and abused the sailors. The City Duma refused to acknowledge the newly formed government of the Council of Peoples' Commissars, and the Committee for Salvation became a focal point for all those who rejected the coup of 7–8 November. When a rumour reached the Duma that the Armoured Car Regiment was wavering, and considered withdrawing their representatives on the MRC, Reed rushed over to the Mikhailovsky Riding School to attend their meeting. He heard Krylenko give an impassioned speech which kept the soldiers loyal to the new government. Later in the afternoon he joined a delegation from the Committee for Salvation which went to the Peter and Paul fortress, where the prisoners from the Winter Palace were being held, to investigate rumours that the prisoners were being tortured. There was no truth in the claims, but the opponents of the Bolsheviks were more than prepared to believe such stories. Late in the night negotiations were underway to form a new government which would specifically exclude the Bolsheviks and their leaders, Lenin and Trotsky.

Reed awoke on Saturday, 10 November, to find the city plastered with posters, denunciations, decrees. He and Williams hurried out to Smolny to obtain passes to go to the Front. Williams was turned down by Lenin. The MRC had moved into larger quarters at Smolny, where Reed found Shatov and learned from him the latest news. The Petrograd proletariat were being summoned to dig ditches and build barricades. Beneath the 'breezy assurance' in the MRC, there was 'a chill premonition, a feeling of uneasiness in the air. Kerensky's Cossacks were coming fast...'(p. 179). Factory whistles could be heard throughout the city. Outside the building, Reed saw the mass mobilisation of workers to defend the revolution. 'They rolled along, torrent-like, companies of soldiers borne with them, guns, motor-trucks, wagons...'(p. 181). They could not accept the decision to keep them away from the battle, and Gumberg, who had joined them at Smolny, coolly got them into a car which was to take Dybenko and Antonov to the Front. Gumberg would not listen to demands that they get out, and in the end they travelled with the People's Commissars for War and Marine to the battle which would settle the fate of the Bolshevik revolution.

The account of this journey, as it appears in *Ten Days,* is among the most delightful passages of comic irony in all of Reed's prose. It was thought necessary by Reed to disguise their presence, so he attributed the account he gave to 'Trusishka', or 'coward'. (He had repeatedly clashed with Gumberg in Petrograd, but it was not until January 1918, when Gumberg played a key role in the withdrawal of Reed's nomination as Soviet Consul in New York, that the dislike he felt soured into rage and bitterness.) They stopped to buy provisions, but neither Dybenko nor Antonov had any money. The unwelcome guests in the car paid for everything. Later, at the Front, when Antonov sought to give an order allowing a military commander to obtain ammunition from the supplies at Smolny, he discovered that no one except the Americans had paper or pens to write out the order. At Tsarskoye Selo they found a city in threatening silence. The commander of the guards at the Imperial Palace told Reed that his pass from Smolny put him in danger. His troops were neutral in the battle, and were merely holding the Palace until Kerensky arrived in the morning. They returned to Petrograd that evening, to find the Committee for Salvation in 'high spirits' at the prospect of Kerensky's arrival. That night Junkers seized control of the Telephone Exchange, arresting an unsuspecting Antonov.

Reed constructed the confusing events of 11 November from Williams, who was at the Telephone Exchange, and who helped free Antonov; and from Bryant, who witnessed an armoured car open fire indiscriminately upon unarmed civilians in the street. Reed went first to the Trade Union headquarters, to find out which way the Railway Union, the powerful Vikzhel, would jump, and then to Smolny. The MRC was 'in full blast, striking and slacking not. Men went in, fresh and vigorous; night and day and night and day they threw themselves into the terrible machine; and came out limp, blind with fatigue, hoarse and filthy, to fall on the floor and sleep' (p. 201). It was a day filled with heroic defiance and last-minute political offers. At Smolny he heard Trotsky talk of the need for 'pitiless struggle' to maintain power for the Soviets. At the headquarters of Vikzhel there was a conference underway of all the socialist parties to form a new government. Dan proposed a new coalition which would exclude the Bolsheviks from power. The crushing of the Junker revolt in Petrograd did much, Reed thought, to encourage moderate socialists to remain in talks about a new government. Everyone was waiting for Kerensky.

The next day, by one of those reversals which impressed every observer of the revolution, Reed found the Smolny silent and nearly empty, while the city Duma and the Committee for Salvation were thronged and noisy. If the Cossacks swept aside the rag-tag ranks of the Red Guard and the ill-led soldiers at Tsarskoe Selo, figures like Mayor Schreider and Shingariov of the Cadets would play a significant role in the future resolution of the political crisis. They were vigorous in their denunciation of the Bolsheviks. Reed talked to Mensheviks and SRs, who were equally as impassioned in their recriminations. In the afternoon he was taken to an apartment where he met SRs who were planning a counter-revolution. At Smolny, he heard Trotsky again address the Petrograd Soviet, warning everyone of the absolute importance of the great battle which was expected at Pulkovo later in the day. Contingents of soldiers flowed in and out as the speeches continued. He waited impatiently for news from the front until 3 a.m. on Tuesday 13 November, when he was handed a cable announcing that the Cossacks under the command of General Krasnov had been defeated at Pulkovo. When he returned to Smolny later in the day he encountered a remarkable scene:

Inside, the long, gloomy halls and bleak rooms seemed deserted. No one moved in all the enormous pile....everywhere on the floor, along the walls, men were sleeping. Rough, dirty men, workers and soldiers, spattered and caked with mud, sprawled alone or in heaps, in the careless attitudes of death. Some wore ragged bandages marked with blood. Guns and cartridge-belts were scattered about.... The victorious proletarian army!

In the upstairs buffet so thick they lay that one could hardly walk. The air was foul. Through the clouded windows a pale light streamed. A battered samovar, cold, stood on the counter, and many glasses holding dregs of tea. [p. 222]

After a visit to the Duma, where there was less talk now of excluding the Bolsheviks from a future coalition government, he asked a driver at Smolny to drive him to the Front. They stopped for lunch at the Battalion Committee of the 6th Reserve Engineers Battalion, where Reed saw another of the scenes which embodied something of the essential nature of the revolution. He was warmly greeted by the soldiers on the committee, who asked him many questions about American life. Their talk was interrupted by the colonel, who hesitatingly requested to enter the room. The man who before the March revolution had been absolute autocrat of the battalion was now completely subordinate to the chairman of the committee.

At Tsarskoe Selo Reed joined a patrol of Red Guards which was heading for the Front, but was separated from it by soldiers who could not fathom his pass from the MRC and who seemed to be on the verge of summarily executing him as a spy. After urgent appeals from Reed, the papers were shown to someone who understood them, and he was taken to the Regimental Committee of the 2nd Tsarskoe Selo Rifles, where he was warmly greeted by a French-speaking officer. (This incident suggests that Reed's *spoken* Russian was still very restricted at this time.) He eventually returned to Petrograd in a truck carrying Red Guards.

News reached Petrograd on 15 November of immense battles in Moscow. After obtaining a pass from Smolny Reed squeezed himself on board a crowded train bound for Moscow. There were substantially more signs of damage to buildings in Moscow than he expected. The supporters of the Provisional government had proved themselves to be better organised in Moscow than in Petrograd. At the Moscow Soviet he was delighted to see Melnichansky, whom he had known at the Bayonne, New Jersey, Standard Oil strike that summer, and who was now secretary of the Metal Workers Union. Melnichansky told Reed about the six-day battle between Red Guards and supporters of the Provisional government for control of Moscow. That evening he attended a special session of the Moscow Bolsheviks to hear the reports of Nogin and Rykov, 'conciliationists' or moderates, who had resigned from the Council of Peoples' Commissars in protest against Lenin's determination that the Bolsheviks remain the majority party in any all-socialist government which might emerge out of the Vikzhel negotiations.[32] He returned to Petrograd after watching the stirring funeral in Red Square of 500 who had died in the fighting for the Kremlin. The vast columns walking in silence through the raining city filled Reed with a sense of the tragic grandeur of the revolution.

With his return to Petrograd, *Ten Days* ceases to be the close record of his day-by-day activities. Chapters XI and XII give an account of the the events of the rest of November, which culminated in meeting of the Peasants' Soviet and the agreement of the Left SRs to join the new government. It was a dramatic moment to end the book. Reed remained in Russia until mid-February 1918, and he finished the manuscript by the end of the year. In other words, the story as he personally witnessed it could have continued at least until the dissolution of the Constituent Assembly on 19 January. Reed planned a second volume, *From Kornilov to Brest-Litovsk*, which would deal with dimensions of the revolution largely missing from *Ten Days:* the collapse of the Russian Army, the attempt to secure an armistice, and the peace negotiations with the Germans. But there was no question of writing the book while he was still so busy in Petrograd covering the unfolding story of the government's attempt to extricate itself from the war. The stacks of *Izvestias* and *Novaya Zhizns*, the posters and leaflets had to be translated; the accounts of others had to be digested. He had seen a vision of the redemption of mankind in Petrograd, but the telling of the story proved to be a more difficult and protracted business than he expected.

"'What counts", Reed remarked to Williams, "is what we do when we go home. It's easy to be fired by things here. We'll wind up thinking we're great revolutionaries. And at home?" He laughed. "Oh, I can always put on another pageant!"'[33] The boundless enthusiasm Reed expressed, his indefatigable energy in pursuit of the revolution, was not without misgivings and even a sardonic self-recrimination. The revolution made him ask whether he was to remain an observer, one of the 'humanitarians, the dilettantes'.[34] 'I have been around a bit', he wrote to Upton Sinclair, 'in Colorado, Bayonne, Lawrence and on the battle-fields of Europe.'[35] But he found an answer to these self-questionings, and to an occasionally sullen mood, when he and Williams were invited by Reinstein to join the Bureau of International Revolutionary Propaganda within Trotsky's Commissariat for Foreign Affairs, where he worked from 1 December 1917 to 7 February 1918. Karl Radek was at first responsible for a German-language daily paper, *Die Fackel*, designed for circulation among Austrian and German prisoners of war. Radek accompanied Trotsky to the negotiations at Brest-Litovsk, where he shamelessly conducted Bolshevik propaganda among the German troops.

At the same time, another section for international revolutionary propaganda had been set up by the Commissariat for Foreign Affairs, and put in the charge of Reinstein. E. H. Carr says that they were meant to produce propaganda in English, which was sent to England in protected Bolshevik diplomatic correspondence.[36] Reed often referred to his propaganda work, but exclusively mentioned propaganda aimed at the German and Austrian Armies. Like the unfortunate incident in the German trenches in 1915, it would have done great harm to Reed in America if it had been known he was involved in Bolshevik propaganda directed towards Britain. Reed and Williams assisted in the preparation of newspapers in a half-dozen languages, as well as pamphlets containing translations from the inflammatory decrees of the Council of Peoples' Commissars and speeches of Lenin and Trotsky. They were widely distributed to prisoners of war. Reed, Williams and Reinstein excitedly devised schemes for their transmission across the lines into the hands of German troops. This seemed to Reed a portent of the new post-imperialist era of conflicts between social systems, which would seek to undermine each other by the power of ideas and ideology. They sent agitators to the front lines and to prisoner-of-war camps. Reed strongly believed that this effort (they were producing half a million newspapers daily) had demoralised and weakened morale among the German front-line troops, and happily recorded the German and Austrian governments' protest at their activities during the Brest-Litovsk negotiations.[37] When the need for troops was at its peak in October 1918, the German High Command regarded those troops which had been stationed in the Ukraine as 'so impregnated with Bolshevik ideas that they would be of no real service in attack, and would threaten the morale of the jaded divisions which had already been defeated'.[38] Lenin agreed to suppress the Bureau of International Revolutionary Propaganda upon signing the treaty of Brest-Litovsk, but the rapid appearance of a Bureau of Foreign Political Literature, under the same direction and with most of the same personnel, was a recognition of their achievements.

Reed's initial $2,000 was largely exhausted by December, and repeated requests to Eastman and the *Masses*, which was over-whelmingly preoccupied with its own demise, failed to produce any further funds. He took temporary employment with the American Red Cross Mission, whose leader, Colonel Raymond Robins, a Bull Moose Republican, was more realistic about the Bolsheviks than the Embassy crowd. Robins had no liking for Marxian socialism, but was determined to persuade the administration in Washington that the American policy of non-recognition of the Soviet government was self-defeating. He wanted the Americans to help the Russians for humanitarian reasons, and also to keep them from signing the peace treaty with the Germans. Reed found him refreshingly free from cant, and readily fell in with a request from Robins to draw up a prospectus for an English-language newspaper in Moscow which would put the American viewpoint, encourage investment in Russia and which would oppose the drift towards a separate peace. No revolutionary would want to have anything to do with such a tainted proposal. Reed would as well have recalled that

American money which had backed Breshkovskaya's Committee on Civic Education in Free Russia in September and October was now being used to discredit her with the Bolsheviks. But a desperate need for cash overrode Reed's scruples. Robins wanted proposals for the use of American aid, and Reed's final report gave him what he wanted. In the dummy issue he prepared he included a warning beneath the masthead: '[t]his paper is devoted to promoting the interests of American capital'.[39]

Living conditions sharply deteriorated in Petrograd in the winter of 1917-18. Of the nearly 800 large-scale industrial enterprises in the city, 265 had closed down; either moved away in the panic of renewed fighting with the Germans, or were simply closed and abandoned. Less than half of the Petrograd workers were in employment. In the spring the population was 1.5 million, down 1 million from the population a year earlier. The daily bread ration was 50g per day. At the 'War Hotel', formerly the Astoria and now taken over by the Peoples' Commissars, Bessie Beatty survived on a diet of cabbage soup, black bread and *rabchik,* a wild bird 'for which we all acquired a deathless hatred'. 'Most of the time', she recalled, 'we were in total darkness. There were no lamps or candles in the halls, and we groped our way up the dark staircases, bumping blindly into one another.' On the streets, former officers were shovelling snow or selling newspapers. The destruction of the bourgeosie had begun in earnest.[40] Reed and Bryant began to make plans for their return to America. Bryant left Petrograd on 20 January with official standing as a 'courier' for the Peoples' Commissar of Foreign Affairs, which enabled her to pass between the lines without inspection. In addition to her own papers, she carried those of Bessie Beatty. The news that Reed had been indicted with the *Masses* editors under the espionage laws made him increasingly impatient to leave, but he remained in Petrograd for the Constituent Assembly, which was due to meet on 18 January, and the Third Congress of Soviets, which was to follow five days later. The dissolution of the Constituent Assembly, which so shocked democratic opinion in America and which did much to discredit the Bolshevik government, left Reed unmoved. He attended its first, and only, session. Its form of political representation seemed anomalous, irrelevant; industrial democracy through the Soviets was something worth fighting for. The most memorable occasion of the meeting was Reed's first meeting with Lenin. On 20 January he joined a patrol of Red Guards which was prepared to defend the Foreign Office from counter-revolutionary attack. He carried a rifle, the first occasion since that unfortunate moment in the German trenches in 1915 when he fired a shot in the general direction of the French. He had just been trying out what it felt like to be a combatant in 1915. Now, in a frozen Petrograd, he was armed and meant it – at least, up to a point. It was also a way to annoy mightily the American Embassy crowd.

At the opening session of the Third Congress of Soviets at the Tauride Palace, Reed was introduced by Reinstein, and gave a little speech promising to bring the news of the victorious Russian proletariat to America in the hope that it would 'call forth an answer from America's oppressed and exploited masses'. In the audience was the American newspaperman Edgar Sisson, representative in Petrograd of George Creel's Committee on Public Information. The appearance of Reed and Williams on the platform was, he wrote, 'the most disagreeable feature of the day' for he had angrily told Reed, after his Bolshevik patrol duty, that such behaviour was 'silly and florid' and that he was simply being used by the Bolsheviks for their propaganda. A contrite Reed accepted the rebuke. He had only gone on the patrol out of journalistic curiosity, he said, and would be more careful in the future. Four days later, he was at it again. Sisson was furious. He felt betrayed, and soon took his revenge on Reed.[41]

Trotsky, in a gesture at once impulsive and humorous, responded to Reed's concern about the safety of his substantial archive by offering to appoint Reed as Soviet Consul in New York. The American government refused to recognise the Bolshevik government, and would certainly have refused to accept Reed's credentials; as an American citizen, however, he could not be refused permission to return home. In prison, he would have given the Bolsheviks some useful publicity. This was the ultimate diplomatic prank, but one which could easily backfire on Reed. He boasted of the appointment, and soon word reached the American Embassy. Chicherin wrote to Ambassador Francis on 29 January announcing Reed's appointment. It enraged Francis, of course. But it also disturbed those like Robins and Sisson who hoped to use the promise of American support to keep Russia in the war, and who hoped that Russian reasonableness would enable relations of some kind to be established with the American government. Everyone in the American community in Petrograd, except Bolsheviks like Reinstein and sympathisers like Williams, regarded the appointment of Reed as a ridiculous blunder.[42] It would certainly have been received with deep hostility in Washington. Secretary of State Robert Lansing had already received enough communications about Reed to regard him as a trouble-maker and potential subversive.

If the leading figures in the American community in Petrograd met to decide what to do about Reed, no record survives of the occasion. But upon the request of Sisson, and certainly with the support of the others, Alex Gumberg directly approached Lenin with a request that the appointment be withdrawn. Gumberg argued that Reed was unsuited for such a post, being impulsive, romantic and idealistic, and he showed Lenin a copy of the prospectus Reed had drawn up for Robins which involved the massive use of American capital for aid in Russia and the setting up of a newspaper to express the American viewpoint on the negotiations at Brest-Litovsk. Reed believed that this report had been stolen by Gumberg from a locked drawer in his desk. Gumberg, who probably received a copy of Reed's proposal from

Robins, said he found it on the top of the desk. The proposal seemed unsavoury to Lenin, and Reed's appointment was withdrawn. 'Thereafter he could not mention Gumberg's name without a string of four-letter epithets'.[43]

Reed left Petrograd in early February 1918 but his troubles with American officialdom were just beginning.

6 *An American Bolshevik 1918-1920*

Reed saw Petrograd in 1917 in the light of events in America. When he returned to New York he found that the standard-bearers of the left wing, soon to be organised into a formal Left Wing Section within the Socialist Party (and thus earning its capital letters), saw America almost wholly in 'Russian' terms. He knew better. Thus the scene was set for a period of sustained political involvement. Reed became a player in the most exciting events which the American left had known for a generation; and it was in his last period in New York that he made a significant contribution to the splitting of the Socialist Party, and the formation of two rival and antagonistic communist parties from the minuscule Left Wing.

On 12 February 1918 the American Military Attaché in London, Lieutenant-Colonel S. L. H. Slocum, forwarded to the Chief of the Military Intelligence Section of the War College Division, Washington, a report from the Embassy in Petrograd announcing Reed's plans to return to the United States. 'He is an anarchist and a Bolshevik sympathiser and is being urged to travel as a Bolshevist Courier by persons in Russia who desire to make trouble with America and believe that in this way an international incident will be created in the case of his arrest.'[1] This was the perception of the American community in Petrograd, where Reed was widely regarded as a fool who failed to understand that he was being used by others for devious ends. Edgar Sisson so distrusted Reed that he refused to believe that the withdrawal of the Consulship was genuine, and suspected that there was a secret plan which would enable Reed to enter the United States with his papers unsearched.[2] Reed's archive loomed large in Sisson's eyes. The State Department instructed its officials in Scandinavia not to 'verify' Reed's passport. In effect, Washington decided to put Reed on ice for the time being. Louise Bryant and Bessie Beatty had already sailed for home, but Reed was caught. He arrived in Christiania, Norway, on 19 February, and was informed by the Consul of his position. A day or two later the Legation obtained a copy of a letter by 'Jack' which he had given to a passenger sailing on 22 February. It was sent to Washington by Diplomatic Pouch (with multiple copies to the Office of Naval Intelligence, United States Postal Censorship and the Military Intelligence Branch of the War College) and contained Reed's explanation that after a thirteen-day journey from Petrograd to Christiania, he now knew that he faced a delay of at least a month. Reed's letters home offered thin pickings for the security services, but they were none the less intercepted and circulated for filing in a dozen government offices. One, forwarded to Washington on 19 April, was found to contain a physical impression from another letter, dated 8 March, to an unnamed comrade. It revealed that Reed had been left with too much time, perhaps, to think about what had happened to him before leaving Petrograd:

> As for the unhappy appointment as Consul and its unfortunate termination, I have only ventured once to timidly refer to that, but nobody wants to search out such disagreeable matters.
>
> When the Germans were advancing on Petrograd, I cabled Petrograd and offered my services, – [stet] to come with volunteers, or anything. I ascertained that the wire reached Petrograd, but of course everybody was too busy.
>
> It does seem such a shame when I have such good will and am willing to give so much, that I cannot be used, but just left here to stew...

Perhaps Reed did not know why the Consulship had so peremptorily been withdrawn. Any intelligence service worth its salt would see this letter was a transparent dodge, and an attempt to deflect attention away from a potentially dangerous radical. Anyone else might see in the letter the pathos of a man who meant well, but who had been rebuffed in Petrograd and ignored in Norway. This fragmentary letter tells us much about Reed's relations with the Bolsheviks in 1918.

While in Christiania, Reed began to draft an introduction for his book about the revolution. The process of composition was an educational experience for Reed: he had been studying Russian history and politics, and his first drafts, heavy with historical explication, gave many signs of the seriousness with which he approached the task of writing about the revolution. When he was not ploughing through his Russian story, or taking long walks (leading his surveillance agents on long rambles through the frozen city), he wrote angry letters to American officials. He finally received his visa in April. The governmental paper trail resumed on 8 May, in a report from Special Agent Wallmo who interrogated Reed upon his arrival in New York aboard the SS *Bergensfjord* on 28 April. 'Mr. Reed says that the only reason he can assign for receiving this appointment was because he was about the only English speaking person available. His appointment was revoked for no special reason except as Mr. Reed said it is the usual way for the Bolsheviki to do business.' When asked about his political opinions, Reed was firm in proclaiming his socialism but cautious about Soviet Russia: 'his reply was that the only thing he could say at the present time was that he would rather see the Germans licked than anything else in the world'. His entire archive was turned over to the censor, and he was allowed to leave the ship. It was Sisson who suggested to the State Department that Reed's papers be seized for leisurely perusal, and when he returned to Washington Sisson found them awaiting his attention (Rosenstone, p. 317).

The day before he arrived in New York the first *Masses* trial ended in a hung jury. The Assistant United States District Attorney immediately announced that the defendants would be retried and so Reed's first task was to appear at the Federal Building on 29 April and post bail of $2,000. New York in May 1918 was a city at war. Petrograd was tired of war, and looked threadbare and hungry; New York was bustling, prosperous and awash with pro-war propaganda, flags, parades and aggressive 100 per cent Americanism. Posters by Howard Chandler Christy and James Montgomery Flagg appealed to patriotic sentiments: 'Hun or Home? Buy more Liberty Bonds.' 'The United States Army builds *Men.*' From a million hoardings pink-cheeked children, white-haired women, brave soldiers and earnest immigrants gestured to the public for supprt. 'Must children die and mothers plead in vain? Buy more Liberty Bonds.'[3]

Reed had been away for nine months, and in the face of a tornado of government propaganda was passionate to begin a campaign to defend the Bolsheviks. Steffens begged Reed to abandon any thought of a national speaking tour, and advised him to accept the need for a time to write for his desk drawer. 'But, Jack, you do wrong to buck this thing... Really, I think it is wrong to try to tell the truth now. We must wait. You must wait.'[4] Reed was temperamentally ill-equipped to accept Steffens's advice. In one respect, however, he had no choice. With all of his papers still at the State Department and no indication of the date of their likely return, he could do nothing about the book he planned to write about the revolution. He wrote letters to the State Department, and appealed to friends within its hierarchy, like William C. Bullitt, who made efforts through Frank Polk and Colonel Edward House, the President's friend and adviser, to have the Reed material returned. He hoped as well that something of what he had to say about Russia might strike a chord among the group, led by House, who were believed to be opposed to intervention. He sent a memorandum to Bullitt, who forwarded it to House on 20 May, in which he argued that intervention, however disguised and on

167

whatever pretext, would be understood in Russia as an attempt to overthrow the Bolshevik government. He argued that the various White governments were 'absolutely unsupported except by the propertied classes and foreign bayonets'.[5] He heard nothing from Washington. The newspapers and magazines were solid in their refusal to print Reed's articles. All that was left to him were the surviving left-wing papers like the *Liberator* and the *New York Call,* and the possiblity of speeches at public meetings arranged by left-wing groups.

He confronted an American public opinion which had turned decisively against the Bolsheviks. The Brest–Litovsk treaty, which took the Russians out of the war, was seen as a betrayal of the one cause – the defeat of the Germans – which was an item of faith in America in the spring of 1918. Reed found the American people desperately ill-informed about Russia. Events were moving so swiftly, and the remoteness and alien character of Russian life for most Americans made an intelligent assessment of Russian affairs notoriously difficult. To be more precise, he believed that they were being fed lies and distortions by those who sought to destroy the Bolsheviks and the radical movement within America. He tried in the *Call* to counter some of this ignorance, particularly concerning the hotly debated question of whether the Russians could in any meaningful sense remain in the war. He argued that the Russian economy was profoundly disorganised by the war, fatally weakened by pro-German treason under the Tsar, and he accepted the Bolshevik propaganda which claimed that there had been extensive sabotage by the bourgeoisie which was designed to discredit the radical forces emerging under the Provisional government. 'Russia, then', he wrote in the *Call* on 2 May, 'was in a state of complete disorganization by the time the Bolsheviks came to power.'[6]

Reed was at the Liberty Defense Union dinner on 10 May, given to honour the *Masses* editors, and to raise funds for their defence.

Morris Hillquit, the socialist lawyer who had defended the *Masses* and many other socialist papers, warned the guests of the likely effects of the 1918 Sedition Law: once it went into effect, criticism of the Constitution and the military will be illegal. Before that threat Hillquit made a little joke ('Congress, it seems, is trying to give us speakers a little vacation').[7] Reed was outraged at what he regarded as the feebleness of the Socialist Party at this moment of tyrannical oppression, and hoped to provide an articulate leadership of its left-wing. Relations within the party were deteriorating, but representatives of its different factions still were prepared to share public platforms. Reed joined the editor of the *Forward,* Abraham Cahan, the socialist New York Assemblyman of the Twenty-Third District (Brownsville), Abraham Shiplacoff, and the socialist lecturer George H. Kirkpatrick at a meeting at Carnegie Hall in New York on 18 May. An agent sent by the New York office of the Military Intelligence Branch secured a seat on the platform, and ten days later wrote an impression of Reed as a revolutionary speaker:

> He is a tall, slender young man of typical American appearance and talk, and spoke entertainingly of what he had seen and heard in Russia, and gave an exhaustive description of the present Soviet (council) government in Russia...

Agent Perkins noted Reed's words:

> The masses supporting Trotsky and Lenin will die before they will submit to Kerensky.
>
> The Soviet government of Russia will not fall if it is left alone. It has faced the malignant hatred of the whole world and withstood it all.
>
> What does the Soviet government expect of you? Do you know what Trotsky said in his first message to the peoples of the world? 'Let all the people bring pressure upon their respective governments to recognize and support our cause.'

> Write to your president to stop this campaign against the Soviet government of Russia!

While explaining the impossibility of continuing the war, and supporting the Soviet government's decision to sign and ratify the Brest–Litovsk treaty (3–16 March), Reed was sometimes equivocal in his public statements about what the Bolsheviks really intended. He was aware that due to sabotage and disorganisation they could no longer remain in the war, while at the same time he drew upon his personal experience of propaganda work to argue that the Bolsheviks continued through the spring and early summer of 1918 to be making a significant military contribution to the Allied cause. Propaganda and fraternisation had created disaffection within large numbers of German troops, who were thus unusable against the Allied offensive which began that summer:

> 'The Russians have not yet begun to fight,' Reed told his audience [at the New Star Casino in New York, on 24 May] when he touched on the stories circulated in this country that the Bolsheviks have surrendered to the Germans.[8]

He repeated this optimistic point, in italics, in an article published in July: '*For the Russian Soviet Government is at war with Germany* – has been at war with Germany since last summer'.[9] He argued that the signing of the Brest–Litovsk treaty gave the Russians 'an opportunity for strengthening the internal regime, and organizing a resumption of the struggle...' long after the idea of a 'revolutionary war' had been abandoned in Russia.[10]

The event which explains Reed's repeated emphasis on the military potential of the Russians was the landing of Japanese troops at Vladivostok on 4 April 1918. This dramatically changed the American perception of the issues at stake in the Russian situation. The American administration did not want an aggressive Japanese Army to seize the whole of Siberia. In May the Trans-Siberian railroad between Irkutsk and the Volga was seized by the Czech

Legion, anxious to be reunited with their comrades then in Vladivostok and to be repatriated to the Western Front. Their fears of attack by armed German and Austrian prisoners of war, and the virtual disintegration of Russia, led President Wilson to accept a limited military intervention. Whatever the pretext, it was great power rivalry which persuaded the Americans to intervene in the rapidly deteriorating situation in Russia. Without privileged access to the policy debates in Moscow or Washington, Reed hoped that American intervention might be avoided if the idea gained ground that the Russians were making a genuine contribution to the war effort. Trotsky's tactic was to use the British and the Americans to counter-balance the aggressive German presence in the Ukraine, and check the blatant imperialist ambitions of the Japanese, thus to play one robber capitalist state off against the others. On 5 March 1918, on the day the Soviet delegation returned from Brest–Litovsk with the final German terms, he met with Raymond Robins and frankly asked if the Americans wanted to prevent the Brest terms being ratified. Robins said that they did, and asked for Trotsky to put in writing their terms to reject the unequal settlement and renew hostilities. The Wilson administration was uninterested in any such arrangement and instructed Robins to say nothing about the offer when he returned that spring to America. This, in Reed's eyes, was an opportunity tragically squandered.[11]

There were good reasons, even for someone as headstrong as Reed, for a degree of caution in his public statements. He was under indictment, and attempts were being made to impress upon President Wilson the unfairness of a resumed prosecution of the *Masses*. Upton Sinclair wrote to Wilson on 18 May. Amos Pinchot, in a letter of 24 May, reminded the President that Reed and the other indicted editors ('men of the finest social feeling') had been among the most idealistic of the president's supporters. 'He antagonized his employers, and took his future in his hands by campaigning for you'.[12] Similar arguments reached the president from others, such as Edward P. Costigan, the Denver progressive lawyer who had worked with Reed in the aftermath of the Ludlow, Colorado, massacre in 1914.[13] Wilson passed this correspondence on to the Attorney-General, Thomas Gregory, for comment, but at a meeting on 6 June 1918 Wilson and Gregory decided to proceed with the prosecution. Reed had contacts in Washington, but they were powerless to intervene on his behalf.

American radicals were as one in opposing the prosecution of Eastman, Art Young and Reed, but many were reluctant to accept some of the arguments Reed offered on behalf of the Bolsheviks. They were quick to pick up his exaggerations and over-statements, his occasional errors of fact, and the resulting exchanges in the *Liberator* and other socialist papers in July and August were ill-tempered. He clashed with Norman Hapgood over his claim that the Russian bourgeoisie had sought to derail the revolution by industrial sabotage, and with Upton Sinclair over Maxim Gorky's attitude towards the Bolshevik revolution.[14]

And when he spoke, the hostility of audiences sent political adrenalin racing through his body. He met aggression with aggression. When socialists in Philadelphia were refused a permit for a public meeting, Reed stood outside the closed hall on 31 May and harangued a crowd of 1,000 until he was dragged away by police. He was charged with inciting to riot, and bailed for $5,000. When Eugene Debs was indicted in June for violation of the Espionage Act, Reed travelled with Art Young to Debs's home at Terre Haut, Indiana, to spend 4 July with the socialist leader.[15] He then travelled to Chicago to attend the first mass trial of IWW militants. Over 100 Wobblies, each charged with more than 100 separate offences, were on trial before the gentlemanly, implacable Judge Kenesaw Mountain Landis.

In the months after his return from Russia Reed had little of the light-hearted gaiety of the old *Masses* crowd about him. He was more aggressively political, more intolerant, more self-destructive.

Eastman cautiously avoided a confrontation with Postmaster-General Burleson over the contents of the *Liberator,* and we have seen how Steffens's strongly advised Reed to hold back and await a better political climate. Reed distanced himself politically from them both. He rejected Steffens' advice, and in August broke with the *Liberator* on a matter of principle: he did not want to appear acceptable in the eyes of Burleson.[16] Reed held talks with Floyd Dell and Frank Harris about the prospects of editing a magazine, to be called *These States*, and which would pick up where *Seven Arts* had been forced to cease publication. It was going to be literary and aggressively modern. But the project foundered when Harris, perhaps showing a more nuanced sense of the literary *Zeitgeist*, rebelled at the prospect of including the poems of Carl Sandburg.[17]

His papers had still not been returned from the State Department, and Reed was increasingly frustrated and angry. He bitterly blamed Gumberg and Sisson for what had happened to him, and told anyone who would listen the story of their perfidy. On his return home, Gumberg found the atmosphere towards himself among radicals in New York to be decidedly chilly. He tried to effect a reconciliation with Reed, or at least to refute some of Reed's damaging stories, by using Eastman as intermediary. Gumberg appealed for help to Raymond Robins, then still in purdah at the behest of the State Department, and the two of them had dinner with Eastman at the Hotel Brevoort. They brought a briefcase full of letters and documents to show the trust Lenin and Trotsky had placed in Gumberg. Eastman invited both Reed and Gumberg to come to his office. The meeting remained vivid in Eastman's memory:

'Jack, Gumberg wants to have a talk with you.'

'Talk!' he said. 'Why talk to that counter-revolutionary son of a bitch?'

He hitched up his pants, gave himself a scratch under the arm, looked at me with a gentle, perhaps a slightly shamefaced smile, and walked out of the room.[18]

Hillquit's little jocular warning in May about the likely effects of the Sedition Law ('Congress, it seems, is trying to give us speakers a little vacation'), was long forgotten when Reed addressed a massive audience at Hunt's Point Palace on South Boulevard in the Bronx on 13 September 1918. Thousands were turned away. It was believed to be the largest demonstration for Bolshevik Russia ever held in the United States.[19] The speakers who preceded Reed had raised the audience to a pitch of enthusiasm, and one in particular, Ben Gitlow, a stocky twenty-seven year old, eloquent with the passionate social concerns of the Yiddish culture of the lower East Side, impressed Reed. They were to work closely together in the next two years. His own speech was billed as an account of present conditions in Russia, but the excitement of the occasion caused Reed to throw caution aside:

> he spoke simply, with conviction and emotion. Although he was no orator, his earnestness and his fighting mood were truly impressive. At times he fairly leaped off the platform as he spoke. Now and again he dropped a few Russian words, which unfailingly drew loud applause and vociferous cheers from the crowd. His words seemed to carry a genuine message from the land of revolution and a challenge to the whole capitalist world.... What was most striking to me was the great impatience that was apparent in his talk. He spoke rapidly, as if in a very great hurry. It seemed that John Reed felt that the revolution was near in America and time must not be lost in preparing for it. John Reed's whole demeanor showed that he was certain of it and was eager to play his part in the momentous events that were to take place.[20]

The day after the speech Reed was arrested for violating the Sedition Act, and freed on $5,000 bail. It was his third arrest since his return from Russia.

The second *Masses* trial brought Reed together with Eastman,

Dell and Art Young, but the issues at stake, whether the defendants had sought to obstruct the draft, were remote from current concerns. If they wished, Reed and the others could have defended themselves in such a way as to guarantee their going to prison. Debs had just received a twenty-year sentence, as had many of the Wobblies: there were good radicals in prison in October 1918. But discretion prevailed, some equivocal answers were given about the intention of certain articles describing the horrors of the war, and the jury again was unable to agree on a conviction. The passionate restatement of Bolshevik integrity made by Ben Gitlow at his trial in early 1920, which secured him a five-to-ten year sentence at Sing Sing after Clarence Darrow had virtually got him acquitted on a charge of criminal anarchy, was not the style of the *Masses* crowd.[21]

Radicals in New York saw Reed as the one who had actually been with Lenin and Trotsky in Petrograd, and as the first anniversary of the revolution approached they wanted his vivid, dramatic accounts of those stirring days. At a memorial meeting for Jacob Schwartz, a young man who died during the course of a trial on a charge of distributing leaflets against military intervention in Russia, Reed gave a picture of the moment when the workers of Petrograd poured out of the city to oppose the approaching Cossacks.[22] At formal celebrations of the anniversary of the revolution on 7 November, Reed, Williams, Eastman and others made the rounds of Hunt's Point Palace, the Brownsville Labor Lyceum and other locations, and were greeted with wild cheering. Reed talked about the events in the Congress of Soviets on 7 November 1917.[23] Both talks reveal that Reed's thinking had changed about the book he planned to write. The early drafts and introduction he had completed in Christiania were analytic and polemical. The brief pieces for the Jacob Schwartz memorial meeting, and for the anniversary celebrations, were descriptive, eye-witness narratives. He decided that for the writing of *Ten Days* he must resume his work as a reporter and a for a time cease to be a political controversialist. The first example of this new approach was 'Kerensky is Coming!', which appeared in the *Liberator* in July 1918. This extended narrative of Reed's visits to the hastily assembled Front at Pulkovo, where the battle was fought which saved the revolution, was quite unlike his earlier pieces on the Rrevolution. In the months during which he was separated from his papers, it became clear to him that the revolution would become comprehensible if readers were allowed to follow the events as Reed had experienced them. His great strengths as a reporter, especially his keen eye for detail, would then be put at the service of a plea for understanding aimed at a wider reading public.

In November, when his papers were finally returned by the State Department, he had before him a large pile of articles sent to the *Masses* and the *Call* from Petrograd, drafts completed in Christiania, notes for lectures delivered in New York and elsewhere, as well as his notebooks, little spiral pads which he bought in Russia and rapidly filled with his sprawling pencil notes. He also had boxes of documentary material, in several languages, only a portion of which had been translated. Reed rented a room above Polly Holliday's restaurant and largely disappeared from sight. Max Eastman saw Reed in the middle of Sheridan Square one day in December 1918: 'He was gaunt, unshaved, greasy-skinned, a stark, sleepless, half-crazy look on his slightly potato-like face – had just come down after a night's work for a cup of coffee.'

> 'Max, don't tell anybody where I am. I'm writing the Russian revolution in a book. I've got all the placards and papers up there in a little room and a Russian dictionary, and I'm working all day and all night. I haven't shut my eyes for thirty-six hours. I'll finish the whole thing in two weeks...'[24]

On New Year's Day 1919, Reed completed the preface to *Ten Days*. 'No matter what one thinks of Bolshevism, it is undeniable that the

Russian Revolution is one of the great events of human history', he wrote. 'In the struggle my sympathies were not neutral. But in telling the story of those great days I have tried to see events with the eye of a conscientious reporter, interested in setting down the truth' (p. xii).

Immediately after delivering the manuscript of *Ten Days* to Boni and Liveright, Reed once again returned to a heavy schedule of public lectures. Local authorities and the police did their best to prevent him from speaking. A meeting scheduled to be held on 3 January 1919 at the People's Forum at Public School 64 had to be hastily rearranged when the city authorities withdrew permission. A hall on Avenue C, in the lower East Side, was booked, but then cancelled after the manager received a warning not to allow the meeting to take place. Rearranged again for a small hall in another building on Avenue C, Reed's words were transcribed by government agents (who pointed out in their report that Reed's speech 'will doubtless be of interest to the United States District Attorney of the Southern District of New York'). Reed's comments were much the same from evening to evening: he proclaimed his family's long roots in the United States, and thus his 'perfect right' to damn the government if he so pleased; he denied that there was democracy any longer in America, and claimed that there was 'economic tyranny'. He openly denounced intervention in Russia, and pointed out how the laws against sedition were being used to suppress socialists and to destroy the constitutional right to freedom of speech:

> Well, the war is finished, comrades, and where in hell is the democracy? Now in New York City free speech is suppressed, socialists are not allowed to meet, the red flag is banned, periodicals are barred from the mails, and all the evidences of Prussianism appear. I want to ask...if you had ever been to a meeting in Germany, a political meeting? Absolutely the same phenomenon is here. The Chief of Police comes to tell you you can't talk about so-and-so, and one

hundred cops in the hall! [speech at Labor Lyceum, Brooklyn, 10 January 1919]

He spoke of the approaching moment when the radical movement would have to go underground; and of the lies and corruption which prevented the truth about the Bolsheviks from appearing in the American press. The venues changed, as did the government agents who attended every talk he gave, but Reed's message remained the same: 'power is the necessity'. He attacked the notion that the election of socialists to the City Hall or New York Board of Aldermen, or the election of socialists like Victor Berger or Meyer London to Congress, was the way to gain power. On the contrary, it was a delusion. And the labour unions were part of the problem:

> we come down here to the East side, and find our workers in organized unions and at the same time socialists. Almost all over the rest of the country we are true Americans, people not of foreign blood but of long American ancestry, who have grown up here. These people are in labor unions which are organised to cut the throat of socialism...[speech at 106 Avenue C, New York, 3 January 1919]

In the *Revolutionary Age*, Reed showed on 18 January 1919 that his criticism of the union movement and the Socialist Party was rooted in a thoughtful interpretation of the mentality of the American working man. Much indeed turned upon this question, for it was central to the defence of the 'practical' and 'pragmatic' anti-socialist policies of the American Federation of Labor that radical ideas and socialism were alien to ordinary workers.[25] To ask in January 1919 why American workers declined to vote socialist suggests that for all of his notorious enthusiasm, Reed's radicalisation had brought out the more reflective side of his nature. David A. Shannon, historian of the Socialist Party, refers in his book to Reed's 'impulsive, wild, undisciplined spirit' which at times made him seem an absurd figure.[26] But his analysis of the mentality of the

American working man in the *Revolutionary Age* shows that Reed was more level-headed, more realistic about the working class, than many of those who joined him in the Left Wing movement within the Socialist Party.

The crucial aspect of Reed's argument was its American emphasis. He advocated the need to conduct propaganda for socialism by following the example of the Bolsheviks:

> First, they found out from the working people what they wanted most. Then they made those wants into an immediate program, and explained how they were related to the other demands of the complete Social Revolution.... Comrades who call themselves 'members of the Left Wing' have an immediate job to do. They must find out from the *American workers* what they want most, and they must explain this in terms of the whole Labor Movement, and they must make the workers want more – make them want the whole Revolution.[27]

Reed's opponents within the Left Wing proposed following the Russian example with ruthless literalness. But, as the great struggle got underway within the Socialist Party, the twin issues of the *Americanness* of the policies of the Left Wing and the example of the Bolsheviks as a guide to policy bedevilled their debates at every turn.

The extent of public misinformation and the profound prejudice of the so-called experts on Bolshevism persuaded Reed, Bryant and Williams to request permission to appear before a sub-committee of the Senate Committee on the Judiciary, chaired by Senator Lee Overman, which was investigating the alleged connection between American brewing interests and German propaganda. On 4 February 1919 the authority of the committee was extended to include Bolshevik propaganda activities in the United States.[28] On 6 February some 60,000 workers in Seattle came out in a general strike, an event which was sensationally reported in the press and which shook the nation. When Bryant appeared on 20–21 February

179

1919, she was furiously grilled on her religious beliefs and political activities, mainly as a way of discrediting her testimony about Bolshevism. She was repeatedly and rudely interrupted. It had been a long, exhausting ordeal, out of which Bryant emerged strong, resilient and honest. It was her finest moment. Reed appeared on the afternoon of 21 February. He was quicker and more subtle than his Senatorial questioners, and in the sparring he could claim that not a glove had been laid on him. But the press reports of his testimony were savage, and continued to distort what he said about Russia. His letter of refutation to the *New York Times* went unpublished. Several weeks later the California novelist Gertrude Atherton wrote in the same paper that 'Bolshevism means chaos, wholesale murder, the complete destruction of civilization.'[29]

Reed went directly from Washington to Philadelphia on 22 February 1919, where he went on trial for his street-corner speech before a closed hall at the end of May. The prosecution tried to prove that by going to the hall after the permit had been denied, Reed was intending to provoke a riot. His defence lawyer put Reed on the stand, and let him tell the story of the speech in his own words. Despite a hostile press, judge and a patriotic address by the prosecutor, Reed's lawyer persuaded the jury that the case was solely about freedom of speech. The jury agreed, and acquitted Reed and his co-defendant.

He returned to New York, where he resumed a heavy schedule of speeches, to a political situation which approached civil war within the Socialist Party. There had been a notional 'left-wing' within the party since its creation in 1901, but it was not until the referendum in 1912 which led to the recall of Bill Haywood from the National Executive Committee that there were signs of a continuity of viewpoint.[30] The dominance of the Old Guard, led by Victor Berger and Morris Hillquit, which was identified with the gradualist electoral strategy of the party, and the determination to eliminate all talk of 'direct action' and syndicalist sabotage, led to a haemorrhage of militants to the IWW. Those activists who remained in the party were leaderless and directionless until war broke out. The party was officially united in its opposition to war, but a sizeable minority, led by intellectuals like John Spargo and A. M. Simons, were from the beginning for the Allies. The majority was strongly opposed to the war, and sought without particular effectiveness to help bring the warring European socialists together. When these efforts failed in 1915, the party opposed preparedness and campaigned to keep America out of the war. After doing poorly in the 1916 presidential election, and failing to make much impact on the national debate about preparedness, the growing left-wing in the party sharply denounced the national leadership. The war gave the left-wing an issue which transcended their narrow powerbase in the party.[31] But it was the Russian revolutionaries within America, and then the Bolshevik revolution, which made possible an organised Left Wing movement within the party.

A meeting of left-wing socialists was held at the Brooklyn apartment of the German-American editor of *New York Volkszeitung*, Ludwig Lore, on 14 January 1917. It was attended by twenty people, including the three leading Russian Bolsheviks then in America – Alexandra Kollontai, Nikolai Bukharin and Lev Trotsky – as well as leading figures on the Left of the Socialist Party – including Louis Fraina, Italian-born Jewish journalist who had learned his radicalism in DeLeon's Socialist Labor Party before joining the Socialist Party, and Louis Boudin, the Russian-born radical lawyer, author of *The Theoretical System of Karl Marx* (1907) and the chief rival within the Socialist Party to Morris Hillquit. (The feud between the socialist lawyers was a feature of party life for more than a decade.) At this meeting the faithful Leninist Bukharin, who had arrived in New York in November 1916 and became *de facto* editor of *Novy Mir* in January 1917, sought to strengthen support among American socialists for the Bolshevik and Zimmerwald view of the war.[32] He proposed that the left-wingers instigate a split from the Socialist Party. Trotsky opposed this tactic, and was supported by Lore, Boudin and Fraina. No consequences followed from this discussion, but the idea had been considered at a high level and the notion of a split had been planted.[33]

The Socialist Party opposed the war at its St Louis convention in April 1917, but the defection of the leading intellectuals and the actions of socialists who held political office did much, in the eyes of those who were passionately opposed, to compromise its stance. In March 1918 Socialist Aldermen in New York voted in favour of the third Liberty Loan. Similar gestures of support for the war were made by nominally socialist bodies in New York such as the United Hebrew Trades, the cloakmakers union and the International Ladies Garment Workers Union. Left-wingers in New York were determined to repudiate these traitors, and by the end of the war the first steps were taken to organize against the Old Guard leadership of the party. The Slavic Federations in Chicago, traditionally hotbeds of radicalism, formed a Communist Propaganda League on 7 November. A week later Local Boston of the Socialist Party issued the first copy of a new bi-weekly left-wing periodical, the *Revolutionary Age*, edited by Fraina. On 30 November the central committee of Local Boston issued a call for an immediate emergency National Convention of the Socialist Party. No such meeting had been held since the St Louis meeting after the declaration of war. The national leadership regarded it as too dangerous in wartime, too likely to be repressed. But now the war was over, opinion within the party was swinging to the left and there was considerable impatience with the delays in summoning the body which would elect a new national committee for the party.

On 19 December 1918, at a meeting in Petrograd, Zinoviev spoke openly of the imminent creation of a Third or Communist International. Reed's old friend, Boris Reinstein, was present at the meeting. The blockade prevented most news from reaching Russia, but Reinstein was optimistic about the revolutionary situation: 'Comrades, in so far as America is concerned, the conditions are ripening...'[34] A safe prediction; but in truth something was beginning to happen. Communications between the left wing in America and Russia were slow, uncertain and sometimes puzzling. A meeting in New York of the Russian and Ukrainian Federations of the Socialist Party and the Union of Russian Workers in January 1919 threatened to divide on a question of tactics, and was addressed in no uncertain terms by the 'International Bureau' of the Comintern, then just in the process of formation: 'There must be no splits or separations' (Lusk, 1, p. 653); but the Manifesto of the Comintern, issued in early March, conveyed the opposite message: 'The indispensable condition for successful struggle is separation not only from the direct servitors of capitalism and enemies of the communist revolution...but also from the Party of the Centre (Kautskians), who desert the proletariat at the critical moment in order to come to terms with its open antagonists' (Lusk, 1, p. 491). Interpreting the Russian approach to immediate tactics was not always easy in the press of heated controversy. Sometimes left-wingers had to feel their way. In early January 1919, at a meeting of the Central Committee of Greater New York Socialist Party, the Left tried to censure the activities of the party members who, as Aldermen, had voted in favour of the Liberty Loan. Were the left correct to choose this as the issue to split the party? The symbolic significance of the Liberty Loans suggests that they were right to see it as crucial. In 1918 the University of Chicago sociologist Robert E. Park explained the relationship of the Loans to the whole question of the war:

> In advertising the Liberty Loan the government has advertised its purposes in this war. People who subscribe to the United States war bonds subscribe at the same time to the aims of the United States, to the principles upon which these aims are founded, and to the methods

of the government in carrying them into effect. In order to sell Liberty bonds to 17,000,000 individuals in the United States it has been necessary to convince the great mass of the people that this is a just war, and to invite their co-operation in carrying it on.[35]

Those socialist Aldermen who supported the Liberty Loan, and who recently had supported the construction of a Victory Arch to commemorate the end of the war, had betrayed every argument, every principle, behind the Socialist Party's St Louis Declaration. But when the left tried to raise the issue, the Old Guard chairman refused. There followed an outraged bolt from the meeting, and an adjournment to another site. Wolfe later argued that 'the left began more as a mood than an organization...'.[36]

The decision was soon taken to form a City Committee of fourteen, which included Reed, Ben Gitlow, Nicholas Hourwich (the leader of the Russian Federation in New York), the Irish trades unionist James Larkin, Jay Lovestone and Bertram D. Wolfe. Reed, at thirty-two, was among the older members. They were immigrants, or the children of immigrants, largely without the middle-class backgrounds, elite educations or social polish which characterised Reed's circle at the *Masses*. He had come far. The tactic of the City Committee was clearly to appeal over the head of the Old Guard directly to the rank and file of the party. Wolfe and Reed were instructed to work on the draft of manifesto and programme written by Max Cohen and Jay Lovestone, and the City Committee authorised the calling of meetings in various boroughs of the city and elsewhere to discuss the formation of a Left Wing organisation. At a meeting on 2 February 1919 the decision was taken to set up as a party within a party: county organisers would be appointed, membership cards issued, and dues of 10c a month were to be charged. How Reed survived the meetings at which such matters were discussed we cannot say. He was not a good committee man. Uninterested in the minutiae of administration, and without the innate deviousness required for political infighting,

Reed was at his best at those moments when bold gestures, not calculation, were required. Others in the Left Wing had ambivalent feelings about Reed. As the author of *Ten Days That Shook the World* he possesed a unique international prestige; in a left wing which was largely 'ethnic' and 'foreign' he was unimpeachably American, and a Harvard man at that. But as a latecomer to left-wing politics, Reed was occasionally resented. However hard he worked at Marxist doctrine, he shared little of the interest in dialectical swordplay of a Lore, Boudin or Fraina. Behind the occasional criticism of Reed was the suspicion that he was using his prestige, and the undoubted enthusiasm with which his lectures were greeted across the nation, as a way to build a personal group within the left.

The manifesto which Wolfe and Reed drafted was a ringing affirmation of the Bolshevik view of class conflict, and an attack on imperialism and 'moderate' socialism. Reed's tone is detectable in the insistence that the Socialist Party 'must preach revolutionary industrial unionism, and urge all the workers to organize into industrial unions, the only form of labor organization which can cope with the power of great modern aggregations of capital' (Lusk, 1, p. 712). The Socialist Party had repeatedly failed to win over the American Federation of Labor to its socialist policies, and then had expelled its syndicalist membership in 1912–13. The Old Guard leadership effectively abandoned the whole question of the party's relation to trades unionism, and pursued a strictly parliamentary or electoral path to power. The National Executive Committee wanted nothing to do with bruising and divisive battles with Samuel Gompers and the American Federation of Labor leadership; and Reed, who retained an abiding affection for the *élan* and style of the Wobblies, regarded the failure 'to arouse the workers to class-conscious economic and political action, and to keep alive the burning ideal of revolution in the hearts of the people' (*ibid.*) as one of the gravest indictments of Socialist Party policy. This was a specific point, a disagreement with the party Old

Guard, rooted in political judgements about the sources of the 'class consciousness' of the working class.

Fraina insisted on re-drafting certain key passages of the manifesto, sharpening its language and inserting the requirement that the immediate struggle for power be conducted through Workmen's Councils, mass organisations of the working class. It was an Americanised version of the Russian 'Soviet'. But for the first time these Councils were alloted the task of destroying the bourgeois state by 'the the mass action of the revolutionary proletariat' (Lusk, 1, p. 713). Gitlow was among those who approved the revised manifesto at the organising convention of the Left Wing, held at St Mark's Place, New York, on 16 February 1919. But he later argued that '[i]t had nothing to do with American conditions'.[37] Reed was elected to the new City Committee of fifteen, and a contributing editor of the *Revolutionary Age*. Fraina stubbornly refused to submit his magazine to the control of the New York Left Wing. Fraina's supporters in the foreign language federations were determined to wait and see which way the new Left Wing was going to jump. Reed became a regular contributor to the *Revolutionary Age*, but the signs of tension between New York and Boston over its fate were a small indication of deeper divisions which emerged later in the year.

The Left-Wing manifesto in its final form appeared in the *Revolutionary Age* on 22 March. Reed, Wolfe, Gitlow and the others took it to every Socialist Party local in the city to which they could gain access. In some the Old Guard kept them away; in others Left-Wing majorities adopted the manifesto and its call for a national convention to implement its policies. The party in New York was in a state of near civil war, as each local was riven by arguments between the regulars and the Left Wing. Men and women who had devoted a lifetime to the party found themselves outvoted by newcomers who espoused policies which were alien to those which the party had so doggedly pursued. Their bitterness at what would

later be called 'entryism' made it virtually impossible for peace-
makers to operate. The Left Wing was undoubtedly gaining the
upper hand in the party across the nation. In a national referendum
held that spring, the Left Wing won twelve of the fifteen seats
contested. Reed defeated Victor Berger, leader of the Milwaukee
local, an elected Congressman on the socialist ticket and for many
years a leading figure on the right of the party. But no one in the
Left Wing doubted that Berger, Hillquit and the Old Guard were
resourceful men, firmly in control of the state party in New York
and the national office.

The counter-revolution began in Albany, New York, on 13
April, when the State Committee passed a resolution affirming its
opposition to the Left Wing Section, and by a vote of twenty-four
to seventeen, with two abstentions, gave the Executive Committee
authority to revoke the charter of any local which affiliated with
the Left Wing.[38] This was a decision taken virtually in despair of
the current political outlook for the Old Guard. On 18 April the
right wing had to stage their own walkout in the Bronx. At the
weekly meeting of the Executive Committee of the Left Wing on
19 April, it was reported that the manifesto had been adopted by
Socialist Party locals in Boston, Philadelphia, Cleveland, Rochester
and Buffalo, and by the state parties in Michigan, Minnesota and
Massachusetts. In the city, it had been adopted by Local Queens
on 3 April (Lusk, 1, pp. 681-2). Were the Old Guard to expel the
whole membership? Victory in the struggle against the Left Wing
might require nothing less – a pyrrhic victory, but feelings were
running so high on both sides in the spring of 1919 that such a final
solution had to be contemplated. On 21 April Julius Gerber
summoned a meeting of the City General Committee at which a
firm decision was taken to 'reorganise' a branch which had fallen
to the Left Wing. As Theodore Draper put it, 'the war in New York
was on'.[39]

On May Day in New York (and in other cities, especially Boston and Cleveland) mobs of uniformed soldiers attacked the offices of radical publications. Socialist meetings were stormed and broken up. At one, the gathered socialists were compelled to sing the 'Star-Spangled Banner'. Demonstrators carrying red banners were assaulted, while the police stood by. No condemnation of these vigilante raids appeared in the *New York Times*.[40] The poet E. E. Cummings was in New York, and wrote sardonically of what he had seen:

> It was tremendously funny – May Day! Cops, Bulls, Stool Pigeons, Fixers, etc. etc. lined 5th Avenue in preparation for the 'Vast Red Plot' fostered *for public consumption* by that charming person & *protegé of Wilson* – Mr. [A. Mitchell] Palmer [the Attorney General]. Not only that, – the government of this great city had a parade of all patriots – taxi drivers, tough guys, gangs, parochial school boys, *down* the Avenue to prevent the granting of a parade-permit to any 'Reds' who might want to march *up* it!!![41]

The American Legion was founded on 5 May 1919 to aid the government in its fight against the reds.

While socialists in New York were nursing their bruises, the Old Guard got busy. On 9 May Reed received a letter that his branch of the Socialist Party was to be 'reorganised'. Members who were not affiliated with any faction, and who 'wish to have a branch in the district free from terrorism, where comrades may come and bring their friends without fear of insult' were welcome.[42] Hillquit, the champion of the gradualist, lawful socialist position, was recuperating at Lake Saranac from a case of tuberculosis while his followers were purging the party. The victory of the Left Wing in the party elections thoroughly alarmed him. In an editorial in the *Call* on 21 May he proposed a clean separation between the warring groups within the party. 'The time for action is near. Let us clear the decks' (Lusk, 1, p. 530).[43] At a meeting of the party's National Executive Committee (NEC) in Chicago a decision was taken to revoke the charters of the Michigan, Massachusetts and Ohio parties, and to expel the foreign-language federations. In total some 30,000 members were removed from membership. At the same time the Old Guard declared null and void the national election to the NEC (which the Left-Wing slate had just won), and decided that the new NEC should be elected at an Emergency Convention to be held in Chicago on 30 August. Expulsions on this scale, and with this determination, stunned the Left Wing.

The day before Reed received the letter announcing the 'reorganisation' of his branch of the party, he began publication of a long series of articles entitled 'Why Political Democracy Must Go'. The Left Wing, grown tired waiting for the *Revolutionary Age* to be placed at its disposal, had decided to create their own organ, which was called *New York Communist*, and which was edited by Reed and Eadmonn MacAlpine. He wanted to show in these articles that the tactics and policies of the Socialist Party had failed, and that the party's electoral strategy had left the American proletariat at the mercy of capitalism and its armed thugs. He remained an admirer of the Wobblies, and shared their harsh scepticism about the likely outcome of playing the electoral game. Like so many things he wrote in 1919, these articles showed Reed's doggedness, his determination to arm himself with historical study and Marxian dialectics for the battles to come. They are, strictly speaking, intramural polemics in the battles between the Left Wing and the Old Guard, and within the Left Wing. Addressing an audience of the converted, he did not hesitate to reiterate his view that socialists had largely misunderstood the psychology of the American worker. Even when writing in the pages of *New York Communist*, Reed did not deceive himself by triumphalism (an ever-besetting tendency on the American left). If anything, he tended to over-state the negative conclusions of quite conservative analysts of the American working class:

> From before the Civil War to this day, the psychology of the American
> worker has been the psychology not of a class-conscious labourer, but
> of a small property holder.... In spite of unending disappointments,
> in spite of the hollowness of all his legislative victories, the American
> worker continues to believe the promises of the capitalism political
> parties, and *vote, vote, vote.*[44]

Between March and June Reed addressed another kind of
audience altogether, when the Press Forum news syndicate invited
him to engage in a debate with Catherine Breshkovskaya on
Bolshevism. Before the debate began Breshkovskaya withdrew and
was replaced by Henry Slobodin, formerly a right-wing member
of the Socialist Party who had resigned over the party's stance
towards the war in 1917. Reed worked hard on these debates, and
the profusion of drafts in the Reed papers at Harvard suggests that
he was particularly concerned to reach the kind of person who
would not normally come into contact with left-wing arguments.
The first drafts, which were begun before the war ended, contain
some interesting material, including a portrait of Lenin as 'a realist
of the coldest and most logical type'. Reed's final arguments reveal
several tendencies in his thought at this time. He had absorbed from
Charles Beard and other radical critics of the framing of the
American Constitution a view of its class bias. *'Apparently democratic
in form, the Constitution of the United States was deliberately framed, by
landlords, traders and speculators, to establish and maintain their property
rights and to thwart the will of the majority of people'* (Reed's italics).[45]
None the less, in an early draft discussion of 'America and Democracy' he seemed to imply that freedom and equality had been lost
by the accumulation of capital, thus negating the basic principle of
the Declaration of Independence that all men were created free and
equal.[46] The issue was whether the republican and democratic
foundations of the American state were part of a 'usable past'.
Could the Left-Wing campaign, as so many radicals in the past had
done, in the name of a restored and purified democracy? Reed's

answer sprawling through page after page of *New York Communist* was negative. He could see no hope in democracy or radical republicanism because the capitalist state functioned in a hegemonic fashion, and with the Bolshevik revolution the dictatorship of the proletariat had finally superseded political democracy.

Few of those who admire *Ten Days That Shook the World*, and Reed's essays in the *Masses* have taken the trouble to track down his political writings in 1919. The only anthology of his essays, *The Education of John Reed*, which was published in 1955, rigorously excludes this material. It is easy to see why: Reed's doubts about democracy, and his defence of the dictatorship of the proletariat sit uncomfortably beside the myths of the 'romantic revolutionary' and 'playboy' which have defined the roles allowed to Reed in American culture. It would be better to look unflinchingly at what Reed has to say, and not because one hopes to find such views acceptable. They remain emphatically against the grain of my own political instincts. Yet, the intertwining of his arguments about democracy and his understanding of the dictatorship of the proletariat explains why, in 1919, Reed played a significant role in the formation of a Communist Party. Without the arguments, the subsequent political struggles seem incomprehensible.

In one of the drafts prepared for the Press Forum debate Reed, writing as a Marxist, tried to show the connection between his several times repeated analysis of the psychology of the American working man and the question of democracy:

> The main purpose of institutions, customs, laws, morals, etc., of modern democratic countries is to create sentiments and conditions which operate to make people support their own oppressors. The working class and groups with similar interests are brought by means of capitalist control over schools, churches, newspapers, science, art and so forth, to act against their own class interests. Only to a limited extent, only to the extent that the capitalist class needs a certain amount of freedom itself, can the workers counteract this control by

means of propaganda and education. This control, not only of the bodies, but also of the minds of the workers, prevents them from exercising even a limited 'democratic' control that they have.[47]

Running throughout the Press Forum debate is Reed's belief that the dictatorship of the proletariat *was* a form of democracy, one which would actually work. 'The power of the capitalist class is based on private property. To secure power the workers must control capitalist property, and abolish ownership. This they can only do by force, – the Dictatorship of the Proletariat. The vast majority of mankind belongs to the working class; a dictatorship of the proletariat is, therefore, a government of and for the majority.'[48] He viewed such a dictatorship as a 'temporary measure' and not a dictatorship in any meaningful sense: 'The only personal liberty denied a citizen of the Bolshevist world is that of living in idleness on the products of the labor of others.'[49] He believed that the class war would be over as soon as the capitalist class ceased to exist:

> This government – the Dictatorship of the Proletariat – will take all measures necessary to eliminate the capitalist class. It will take away their property and disenfranchise all who do not work. When this process is completed, the war between the capitalist class and the working class will be over, classes will have disappeared, and democracy follows, based upon equality and the liberty of the individual.[50]

With the coming to power of the Bolsheviks, the idea of the 'dictatorship of the proletariat' had passed from the realm of theory to practice, and Reed had observed only the first four chaotic months of the new Soviet state. The very haziness of the concept, and the absence of sustained discussion of it in the works of Marx and Engels left Reed to envisage the 'dictatorship' in the passage quoted above as the *government* which presided over the transition to socialism, the government created by the Soviets. Reed had seen the proletariat intervene in the political and military struggle which followed the overthrow of the Provisional government and save the revolution. But of the complex questions of the relations of the Bolshevik Party to the proletariat, of the need to reconstruct a functioning social system, and of the actual course of civil liberties under the 'dictatorship', Reed in early 1919 had little understanding. But he fervently believed that the true democracy which would emerge would be 'based upon equality and the liberty of the individual'.[51]

The Left Wing could respond to the attack by the Old Guard, whose actions were of doubtful legality and were highly undemocratic. But the attentions of the Justice Department posed a more sweeping threat. The Immigration Act of 1918 gave the government the power to deport aliens for their beliefs. It was an administrative measure, against which there was no legal redress. A bomb attempt on the Attorney-General's life on 2 June triggered off a Justice Department decision, taken on 17 June, for the mass round-up and deportation of alien radicals. J. Edgar Hoover, promoted at the youthful age of twenty-four to Special Assistant to the Attorney-General, was placed in complete charge of the attack on radicalism in the summer and autumn of 1919. Hoover selected the targets (Emma Goldman, Alexander Berkman, C. A. K. Martens) and groups which were to be seized, he wrote the briefs which justified the deportations, organised the Radical Division (an interdepartmental task force, with its own budget and administrative staff), and hired its experts and translators.[52] The raids which Hoover planned were executed on the night of 2-3 January 1920, when 10,000 radicals were arrested. These efforts were duplicated on a local and state level. The Lusk Committee of the New York State Assembly was immediately disruptive of the Left Wing. The Lusk Committee obtained warrants for raids upon the offices of various groups which were sympathetic to Bolshevism, beginning on 12 June 1919 with the Russian Soviet Bureau, which had its files and correspondence seized. This was followed with raids on 21 June at the Rand School for Social Science, the headquarters of the Left-Wing Section of the Socialist Party, and the New York headquarters of the IWW. Warrants were executed against the Union of Russian Workers on 14 August. On the basis of materials seized, prosecutions were launched against many figures on the Left (seventy-five individuals are named in the Lusk report, 1, pp. 24-6).

Reed became increasingly secretive about some of his activities. While he would gladly risk arrest for speaking in public, he was anxious to maintain the privacy of his communications with Russia and with left-wing socialists in Europe. Inspection of his papers had ended in November 1918. Reed was unaware that his correspondence continued to be opened and copied. More direct approaches were made to find out what Reed was up to. An agent of the Office of Naval Intelligence approached Reed saying that he had just returned from abroad and would like to talk. He was invited on 14 March to Reed's small room on Patchin Place, and was asked about his credentials. Affiliation with the 'Norwegian Working Party' (*sic*) met with Reed's approval, and they talked for some time about matters of interest to Naval Intelligence. Reed admitted that American Bolsheviks had no reliable means to secure information from Russia, other than by underground channels. He hoped that some connection might be established through the Scandinavian countries, and mentioned that the postmaster in Stavanger was 'keenly interested' in Bolshevik activities. Reed explained that he planned to secure the services of a few sailors who regularly travelled between Holland and America. He seemed pleased to learn that the visitor, who claimed he had been an active Bolshevik, was soon returning abroad. He planned to prepare a statement which the visitor could take with him about the best way to improve communications, and asked the visitor to write a report of conditions in Scandinavia, which might be published under an assumed name. Copies of the report were sent to the State Department, Military Intelligence and to the Bureau of Investigation in the Justice Department – the agencies which competed for jurisdiction over loyalty and espionage cases.[53]

On 21-4 June 1919 the conference which organised the National Left Wing Section was held in New York. Held at the suggestion of Fraina and Ruthenberg, it was the Left's response to Hillquit's demand to 'clear the decks'. Delegates from newly expelled states and the foreign language federations were strongly represented. But when the National Council of nine was elected, the federations were omitted from the leadership. Nicholas Hourwich demanded that the federations be represented on the National Council in proportion to their membership strength. But this masked a sharp divergence on the future policy of the Left Wing. Hourwich was determined to break away and found a Communist Party; the others saw the Left Wing as a vehicle for taking control of the Socialist Party. This disagreement was over more than tactics. The language federations were made up of immigrants, with no roots in the American working class and no likelihood of assuming leadership of a national political party; they were distrustful of the reliability of American radicals. Their opponents, equally as likely to have immigrant parents or to have been immigrants themselves, were more clearly assimilated and more 'American' in outlook. It is significant that Irish trades unionists like Larkin, MacAlpine and Carney, whose roots were in the traditions of British social radicalism, were on the side of the 'Americans' in this dispute. The language federations were the big battalions. Two-thirds of the 70,000 members expelled or suspended by the Socialist Party were in federations represented by the thirty-strong group which Hourwich led out of the congress in protest. The National Council included Fraina, Ruthenberg, Larkin, Gitlow and Wolfe. It was an administrative body, given carefully defined duties with no power to make policy. Fraina was instructed to write a new manifesto.

On 26 June the National Council met in New York, where it approved and ordered the publication of the manifesto in the *Revolutionary Age*, which had now been relocated in New York and amalgamated with the *New York Communist*. Reed did not come through these meetings with particular distinction. He was elected to the committee on labour of the National Council, but was dropped from the staff of the *Revolutionary Age*. Only on Fraina's suggestion was he made a contributing editor, and given a small salary. The National Council was instructed to prepare a national conference to be held in Chicago on 1 September. With the language federations in opposition to the National Council, they were somewhat in the position of leaders without followers.

The Left Wing had decided against directly forming a Communist Party, and planned to pressurise the Socialist Party and then to take it over at the end of August. But when the language federations issued a formal call for a national conference to organise a Communist Party in the 7 July issue of *Novy Mir*, and denounced the Left Wing majority as 'centrists', elements of the Council (specifically Fraina, Ruthenberg and Lovestone) began secretly to negotiate with the leadership of the language federations. There was astounding duplicity in this move. Gitlow believed from this betrayal 'began the era of double dealing, lying, disregard of decisions, breaking of promises, and horsetrading for personal gain and position'.[54] These same people played out the farce of assembling in Chicago on 27 July to proclaim themselves the 'real' NEC of the Socialist Party. Victorious in the spring postal ballots, Fraina, Ruthenberg and Wagenknecht were elected national delegates. The new majority demanded that the national headquarters be turned over to themselves, and they voted to reinstate the expelled and suspended affiliates. They also requested all locals to ignore the expulsions and to send delegates to the Chicago convention. The Old Guard refused to accept the validity of the elections which had created this new NEC, and held tight to the offices and publications under their control. Reed took part, sincerely, in this farce. Fraina and the others did so in bad faith, having already determined to go where the numbers, and the power, really lay: with the language federations. On 28 July, Isaac Ferguson and Gitlow, representing the National Council, attended a meeting in New York to discuss the differences between the language federations and the Left Wing. The meeting ended in failure. They would not accept any of the proposals of the National Council, and demanded complete capitulation to the language federations, which would mean abandoning the plan to participate in the Socialist Party Emergency Convention. Gitlow was dismayed at the tactics employed (they spoke between themselves in Russian, and would provide no translator), and was even more alarmed when Ferguson revealed that he favoured capitulation. He felt the Russians knew more about revolution than anyone else.[55]

One day later, on 29 July, the National Council of the Left Wing received the demands of the language federations conveyed by Gitlow and Ferguson. This was the moment when the duplicity was revealed. In the ballot on the federations' demands, five voted to go to Chicago for the sole purpose of organising a Communist Party (Ruthenberg, the leader of the Cleveland Left Wing, John Ballam, Ferguson, Wolfe and Maximilian Cohen), and two (Gitlow and Larkin, joined by Reed, Wagenknecht and MacAlpine) voted to continue with National Council policy and attend the Socialist Party convention. Neither editor of the *Revolutionary Age* voted, but it was clear that Fraina had been the chief conspirator of this reversal of policy.

Reed, Gitlow and Larkin, like the socialist Old Guard, thought they had been betrayed, and were determined to strike back with whatever force they could muster. On 15 August the first issue of *The Voice of Labor* appeared, edited by Reed. It was the journal of the labour committee of the Left Wing Section, and a rallying point for loyalists. It soon had a circulation of 25,000. Eight days later, on the 23 August, the *Revolutionary Age* carried a joint call for a Communist Party convention, signed by Fraina, Wolfe and the others. The same issue also carried the announcement of the resignation from the staff of the paper by Reed, Gitlow and MacAlpine, in protest against the actions of the National Council. In the early summer the Left had fought and largely won the battle in the New York locals against the Old Guard. Now Reed returned to these same locals, in a renewed struggle for the loyalty of the party membership. He no longer hoped to succeed in Chicago by sheer weight of delegate support. The split in the Left Wing made defeat certain, but Reed and Gitlow, who worked intimately together, were determined to create out of the wreckage of Chicago a Communist Party which would be *American* in orientation. They knew that they were in a minority on the Left, and perhaps regarded the struggle as one of principle, and also of powerful symbolism. They could not conceive of a party led by the sectarian Hourwich and the untrustworthy Fraina as having credibility with the American working class. But the political differences between the Left Wing and Reed's group was slight: they were both violently against 'laborism' and 'moderate' socialism; they hoped to encourage splits in the American Federation of Labor unions; and were determined to destroy bourgeois democracy. It is easier to see a common programme uniting them than agreement on a common leadership. Fraina regarded Reed's split as being sectarian in origin, owing more to ambition than principle.

Reed, Larkin and Gitlow travelled together to Chicago.[56] Despite their realistic assessment of the prospects of success, Reed's spirits rose at the prospect of a good fight. He 'was as jubilant as a college boy going to a football game'.[57] The Socialist Party convention was to meet at Machinists' Hall, 113 S. Ashland Avenue, in the main auditorium on the second floor. The Left Wing met on 29 August, in a room on the ground floor of Machinists'

Hall. They were fifty-two strong, and elected a steering committee composed of Reed, Gitlow, Ruthenberg and Katterfeld.[58] They were preparing for serious battle, and agreed to vote as a unit. Reed's plan was to arrive early on 30 August, take their place in the hall and defy the organising committee's attempt to rule their credentials invalid. They correctly assumed that the Old Guard would use the question of credentials to control the convention. Notes of their plans for the following day were unaccountably left in the room where they met, and a politically alert janitor turned them over to Julius Gerber, Secretary of the New York County Socialist Party, who was the chief organiser of the convention. Thus they lost any hope of tactically surprising the Old Guard. All delegates were required to register at the Socialist Party National Headquarters, elsewhere in Chicago, for credentials to be admitted to the convention. Uncontested delegates would be issued with white cards. Reed and the Left Wing had been elected as delegates by locals which had been suspended or 'reorganised', and thus their credentials were invalid. Reed and his group barged into the hall, but were confronted by Gerber. Angry words were exchanged, which ended with Reed holding Gerber in the air, upside down, and insisting that they be allowed to remain. Gerber had anticipated the dispute, and instructed the Chicago policemen he had requested to clear the hall and only re-admit delegates with white cards. The Left Wing angrily went downstairs, followed by accredited Left-Wing delegates who bolted the convention when the majority refused to take immediate action on the exclusion of Reed and the others. He cabled home to Bryant at Patchin Place: 'Wonderful convention. Everything going fine.'[59]

Later that day eighty-two delegates formed a Communist Labor Party (CLP). Wagenknecht was elected Executive Secretary. Neither Reed nor Gitlow was on the National Executive, but their influence upon the CLP was manifest. Without them, the party would not have come into existence. Gitlow confined himself to membership of the labor committee, and Reed was selected international delegate. His worldwide prestige as the author of *Ten Days That Shook the World* would strengthen their case for recognition by the Communist International. It was probably clear to Reed from 30 August that he would again be travelling back to Russia. On 1 September the language federations and the majority of the Left Wing National Council met in Chicago and formed the Communist Party. Suggestions from Ruthenberg for an early amalgamation came to nothing, despite the fact that there was no longer any major issue dividing them. The rival manifestos were virtually interchangeable. Reed angrily stated that the Russian federation would have to 'come crawling on its knees' if it wanted unity.[60] And so, within a week, the Socialist Party was gutted, and two rival communist parties were born. Hostilities broke out almost at once.

When Reed returned to New York he told Bryant of the need to go to Russia (and to get there before Fraina). She was furious. Each time he went away it was an abandonment, increasingly hard to endure. He was too busy to argue. For three weeks he worked on future issues of the *Voice of Labor*, and discussed with Larkin the best way to depart without attracting the attention of the detectives, special agents, policemen and others who followed known radicals everywhere in the city. Forged seaman's papers in the name of 'Jim Gormley' were obtained, and Reed, dressed in workman's worn clothes, boarded a Scandinavian freighter in early October. Characteristically, he insisted that a few close friends see him off, and laughed at their alarm at the dangers of police surveillance.

He worked as a stoker during the voyage, and when he landed at Bergen he was given shore leave and promptly disappeared. Socialist comrades took Reed to Christiania, and on 22 October he crossed the border into Sweden. The civil war in Russia, and the threat of White terror in Scandinavia, made the organisers of his travel cautious. He was put on board a ship bound for Abo in Finland, and then travelled to Helsingfors, where he stayed with the writer Hella Wuolijoki – at each stage hearing news about Bolshevik defeats at the hands of the White generals Yudenitch and Denikin. Police raids prevented travel beyond Helsingfors. 'I can go neither forward nor back', he wrote to Bryant on 9 November (Rosenstone, *Romantic Revolutionary*, p. 361). When it was safe to move, they reached the border by sleigh and on foot. He caught the first available train for Moscow, and made his report to the Executive Committee of the Communist International (ECCI). Living modestly in a worker's house (a decision which impressed Lenin), he awaited the decision of ECCI which could send him back to New York. Reed once again began to function as a journalist, interviewing Trotsky (who seemed to Reed 'calmer, warmer, more genial') and Lenin (to whom he presented a copy of *Ten Days That Shook the World*); he also talked to Kamenev, and scribbled down in his notebook that he was plumper now, looking more than ever like a cocker spaniel.[61] Lunacharsky tried to explain to Reed the Bolshevik ideals in Soviet education, and he observed with great sympathy the work of the Proletcult. He was introduced to Mayakovsky. Despite the coldness of the winter of 1919-20 and the difficulty of securing transportation, Reed dressed in a long fur coat and fur *shapka,* which made him look like a visitor from the Caucasus, and began to travel outside Moscow to see factories, communes and villages. Angelica Balabanoff, who was then Secretary of the ECCI, recalled that 'I do not think than any foreigner who came to Russia in those early years ever saw or came to know as much about the conditions of the people as did Reed in the spring and summer of 1920.'[62] He filled numerous small notebooks with random notes and observations. Nothing systematic or profound, but the kind of thing which he could use later to write about the condition of Russia. He had an affair with a Russian girl.

201

On the surface Reed remained a dedicated supporter of the regime, but some of those who met him in Russia in 1920 have left contradictory accounts of his attitude towards the revolution. He met Emma Goldman, recently arrived on the *Buford*, the 'Red Ark' which carried radical deportees from the United States, in January. Despite her delight at seeing Reed, she was disturbed by much of what she had seen in Russia. It seemed to Goldman very far from being a society built on justice and freedom. 'The situation is such that we are now going through the deepest spiritual conflict in our lives', she wrote to a friend.[63] Goldman expressed some of her doubts to Reed, especially concerning the functioning of the Cheka. Reed had made several entries in his Russian notebooks about the counter-terror of the Cheka, without indignation. There were real conspiracies, and assassination attempts had been made; the Cheka dealt with enemies of the revolution. Others, regrettably caught up in their zeal, could not be helped. He was particularly bloodthirsty while talking to Goldman about the SRs and socialists who had allied with the White forces in opposition to the Bolsheviks. By implication he may have seen Goldman heading in the same direction and wished to give her a vivid warning. 'I don't give a damn for their past. I am concerned only in what the treacherous gang has been doing during the past three years. To the wall with them! I say. I have learned one mighty expressive Russian word, "*razstrellyet*"! (execute by shooting).'[64] Goldman found this reasoning outrageous, and said so. He accused her of failing to understand the reality of revolution. They parted angrily. Before he left Reed suggested that Goldman might want to call on Angelica Balabanoff in Moscow.[65] By this Reed certainly meant more than a good contact or helpful hand for the newly arrived Goldman. He had been seeing Balabanoff about the ECCI discussions of the American situation, and they had soon come to trust each other. Trust was one of the many commodities in short supply in Moscow in 1920. He had said things to Balabanoff which he felt he could share with no one else in Russia. She recalled Reed's depression at the suffering he had seen on his travels in Russia, a disorganisation far worse than that which he had seen in 1915 or 1917 and which was made worse by the cynical indifference of the bureaucracy. His irritation and discouragement were not specifically directed against the government. 'Sensitive to any kind of inequality and injustice', she wrote, 'he would return from each of his trips with stories that were heartbreaking to both of us'.[66] In one of his Russian notebooks, he wrote:

From
Dying village we hear cry and aweful sigh
A sigh which cried 'Land Land'
It grows & widens to the cities he cries 'Understand me!' In this awful cry so much bitterness and pain so much pain lonesomeness and tears as if millions of pale arms – hands Faces which clouded without home without…[67]

When they met Goldman was surprised by Balabanoff's frankness about the reality of conditions in Russia. She was the first Communist who did not repeat the 'old refrain' and blame everything on sabotage and the civil war.[68] Reed wanted Goldman to share the sense he and Balabanoff had of the complexity of conditions, and not to fall into destructive outright opposition. His provocative words to her about executions were those of a friend, if only Goldman had the subtlety to understand correctly what he was trying to say.

The ECCI decision about the recognition of the American parties was made in February. They called on the Communist Labor Party and the Communist Party to hold a merger convention; that the merged party was to be called the United Communist Party of America; and that the foreign language federations were to be subordinated to the central party organisation. Reed had heard nothing from America since entering Russia, but the little news which arrived was of mass arrests and repression of the Left. (Communications were so difficult that a Comintern circular dated 1 September 1919 was not received in New York until January 1920.[69]) It was clear that a unity convention would be highly vulnerable to government raids, but there was nothing to do but to prepare for an arduous journey across Scandinavia to find a place once again on a ship heading for New York. There were other reasons for leaving as quickly as possible. He missed Bryant and had heard nothing from her since leaving New York in the autumn. The last time he was in Russia he faced a criminal trial on his return. He faced another trial if he returned, for he had been charged with criminal anarchy in Illinois along with three dozen other CLP leaders and a much larger number of CP members. His friends Ben Gitlow and Jim Larkin had been convicted and sentenced to long terms in prison on criminal anarchy charges, and Reed would necessarily have assumed that he too would go to prison if he returned home. None the less he persisted in planning his return. The ECCI gave him some jewels (102 small diamonds worth about $14,000) and cash to the value of $1,500 to carry with him back to America for the communist movement. It was a small sum, but Russian couriers had repeatedly been arrested.

His first attempt to leave Russia in February was made through Latvia. He grew a moustache for the occasion, and carried seaman's papers in the name of 'Jim Gormley'. In addition to the jewels, he carried a packet containing letters from *Buford* deportees, notebooks, autographed photographs and a brief introduction which Lenin had written in English for *Ten Days That Shook the World*. But a sudden turn of fortune for the Red Army left him waiting in a deserted railway station for a train to the coast which never came. He eventually returned in the box car of a military train bound east, and reappeared in Petrograd frozen and exhausted.

A second trip in March was arranged by Finnish ship bound for

Sweden – the traditional coal box route which Bolsheviks used to reach Stockholm. He crossed the Finnish border and reached Helsingfors, where he had friends among the local radicals. At the port of Abo Reed was hidden in the hold of a freighter on 13 March, but was found in the coal bunker by customs officials during a routine inspection. He was taken to the police station. He stood up to intense police interrogation with great fortitude, maintaining that he was in truth Jim Gormley. But the jewels, photographs, letters and false documents rendered his story untenable, and he readily gave the Finnish authorities his name. Despite being beaten several times and threated with torture, throughout April and May he refused to give the Finnish authorities the names of his contacts in Helsingfors. He talked with great enthusiasm about conditions in the United States and Russia, but clammed up when they asked about his local friends. Tiring of this, he decided on a policy of non-communication. Had his links with Finnish socialists been revealed, he would have faced a trial for treason. Unable to try him on the more serious charge of treason, Reed was tried and convicted for smuggling, and the jewels were confiscated.[70] The Finns would have preferred to keep the whole case a secret, but word soon leaked out and stories appeared in the Finnish press about the mysterious 'man in the coal box'. The American press carried an announcement of his arrest on 17 March.

The American Secretary of State was satisfied that Reed had been arrested. The legation in Helsingfors would certainly have received reports of Reed's presence in Moscow, and there was intense pressure upon the Finnish authorities to grant access to Reed's papers. The Finnish Ambassador in Washington was summoned to the State Department to receive the formal American request for this material. The American Chargé d'Affaires in Helsingfors eventually obtained copies of Reed's letters and other papers, which were then forwarded to Washington. There was no basis for extraditing Reed to America (the charges pending in Illinois were for violation of state and not federal law), and no treaty with the Finns even if there had been. Otherwise, the American authorities remained indifferent to Reed's fate, and he declined to ask for their diplomatic assistance.

Reed's friends in Helsingfors, who provided him with legal support and reading matter, allowed the story that Reed had been executed by the Finns to reach the Associated Press correspondent. When this news reached America on 9 April Reed's friends, orchestrated by Bryant, bombarded Washington with demands that the government investigate the story. These friends included Jane Addams, Carl Hovey and H. J. Whigham from the *Metropolitan*; Fred Howe, Louis Post, Arthur Garfield Hays and even Bernard Baruch made representations to the State Department.[71] A denial was soon forthcoming, but the Chargé d'Affaires was strictly instructed not to involve himself in Reed's plight. When news of his arrest reached Russia, approaches were made, using an American journalist as intermediary, to enquire whether the Finnish authorities would exchange Reed for a Finnish general and his son taken prisoner at the end of February 1920. Nothing came of this vague approach. After payment of the fine for smuggling, no charges were pending against him, and his continued detention was clearly illegal.

As the weeks dragged on Reed's physical condition and state of mind deteriorated sharply. He remained uncooperative with the authorities, but was suffering from insomnia and depression, and his letters to Bryant were alarming. In despair, on 18 May Reed threatened to go on hunger strike if he was not released. On 2 June he wrote to Bryant that he had still heard nothing from Estonia, where his friends had sought permission for him to travel on to Russia. 'It is dreadful to wait so, day after day – and after three months, too. I have nothing to read, nothing to do. I can only sleep about 5 hrs. and so am awake, penned in a little cage, for 19 hrs. a day.'[72] The Finns suddenly decided to release Reed, providing he could obtain permission to enter another country. The State Department refused Reed's application in May to issue him with a new passport, and hoped that Reed would voluntarily surrender himself to the American authorities. Reed's friends in Helsingfors finally secured Estonian permission and on 5 June he sailed to Reval. Two days later he travelled to Petrograd, bringing with him some of his papers, including the text of Lenin's introduction to *Ten Days*, but the rest were retained by the Finnish authorities and subsequently disappeared. He was put up in the Hotel International to recover. Emma Goldman heard that Reed was alone and without proper care. When she visited him he seemed in a bad state. He had been fed almost exclusively on a diet of dried fish by the Finns and was badly malnourished and suffering from scurvy. His spirits seemed high.[73] By the end of the month he was sufficiently recuperated to travel south to Moscow. He sent three messages to Bryant by courier, but repeatedly advised her to await definite word before coming to join him. It is possible that he still hoped to leave Russia, and to meet her somewhere else. He did not want to put her at risk until plans were perfected; but he said nothing definite and Bryant tensely awaited the couriers who hand delivered each letter. She finally sailed on a Swedish tramp steamer on 30 July and landed at Gothenburg on 10 August.

The second Congress of the Communist International was scheduled to be held in July. Reed was housed in the hotel near the Kremlin set aside for delegates, and greeted old friends and strangers to Moscow with enthusiasm. There were some 200 delegates gathered for the Congress, from thirty-five countries. With the arrival of Fraina in Moscow the American representation would be at a high level. They were not personally close, but when confronted with the Comintern thinking about American trades unions the areas of agreement far outweighed any disagreements. With the other delegates Reed was jovial, charming, persuasive and as boisterous as ever. 'The famous American revolutionary was indeed like an over-grown boy – tall, powerfully built, with a handsome face and extremely friendly manners', recalled the Indian revolutionary M. N. Roy.[74] But photographs taken of Reed at this time show that he was much thinner, and his face was lined. The experiences of the past year had taken a great deal out of him. He looked weak and sallow and when the mask of enthusiasm slipped he was an exhausted man.

The Congress began with ceremonial sessions held in Petrograd, and then shifted back to Moscow for extended working sessions in the Coronation Hall. The procedure adopted was for the election of committees at the first plenary session on 23 July which would report back draft theses for discussion and adoption by the delegates. Karl Radek, as Secretary of ECCI (where he replaced Balabanoff), had control of the agenda and speakers chosen, and this control was exercised with ruthless effectiveness. The worldwide respect for the Russian revolutionaries, and for the success of the Red Army (which was sweeping westward through Poland when the Congress began), led to the same behaviour which had outraged Reed in the Left Wing section of the Socialist Party in America: he was continually alarmed at the willingness of hardened revolutionaries meekly to defer to Russian wishes. Reed was made of sterner stuff, and did not hesitate to argue his views about the correct revolutionary tactic for the United States. The Congress line, laid out in Lenin's *Left Wing Communism: an Infantile Disorder*, assumed that the tide of revolutionary ferment which coincided with the end of the war had now ebbed, and that in the future it was the duty of communists to work within existing political and trades union institutions. In Reed's opinion, this was a disastrous policy. The Socialist Party had utterly failed to capture the American Federation of Labor, and the policy Reed advocated for the Communist Labor Party was designed to split off the radical elements from American Federation of Labor unions and to carry the fight for radical unionism to unorganised workers in the tradition of the Wobblies. Reed believed that the Russians had failed to grasp the utterly reactionary nature of the American Federation of Labor, and he gathered together a group of two dozen delegates who consisted of all the Americans, the English and assorted adherents of syndicalism among the other European delegations. They made two requests: that the trades union question be given priority and that English be included among the official languages. Both requests were brushed aside by Serrati for the Presidium.[75] He was appointed to the commission on National Minorities, and on Trade Union Activities. Reed's contribution to the former came on 25 July, when he argued that policy towards the American Negro should be based upon their demands for social and political equality, that they should be organized into the same unions as whites and treated in every other respect as workers (*Minutes*, 1, pp. 120-4).

The trades unions question loomed as the cause of the greatest conflict between Reed and the ECCI. The official theses on trade unions were introduced by Radek, and followed the ninth of Lenin's nineteen conditions for affiliation to the Communist International. The official view was that it was the job of communists to infiltrate established trade unions in order to transform them into organs of revolutionary struggle. The British and American delegates took the lead in opposing this. In the United States, in particular, where only 20 per cent of the labour force was within unions affiliated to the American Federation of Labor, a policy which concentrated upon winning over the labour aristocracy and which effectively ignored the rest was self-evidently inadequate. They also argued that Gompers's bureaucracy was unchallengeable. They wanted to destroy the American Federation of Labor, and to concentrate upon the vast number of unorganised workers. The two strategies were scarcely reconcilable. The Russians would only accept work within such bodies as the Trades Union Congress (TUC) and the American Federation of Labor.

English-speaking delegates denied that such a policy was possible. Fraina shifted towards the Comintern view during the debate, thus strategically positioning himself *against* dual unionism and *against* smashing the old unions. Radek and his lieutenants did their best to keep the bitter disagreements from the knowledge of the Congress by asserting that essential agreement had been reached. They tried to overcome objections by sheer force of lung-power and oratory, and then by sharp procedural practice by calling for a vote before the debate had finished. Reed saw in their tactics an attempt to shut out the English and American delegates. They were not prepared even to debate the question. He pointed out that Radek had misrepresented the debates in the committee sessions, at which Radek accused Reed of impudence and of being a liar (*Minutes*, 2, pp. 90-1). Despite interventions by Eadmonn MacAlpine and Willie Gallagher, all they could wrest from Zinoviev was a delay until the session of 5 August, at which point the Leninist theses were overwhelmingly approved. Reed did not vote. 'We can't got back to America with that', he told Rosmer. But there was little choice.[76] In the eyes of Radek and Zinoviev, Reed had been the chief troublemaker at the Congress, and there was not the slightest hint that he either regretted his opposition or planned to conform in the future. None the less, at the end of the Congress he was named the American representative on ECCI. He continued his awkward behaviour within ECCI, and fully intended to demand the reversal of the theses on trades unions at the next Comintern Congress. He was contemptuous of Radek and Zinoviev, and after one particularly unsatisfactory meeting he offered to resign. This in turn was branded as 'petty bourgeois' behaviour, and Reed withdrew. But the reality was that he did not like what he had seen of the Comintern and its leadership. Like Balabanoff, he was inclined to blame Zinoviev for the autocratic and manipulatory way the organisation was being run. The fault lay in the man and not the system.

Zinoviev did not wait long to take his revenge. A call to the 'Enslaved Peoples' of the East had appeared in *Izvestia* on 3 July 1920, before the Comintern Congress. A large anti-colonialist Congress was to be held on 15 August at Baku, the great oil port on the Caspian Sea and revolutionary centre of the Caucasus. The Congress was a symbolic gesture of defiance against the British, who had seized the oil fields during the civil war; and an affirmation of common cause between the western industrial proletariat and the eastern colonial peoples. M. N. Roy, who had played an important role in the Congress discussion on colonialism, opposed the idea. He felt it was premature, and that revolutionary parties in the east were too disorganised. When pressed by Zinoviev (who with Radek and the Hungarian Bela Kun were the ECCI delegates to Baku), Roy described the Baku meeting as a wanton waste of time and energy, and referred to it as 'Zinoviev's Circus'.[77] Radek turned his formidable powers of sarcasm on Roy; Borodin lectured him on Bolshevik discipline and Chicherin argued the case for going with gentle persuasiveness – all to no avail. He refused to go, and busied himself with plans to set up a Central Asiatic Bureau of the Comintern based at Tashkent.

The case of M. N. Roy is an interesting example of the limits of individual dissent within the early Comintern. There were, if one knew the inner life of Bolshevik Moscow, other examples of such tactics. Early in 1920 Balabanoff, then secretary of ECCI, was ordered by Zinoviev, newly appointed President of the Comintern, to take charge of a branch of the Comintern which they proposed to open in the Ukraine. Despite Lenin's specific wish that she should go, Balabanoff refused. The Bolshevik Party Central Committee then ordered her to take a rest at a sanitorium. Despite the unique privilege being offered, Balabanoff refused. She was then ordered by Zinoviev to head a propaganda train which was to be sent to Turkistan. It was also a period when powerful delegations were expected from Britain and then from Italy, which included her oldest friends and comrades. Reed understood what Zinoviev was doing, and tried to warn Balabanoff:

> 'They want to get rid of you,' he told me after my return from Petrograd, 'before the foreign delegations arrive. You know too much.'
>
> 'But surely', I replied, 'they don't doubt my loyalty.'
>
> 'Of course not, but neither do they doubt your honesty. It is that they are afraid of.'[78]

She once again refused to go to Turkistan. And for this she was excluded from the workings of ECCI, and then removed from her position as Secretary.[79]

Reed's warning long preceded the Comintern Congress, but it confirms that before his angry conflicts with Zinoviev and Radek he had drawn firm conclusions about what kind of people they were, and what might be expected from them. It alerted him to the procedural tricks and bullying tactics he encountered at the Congress, and it made him doubly wary when Zinoviev insisted that Reed be one of the delegates to the Baku Congress. The plan was for delegates from countries with colonies to be given special prominence in the Congress's anti-colonialist propaganda: Jansen from the Netherlands, Rosmer from France, Quelch from Britain and Reed were selected for this role. (Quelch and Rosmer had signed the original call for the conference, as had Fraina. The decision to require Reed to attend looked suspiciously like Zinoviev's retribution.) It was a long journey, five days by train, through countryside devastated by the civil war, and infected by typhus. Reed was reluctant to make the trip. He had planned to go to Petrograd to meet Bryant, who was travelling from Murmansk, but Zinoviev refused to allow him to travel to Baku later, after meeting Bryant. He insisted that Reed go on the official train. His precise words, as preserved by Gitlow, were 'Die Kominturn hat ein Beschluss gemacht. Gehorchen sie'[80] – the

Comintern has made a decision. Obey. Reed was not used to being spoken to in such language, and with such obvious contempt, and one can easily imagine the aggressive and rebellious response which in other circumstances he would have made. But there were other considerations. He was far more dependent on Bolshevik goodwill than Roy, due to the sheer difficulty of travel; and unlike Balabanoff he was not yet prepared to break completely with the Comintern. An additional factor was Bryant. She had sought to communicate with Reed through ECCI, but her letters were not forwarded. Reed did not know precisely where she was, nor where they might meet. He was, in the end, not free to do other than Zinoviev demanded.

Long after his abandonment of communism, Ben Gitlow wrote of Reed as 'the prisoner of a movement that advocated the suppression of liberty and held individualism in contempt'.[81] If such a picture of Reed was ever correct, it applied to the moment when he received his orders from Zinoviev. But there was more than one ideology which justified the suppression of liberty and dealt in a cavalier manner with human rights, if not theoretical individualism. And there were many different kinds of prisoner in 1920. As the world looked to Reed, to be free at the discretion of Albert Burleson, the Postmaster-General, or Judge Landis did not ultimately seem preferable to accepting orders from Zinoviev. He had taken the side of the proletariat in the greatest issues of the day, and that was perhaps the most important imprisonment of all. It was a commitment which he accepted even at the high cost of the loss of personal liberty. He once remarked to Arno Dosch-Fleurot: 'Perhaps it is time some one went to jail. It may be the best thing I can do to advance the cause.'[82]

And so, with great reluctance, he went to Baku. Accounts of this expedition vary greatly in detail and emphasis, and are also strongly coloured by the attitude of the source towards the Communist International, and towards the question of Reed's last illness and alleged disillusionment with communism. Gitlow

published two memoirs of his experience of American communism, in the second of which, *The Whole of Their Lives* (1948) appears
'Louise Bryant's Story', which he claims was told to him in 1921
or 1922 by Bryant while Gitlow was still in prison. This text has
remained central to the argument that Reed died in bitter
disillusionment with the Communist movement.[83] In addition to
containing the allegation that Reed suspected that he had been
betrayed by Zinoviev to the Finnish police, Bryant gave a
description of the Baku journey that revealed Reed's sense of
outrage at the corruption of the Comintern leadership and the
demagogy of its policies. In particular, she claimed that while the
Russian people were starving, the delegates were lavishly provided
with expensive foods and liquors, that 'old Mohammedan women'
boarded the train and offered their daughters, disrobed, to the
delegates. What followed was an 'orgy of drunken lasciviousness'
in which Radek played a leading part. The conference itself, as
Bryant recounted it, was characterised by the extreme cynicism and
demagogy of Zinoviev and Radek, who would say anything to
arouse the participants but who allowed only a carefully sanitised
account of the speeches to be broadcast to the world.

Rosmer, a French communist delegate at the Second Congress
of the Comintern and like Reed a member of ECCI, was a delegate
to the Baku Congress and included an account of the journey in his
Moscou sous Lénine (1953), published long after his own break with
the Comintern. He would, in other words, have as little reason as
Gitlow to cover up disgraceful events on such an occasion. But he
has the peasant women offering the travellers fruit, not their
daughters. In other respects, the omissions in Rosmer's account are
striking. He said nothing about Reed's weakened physical state or
illness, nor of Reed's conflict with Zinoviev. On the other hand,
he gave a truthful sense of Reed's poverty and adventuresomeness,
and quotes a sentence from Reed's speech which undoubtedly
captures the man: 'Don't you know how Baku is pronounced in

American? It's pronounced *oil*!'[84] What Reed did and thought on the journey to and from Baku, and during the Congress, remains conjectural. He was outraged at the behaviour of Zinoviev and Radek before he left, and nothing occurred which changed his mind on that score. The receipt of a telegram from Bryant, announcing her arrival in Moscow, would have made him doubly impatient to return.

Reed arrived in Moscow on 15 September, and he at last was able to tell Bryant something of what had happened to him over the past eight months. He seemed to Bryant a man transformed:

> I found him older and sadder and grown strangely gentle and aesthetic. His clothes were just rags. He was so impressed with the suffering around him that he would take nothing for himself. I felt shocked and almost unable to reach the pinnacle of fervor he had attained.[85]

He took Bryant to meet Lenin, Trotsky, Kamenev and other leading Bolsheviks, and they went to the ballet and visited Moscow's art galleries. Reed was determined to return home, and despite Bryant's pleas that he at least rest and regain his strength, there was a frightening intensity about him. When she was briefly out of the room, he would shout for her, and hold her hand tightly when she returned. On 25 September he fell ill with a high temperature and dizziness which the doctors at first diagnosed as influenza. Reed was moved to the Marinsky hospital on the 30 September, where a further diagnosis revealed that he was suffering from spotted typhus. Bryant spent every moment trying to make him more comfortable, but the Allied blockade was effective and there were no medicines to be obtained. His mind wandered back to their earlier lives together, when they were both very brave. And then he lost the use of the right side of his body, and could no longer speak. Bryant was holding his hand on 17 October 1920, three days before his thirty-third birthday, when he died.

Bryant preserved Reed's papers for many years, only to succumb to alcoholism, Dercum's disease and a cerebral haemorrhage in Sèvres in 1936. She was never interviewed by Reed's first biographer, Granville Hicks.

The others who had known Reed dispersed across the globe. Carranza died in 1920, murdered by a rival for power. Villa was assassinated in 1923. Lenin and Wilson, stricken men, died in 1924, as did 'Jig' Cook, who had gone to live in Greece. 'Big Bill' Haywood jumped bail and fled to Russia, where he died a forgotten man in 1928. Hillquit, still loyal to the Socialist Party, died in 1933. Steffens, feted by communists in his last years, died in 1936. Zinoviev, Stalin's ally in the struggle against Trotsky in the 1920s, was accused of treason and executed by Stalin in 1936. Radek supported the Trotskyite opposition until 1929, and then capitulated to Stalin. Arrested in 1936, he was the chief defendant in the second show trial in 1937 and probably died in prison in 1939. Trotsky was expelled from the Communist Party in 1927, exiled from Russia in 1929 and assassinated in Mexico in 1940. Hutchins Hapgood, largely forgotten as a writer, died in 1944. Reinstein survived the worst of the purges to die in Russia of natural causes in 1947. Eugene O'Neill, the greatest American playwright, died in 1953, as did Louis Fraina, who, after his expulsion from the Communist Party, adopted the name 'Lewis Corey' and made a second career as an academic economist. Mabel Dodge turned away from Greenwich Village, married a Native American, Tony Luhan, and lived for many years in Taos, New Mexico, where she died in 1962. Albert Rhys Williams, who never joined the Communist Party after all, completed the manuscript of his second book on his experiences in Petrograd, *Journey into Revolution,* before his death in 1962. His last article, 'a magnificent reaffirmation of his socialist faith' (Joshua Kunitz), was a piece requested by *Izvestia* to mark the forty-fourth anniversary of the Bolshevik Revolution. Balabanoff returned to Italy after the fall of Mussolini, and worked for the right-wing Social Democratic Party of Saragat. She died in 1965.

Eastman, who had become a Goldwater Republican and a regular contributor to the *Reader's Digest*, died in Barbados in 1969. He and Gitlow had been prominent anti-communists since the 1920s. Kerensky, for many years exiled in the United States, died in 1970. Walter Lippmann died in 1974. He had become the most eminent of conservative commentators on public affairs. Reed had a hero's funeral, and was buried in the wall of the Kremlin.

Notes

Introduction

1 Anatoli Rybakov, *Children of the Arbat*, trans. Harold Shukman, London, 1988, p.282.

2 Joseph Freeman, 'Review and Comment', *New Masses*, 16 June 1936, pp.23-4.

3 Eugene C. Dolson, 'John Reed', *Poetry*, 30 (August 1927), p.265. See also Michael Gold, 'John Reed and the Real Thing', *New Masses*, 3 (November 1927), pp.7-8.

4 First published by Dos Passos as 'John Reed', *New Masses*, 6 (October 1930), pp.6-7. See also Alan Calmer, 'John Reed', *The Left*, 1 (Spring 1931), pp.22-7.

5 Granville Hicks, *One of Us: The Story of John Reed*, New York, 1935, section 30 (unpaginated).

6 Louis Fischer, *The Life of Lenin*, New York, 1964, p.124.

Chapter 1

1 E. Kimbark, MacColl, *The Shaping of a City: Business and Politics in Portland, Oregon 1885-1915*, Portland, 1976, pp. 64-5.

2 'Almost Thirty' was first published in two parts in *The New Republic*, 86 (15, 29 April 1936), pp. 267-70, 332-6. It is most conveniently available in Reed's *Adventures of a Young Man: Short Stories from Life*, San Francisco, 1975.

3 Granville Hicks, *John Reed: the Making of a Revolutionary*, New York, 1936, p. 18. Further references to Hicks will appear in the text.

4 MacColl, *The Shaping of a City*, pp. 290-8; Steffens, *Autobiography*, 1 vol. ed. , New York [1958], pp. 544-5, gives a brief account of the Oregon timber frauds.

5 MacColl, *The Shaping of a City*, p. 298.

6 Barrett Wendell, *English Composition: Eight Lectures Given at the Lowell Institute*, New York, 1891, pp. 196, 200.

7 M. A. De Wolfe Howe, *Barrett Wendell and His Letters*, Boston [1924], pp. 68, 327.

8 William R. Castle, 'Barrett Wendell – teacher', *Essays in Memory of Barrett Wendell, by His Associates*, Cambridge, Mass., 1926, p. 7.

9 William James, *The Varieties of Religious Experience* (1902) in *Writings 1902-1910*, ed. Bruce Kuklick, New York, 1987.

10 Eliot's 'The humanism of Irving Babbitt', *Forum*, July 1928, appears in his *Selected Essays*. On Eliot's reaction to Babbitt while still at Harvard, see Herbert Howarth, *Notes on Some Figures Behind T. S. Eliot*, London, 1965, pp. 127-35. Eliot took Copeland's English 12, and his experiences are recorded in J. Donald Adams, *Copey of Harvard: a Biography of Charles Townsend Copeland*, Boston, 1960.

11 Robert Rosenstone, *Romantic Revolutionary: a Biography of John Reed*, New York, 1975, p. 40. Further references to Rosenstone will appear in the text.

12 Ronald Steel, *Walter Lippmann and the American Century*, London [1981], p. 14.

13 *Ibid*. , p. 24.

14 *Ibid*. , p. 28

15 John S. Reed, 'Interesting people: Charles Townsend Copeland', *The American Magazine*, 68 (November 1911), pp. 64-6.

16 Lippmann, quoted in A. Scott Berg, *Max Perkins: Editor of Genius,* London [1979], pp. 31-2.

17 Reed, 'Copeland', p. 65.

18 Brooks, *Scenes and Portraits: Memories of Childhood and Youth*, New York, pp. 118-19.

19 Walter Lippmann, 'Legendary John Reed', *The New Republic*, 1 (26 December 1914), pp. 15-16; reprinted in Lippmann, *Early Writings*, with an Introduction by Arthur Schlesinger, Jr, New York, 1970, pp. 293-6.

20 John Reed, *Collected Poems*, ed. Corliss Lamont, Westport, Conn., [1985], pp. 25-6.

21 T. S. Eliot, *Poems Written in Early Youth*, London, 1967, p. 20.

Chapter 2

1 Floyd Dell, *Homecoming: an Autobiography*, New York [1933], p. 250; William Brevda, *Harry Kemp: the Last Bohemian*, Lewisburg, Pa [1986], p. 82.

2 John Reed, 'The Day in Bohemia', in *Collected Poems* (*CP*), ed. Corliss Lamont, Westport, Conn. [1985], p. 68. All further references to Reed's verse will appear in the text.

3 *The Autobiography of Lincoln Steffens*, New York [1958], p. 653.

4 Lincoln Steffens, obituary of John Reed in the *Freeman*, 3 November 1920, reprinted in *Lincoln Steffens Speaking*, New York, 1936, p. 313.

5 H[arriet]. M[onroe]. , 'The City and the Poet', *Poetry*, 10 (April 1917), p. 34.

6 John Gould Fletcher, *Irradiations Sand and Spray*, Boston, 1915, p. 7.

7 'The Wanderer: A rococo study', the *Egoist*, 1 (16 March 1914), pp. 109-11.

8 'Preludes', *Blast*, 2 (July 1915), pp. 48-51.

9 John Reed, *Adventures of a Young Man: Short Stories from Life*, San Francisco, 1975, pp. 138-9.

10 Martin Green, *New York 1913: the Armory Show and the Paterson Strike Pageant*, New York [1988], pp. 42-3.

11 John Gould Fletcher, *Life is My Song*, New York, 1937, pp. 71-2.

12 Lloyd R. Morris, *The Young Idea: An Anthology of Opinion Concerning the Spirit and Aims of Contemporary American Literature*, New York, 1917, p. 38.

13 Alfred Kreymborg, *Troubadour: an Autobiography*, New York, 1925, p. 221; Orrick Johns, *Time of Our Lives: the Story of My Father and Myself*, New York, 1937, p. 226.

14 Kreymborg, *Troubadour*, p. 239.

15 This theme is most effectively developed in C. K. Stead, *The New Poetic*, London [1964].

16 See Eric Homberger, *American Writers and Radical Politics 1900-39: Equivocal Commitments*, London [1986], pp. 189-96.

17 See Michael D. Marcaccio, *The Hapgoods: Three Earnest Brothers*, Charlottesville [1977].

18 The link between progressivism and the protestant mind has long been debated. Margaret Vance in Howells's *A Hazard of New Fortunes* (1890) suggests the type. See Richard Hofstadter, *The Age of Reform from Bryan to F.D.R.* , New York, 1955, 203 ff.; Roy Lubove, *The Progressives and the Slums: Tenement House Reform in New York City 1890-1917*, Pittsburgh, 1962; Allen F. Davis, *Spearheads for Reform: the Social Settlements and the Progressive Movement 1890-1914*, New York, 1967, ch. 2; Robert M. Crunden, *Ministers of Reform; the Progressives' Achievement in American Civilization 1889-1920*, Urbana and Chicago, 1984, ch. 1. On Poole see his *The Bridge: My Own Story*, New York, 1940; and Truman Frederick Keefer, *Ernest Poole*, New York, 1966.

19 Quoted Hicks, *Reed*, p. 107; see William James, *The Varieties of Religious Experience* in *Writings 1902-1910*, ed. Bruce Kuklick, New York, 1987, p. 86.

20 Art Young, *Art Young: His Life and Times*, ed. John Nicholas Beffel, New York, 1939, p. 271.

21 Piet Vlag, 'Sensationalism', the *Masses*, 1 (December 1911), p. 8.

22 Dell, *Homecoming*, pp. 248-9.

23 Louis Untermeyer, *From Another World*, New York [1939], pp. 41-2.

24 Eastman's version of the offer ('You are elected editor of the *Masses*. No pay. ') appears in his *Enjoyment of Living*, New York [1948], p. 394. See also Art Young, *Art Young*, p. 274, who claims that he was the one to approach Eastman to edit the *Masses*.

25 Eastman, *Enjoyment of Living*, p. 404.

26 *Ibid.* , p. 406.

27 *Ibid.* , p. 406.

28 The *Masses* remains the most-admired, and most assiduously studied, of the American 'little' magazines. There is a remarkably generous anthology of its articles and artwork, *Echoes of Revolt: 'The Masses' 1911-1917*, ed. William L. O'Neill, Chicago, 1966. Among the studies of the magazine, Rebecca Zurier, *Art for The Masses (1911-1917): a Radical Magazine and its Graphics*, New Haven, 1985, stands out for the quality of its research.

29 Max Eastman, 'New Masses for old', *Modern Monthly*, 8 (June 1934), pp. 292-300.

30 Ezra Pound, 'The new sculpture', the *Egoist*, 1 (16 February 1914), p. 68.

31 Max Eastman, 'John Reed and the Russian Revolution', *Modern Monthly*, 10 (December 1936), p. 16.

32 Mabel Dodge Luhan, *Intimate Memories*, 3, *Movers and Shakers*, New York, 1936. The four volumes of *Intimate Memories* were reprinted in two bulky volumes by Kraus in 1971, which retain the pagination of the original editions. Further references to this edition will appear in the text. There have been two biographies: Emily Hahn, *Mabel: a Biography of Mabel Dodge Luhan*, Boston, 1977; and Lois Palken Rudnick, *Mabel Dodge Luhan: New Woman, New Worlds*, Albuquerque [1984]. Both follow *Intimate Memories* closely, though Palken is based upon the more solid archival research. See Christopher Lasch, *The New Radicalism in America (1889-1963): the Intellectual as a Social Type*, New York, 1966, pp. 104-40.

33 *Intimate Memories*, 3, pp. 5-6. Further references to *Intimate Memories* will appear in the text.

34 Orrick Johns, *Time of Our Lives*, p. 217.

35 Edith Wharton, *A Backward Glance*, New York, 1934, pp. 106-7. Wharton's *The Decoration of Houses* (1897) made a dignified case for restraint, but seemed hopelessly old-fashioned by the standards of Mabel Dodge's apartment.

36 See Milton W. Brown, *The Story of the Armory Show*, New York [1963]; and Green, *New York, 1913*.

37 Eastman, *Enjoyment of Living*, p. 523; and Steffens, *Autobiography*, p. 655.

38 Melvyn Dubofsky, *We Shall Be All: a History of the Industrial Workers of the World*, New York, n. d. , p. 277.

39 Hapgood, quoted by Peter Carlson, *Roughneck: the Life and Times of Big Bill Haywood*, New York [1983], p. 210.

40 Reed's principal contributions to the *Masses* have been collected in *John Reed for 'The Masses'*, ed. James C. Wilson, Jefferson, North Carolina and London [1987], and will referred to by date of publication in the text.

41 Reed to Edward Eyre Hunt, n. d. , John Reed Papers, Houghton Library, Harvard University; quoted Robert E. Humphrey, *Children of Fantasy: the First Rebels of Greenwich Village*, New York [1978], p. 131.

42 Carlson, *Roughneck*, p. 213.

43 Rosenstone, *Romantic Revolutionary*, pp. 126-7n, discusses the origins of the pageant. See Green, *New York 1913*, pp. 195-7.

44 'The Paterson Strike Pageant', the *Independent*, 74 (29 May 1913), pp. 1190-2; 'Pageant of the Paterson Strike', *Survey*, 30 (28 June 1913), p. 428; Hapgood, quoted in Green, *New York 1913*, p. 204. Green's account of the pageant, and reactions to it in the press, is a fascinating piece of cultural archaeology.

45 I owe this insight to George Abbott White, whose comments on a draft of the manuscript of this book were very insightful.

46 Reed to Walter Lippmann, 8 September [1913], Walter Lippmann Papers, Sterling Memorial Library, Yale University; Steve Golin, 'Defeat becomes disaster: the Paterson Strike of 1913 and the decline of the I.W.W. ', *Labor History*, 24 (Spring 1983), pp. 223-48. .

47 Hutchins Hapgood, *A Victorian in the Modern World* (New York, 1939); reissue, ed. Robert Allan Skotheim, Seattle and London [1972], p. 353

48 Rudnick, *Mabel Dodge Luhan*, p. 96, following Hicks, *Reed*, p. 111.

49 Mabel Dodge to Neith Boyce, Yale University Library, quoted in Rudnick, *Ibid.* , pp. 96-7.

50 This was virtually the programme of the *Masses*. 'So far. . . as I shaped its policy', wrote Max Eastman (*Enjoyment of Living*, p. 420), 'the guiding ideal of the magazine was that every individual should be made free to live and grow in his own chosen way. . . Even if it can not be achieved, I would say to myself, the good life consists in striving towards it. ' Mabel Dodge did not necessarily endorse all of the *Masses* ideals, but they – and many others – would have agreed on the imperative of self-fulfillment.

51 As the above discussion indicates, I find their relationship of far more than 'secondary importance' for Reed's development. This emphasis is largely

contra Jim Tuck, *Pancho Villa and John Reed: Two Faces of Romantic Revolution*, Tucson, 1984.

Chapter 3

1 Walter Lippmann to John Reed, 25 March [1914], Lippmann Papers, Yale University Library; and Lippmann, 'Legendary John Reed', *The New Republic*, 1 (25 December 1914), pp. 15-16.

2 J. R. D[os]. P[assos]. , review of *Insurgent Mexico, Harvard Monthly*, 59 (November 1914), pp. 67-8.

3 Kipling quoted in Virginia Gardner, *'Friend and Lover': the Life of Louise Bryant*, New York [1982], p. 62.

4 Jim Tuck, *Pancho Villa and John Reed: Two Faces of Romantic Revolution*, Tucson, 1984, p. 104.

5 Reed, *Insurgent Mexico*, with a preface to the new edition by Renato Leduc, New York, 1969, p. 34. Further references to *Insurgent Mexico* will appear in the text.

6 Richard Harding Davis, *Notes of a War Correspondent*, New York, 1911, p. 67. The comment on 'trivial details' appears on p. 193.

7 *Adventures and Letters of Richard Harding Davis*, ed. Charles Belmont Davis, New York, 1918, pp. 355, 365.

8 Tamara Hovey, *John Reed: Witness to Revolution*, Los Angeles, 1982, p. 129.

9 Davis, *Adventures and Letters*, p. 408.

10 Eugene O'Neill helped circulate this anecdote. See Arthur and Barbara Gelb, *O'Neill*, London, 1962, pp. 262-3.

11 Roosevelt quoted in David M. Kennedy, *Birth Control in America: the Career of Margaret Sanger*, New Haven and London, 1970, pp. 68, 42.

12 Lloyd C. Gardner, 'Woodrow Wilson and the Mexican Revolution', *Woodrow Wilson and a Revolutionary World*, ed. A. S. Link, Chapel Hill [1982], pp. [3]-48.

13 Their attempts to draw Mexico into an alliance, and thus to distract the United States from involvement in the European war, has been vividly told by Barbara Tuchman, *The Zimmermann Telegram*, London, 1981 ed.

14 H. Hamilton Fyfe, *The Real Mexico: a Study on the Spot*, London, 1914, p. 17.

15 Ivie E. Cadenhead, Jr, 'The American socialists and the Mexican Revolution of 1910', *The Southwestern Social Science Quarterly*, 43 (September 1962), pp. 103-17; *The Autobiography of Lincoln Steffens*, New York [1958], pp. 712-40.

16 Lippmann, 'Legendary John Reed'.

17 *Ibid.*

18 Tuck in *Pancho Villa and John Reed* stresses this side of Carranza and Obregón.

19 Reed to William Phillips, 4 June 1914, *The Papers of Woodrow Wilson*, ed. A. S. Link *et al.*, 30 (6 May–5 September, 1914), pp. 156-7.

20 John Reed, 'The causes behind Mexico Revolution', *New York Times*, 27 April 1914.

21 Arthur S. Link, *Wilson: the New Freedom*, Princeton, 1956, p. 395.

22 Reed, 'The causes behind Mexico Revolution'.

23 Wilson to Walter Hines Page, 18 May 1914, *The Papers of Woodrow Wilson*, ed. A. S. Link *et al.*, 30 (6 May–5 September, 1914), Princeton, 1979, p. 42.

24 See Eric Homberger, 'Greenwich Village intellectuals and the Ludlow massacre, 1914', in *American Writers and Radical Politics, 1900-39: Equivocal Commitments*, London, 1986, pp. 59-79.

25 Max Eastman, 'Class lines in Colorado', *The New Review*, 2 (July 1914), pp. 381-87.

26 Max Eastman, 'The nice people of Trinidad', *Masses*, 5 (July 1914), pp. 5-8.

27 See *Mother Jones Speaks: Collected Writings and Speeches*, ed. Philip S. Foner, New York, 1983, pp. 222-63.

28 'Class war in Colorado', *Masses*, 5 (June 1914), pp. 5-8; 'Class lines in Colorado' (n. 25); 'The nice people of Trinidad' (n. 26).

29 Lippmann to Reed, 25 March [1914], John Reed Papers, Houghton Library, Harvard University.

30 Edgcumb Pinchon to Reed, 26 July 1914, John Reed Papers, Houghton Library, Harvard University.

31 Reed to William Phillips, 4 June 1914, *The Papers of Woodrow Wilson*, ed. A. S. Link *et al.*, 30 (6 May–5 September, 1914), pp. 156-7; the same motive – the desire to explain the president's policy – is evident in Reed to Wilson, 18 June 1914, *Papers*, 43, pp. 192-3.

32 Steffens to Reed, 6 June 1914, *The Letters of Lincoln Steffens*, ed. Ella Winter and Granville Hicks, 2 vols., New York [1938], 1, p. 342.

33 Date of the interview: Reed to Upton Sinclair, 18 June [1914], Sinclair Papers, Lilly Library, Indiana University; initial White House reaction: Joseph Patrick Tumulty, memorandum to the President, 22 June 1914, and Wilson to Tumulty, 29 June 1914, *Papers of Woodrow Wilson*, 43, pp. 202, 223.

34 The text of the final draft was published for the first time in *Papers of Woodrow Wilson*, 43, pp. 231-8.

35 Floyd Dell, *Homecoming: an Autobiography*, New York [1933], p. 260.

36 Hutchins Hapgood, *A Victorian in the Modern World*, New York, 1939,

reissued Seattle [1972], p. 385.

37 Max Eastman, 'John Reed and the old Masses', *Modern Monthly*, 10 (October 1936), pp. 20-1. Hicks gives a significant role to Boyd in the shaping of Reed's radicalism, a view emphatically not shared by Eastman.

38 *Ibid.*, pp. 385-90.

39 Irving Werstein, *Sound No Trumpet: the Life and Death of Alan Seeger*, New York, 1967, pp. 46-58.

40 Seeger to his mother, 17 October 1914, *Letters and Diary of Alan Seeger*, London, 1917, p. 7.

41 Harold D. Lasswell, *Propaganda Technique in the World War*, New York, 1938, p. 126, discusses the dominant position afforded the British by their control of transatlantic cables. M. L. Sanders, 'Wellington House and British Propaganda during the First World War', *The Historical Journal*, 18 (1975), pp. 119-46.

42 See Rosenstone's insightful discussion of their relationship at this time in *Romantic Revolutionary*, 189 ff.

43 Richard Harding Davis, *With the Allies*, London, 1915, pp. 227-8, 238.

44 Philip Gibbs, *Realities of War*, rev. ed. , London [1936], pp. 17-8.

45 Roosevelt to Gray, 22 January 1915, quoted Harold D. Lasswell, *Propaganda Technque in the World War*, pp. 136-7.

46 See Tamara Hovey, *John Reed: Witness to Revolution,* p. 122.

47 Steffens to Reed, 19 November 1914, *Letters*, 1, p. 350.

48 A somewhat different version of Reed's affair with Freddie Lee, from Andrew Dasburg, appears in Virginia Gardner, *'Friend and Lover': the Life of Louise Bryant*, New York [1982], p. 177. It is equally as discreditable to Reed.

49 He published an account of this interview as 'Karl Liebknecht's Words' in the *Revolutionary Age*, 1 February 1919, after the murder of Liebknecht and Rosa Luxemburg.

50 Dunn's article appeared in the *New York Evening Post*, 27 February 1915. Steffens sought to minimise the damage with a letter in the same periodical on 16 April (see his *Letters*, 1, pp. 353-4). Reed's most detailed account of this incident occurs in his testimony before the Overman Committee on 21 February 1919 (*Brewing and Liquor Interests and German and Bolshevik Propoganda: Report and Hearings of the Subcommittee on the Judiciary, United States Senate, submitted pursuant to S. Res. 307 and 439, 65th Cong.*, 3 vols, Washington, DC, 1919, 3, p. 587.) See also on this incident Robert Dunn, *Five Fronts: On the Firing-Lines with English, French, Austrian, German and Russian Troops*, New York, 1915, pp. 163-200; and Rosenstone, *Romantic Revolutionary*, p. 211.

51 Quoted Hovey, *John Reed: Witness to Revolution*, p. 128, precisely echoing Lippmann's praise of Reed's first articles about Mexico in the *Metropolitan*.
52 This theme is very interestingly developed in Roland N. Stromberg, *Redemption by War: the Intellectuals and 1914*, Lawrence, Kans., 1982.
53 H. C. Peterson, *Propaganda for War: the Campaign Against American Neutrality, 1914-1917*, Norman, Okla., 1939, p. 245.
54 A. M. Schlesinger to John Spargo, 3 June 1917, Butler Library, Columbia University, quoted in David M. Kennedy, *Over Here: the First World War and American Society*, New York, 1980, p. 40. A similar suggestion had appeared in William English Walling, ed. *The Socialists and the War*, New York, 1915, to the almost universal derision of other socialists.
55 Letter, 4 April 1915, quoted Rosenstone, *Romantic Revolutionary*, p. 213.
56 Reed, *The War in Eastern Europe*, New York, 1916, p. 281. Further references will appear in the text.
57 Lasswell, *Propaganda Technique in the World War*, p. 98.
58 W. Bruce Lincoln, *Passage Through Armageddon: the Russians in War and Revolution 1914-1918*, New York, 1986, pp. 128-9.
59 Roman Vishniac, *A Vanished World*, with a Foreword by Elie Wiesel, Harmondsworth, 1986; Roland Barthes, *Camera Lucida*, trans. Richard Howard, London, 1984, pp. 94-7.
60 *The Autobiography of Arthur Ransome*, ed. Rupert Hart-Davis, London [1976], pp. 189, 191.
61 Negley Farson, *The Way of a Transgressor*, London, 1935, pp. 137-8.
62 Reed's thoughts about Russia were recorded by Charles Erskine Scott Wood to Sara Bard Field, 6 December 1915. Wood Collection, Box 250, item 4, Huntington Library, Pasadena, Calif. Robert Hamburger, Wood's biographer, kindly drew my attention to this letter.

Chapter 4

1 Reed to Sally Robinson, December 1915, quoted Rosenstone, *Romantic Revolutionary*, p. 239.
2 *Ibid.* Others who knew them both thought Bryant had reason for caution. Charles Erskine Scott Wood saw Reed as supremely a man of the modern moment, who, like a Nietzschean, would ruthlessly leave Bryant to look after herself when his interests moved on. Wood to Sara Bard Field, 25 January 1916. Wood Collection, Box 250, item 6, Huntington Library, Pasadena, Calif. Robert Hamburger, Wood's biographer, kindly called this letter to my attention.
3 Rosenstone, *Romantic Revolutionary*, p. 242; Alice Wexler, *Emma Goldman:*

an Intimate Life, London [1984], pp. 213-15.

4   H. C. Peterson, *Propaganda for War: the Campaign Against American Neutrality, 1914-1917*, Norman, 1939, pp. 126-7. Peterson estimates that by 1916 there were 10, 000 American writers, publicists, preachers and lecturers who were advocating the Allied cause (p. 233).

5   Mary Heaton Vorse, *A Footnote to Folly: Reminiscences*, New York [1935], p. 128.

6   Walter Lippmann, *Drift and Mastery: an Attempt to Diagnose the Current Unrest*, New York, 1914, pp. 314-15.

7   Quoted Ronald Steel, *Walter Lippmann and the American Century*, London, 1981, p. 95.

8   John Reed, 'Bryan on tour', *Collier's*, 20 May 1916.

9   Rosenstone, *Romantic Revolutionary*, p. 254, argues that Reed supported Wilson 'almost by default'. His attempt to influence Wilson's Mexico policy, and the role he hoped the government would play in industrial conflicts, suggests, in 1916, a stronger rationale behind his decision to support Wilson's re-election.

10 John Reed, 'Bandit in mountains can hold his retreat', *New York American*, 13 March 1916. 'Fumble' comment in Barbara Tuchman, *The Zimmermann Telegram*, London, 1981 ed. , p. 94.

11 Grace Potter to Reed, 8 May 1916; and Hiram Kelly Moderwell to Reed, 9 June 1916, John Reed Papers, Houghton Library, Harvard University; Hicks, *Reed*, pp. 213-14.

12 See Mary Heaton Vorse, *Time and the Town: a Provincetown Chronicle*, New York, 1942.

13 Barbara Gelb, *So Short a Time: a Biography of John Reed and Louise Bryant*, New York [1973]), p. 93.

14 Orrick Johns, *Time of Our Lives: the Story of My Father and Myself*, New York, 1937, p. 236.

15 John Reed, 'Roosevelt sold them out', *Masses*, August 1916.

16 Walter Lippmann, 'At the Chicago conventions', *New Republic*, 17 June 1916.

17 See Arnold Goldman, 'The culture of the Provincetown Players', *Journal of American Studies*, 12 (December 1978), pp. 291-310, and C. W. E. Bigsby, *A Critical Introduction to Twentieth-Century American Drama*, 3 vols, 1, 1900–40, Cambridge [1982].

18 The affair between O'Neill and Bryant was not known to Hicks (or omitted by him). It appears in memoirs of the period, Arthur and Barbara Gelb, *O'Neill*, London [1962]; Barbara Gelb's book about Reed and Bryant,

Rosenstone's *Romantic Revolutionary* and Virginia Gardner, *'Friend and Lover'*: *the Life of Louise Bryant*, New York [1982].

19 Gardner, *'Friend and Lover'*, pp. 38-9.

20 Max Eastman, 'The Masses at the White House', *Masses*, 7 (July 1916), pp. 16-17.

21 Ronald Steel, *Walter Lippmann and the American Century*, London [1981], p. 107.

22 George Creel, *Rebel at Large: Recollections of Fifty Crowded Years*, New York [1947], p. 153; and Rosenstone, *Romantic Revolutionary*, p. 255.

23 David Montgomery, *The Fall of the House of Labor: the Workplace, the State and American Labor Activism, 1865-1925,* Cambridge and New York [1987], p. 361; see pp. 360-5 for a brief account of the itinerary which led Walsh to support Wilson in the 1916 election.

24 Emma Goldman, *Living My Life*, 1 vol. ed. , Garden City, NY [1934], p. 586.

25 Joseph Freeman, *An American Testament: a Narrative of Rebels and Romantics*, New York [1936], p. 90.

26 Blanche Wiesen Cook, 'Introduction', *Crystal Eastman on Women and Revolution,* Oxford and New York, 1978, p. 16.

27 Reed, 'The Mexican tangle', *Masses*, June 1916.

28 Reed to the Socialist Party NEC, 13 October 1916, Socialist Party Collection, Duke University, quoted David A. Shannon, *The Socialist Party of America: a History*, New York, 1955, p. 92.

29 Bigsby, 1, p. 12.

30 Reed, *Collected Poems*, pp. 102-7.

31 Fred Boyd to Reed, 28 November 1916, and Edward Eyre Hunt to Reed, 24 December 1916, John Reed Papers, Houghton Library, Harvard University.

32 Gardner, *'Friend and Lover'*, pp. 56-7; Barbara Gelb, *So Short a Time,* p. 113.

33 Quoted Tamara Hovey, *John Reed*, pp. 153-4.

34 See, for example, John Heaton, *Cobb of 'The World'*, New York [1924], pp. 265-7, which reprints an editorial from 4 February.

35 Leon Trotsky, *My Life: an Attempt at an Autobiography*, with an introduction by Joseph Hansen, Harmondsworth, 1975, pp. 285-6.

36 Reed, 'The fall of the Russian Bastille', *New York Tribune*, 25 March 1917.

37 Reed, 'Whose war?', *Masses*, April 1917.

38 H. C. Peterson and Gilbert C. Fite, *Opponents of War 1917–1918*, Seattle and London [1968] ed. , p. 7; Russell in the *New York World*, 7 September 1917, quoted in Christopher Lasch, *The American Liberals and the Russian*

Revolution, New York [1962], p. 39.

39 Heaton, *Cobb of 'The World'*, pp. 268-70. Wilson's words were reported by Cobb to Laurence Stallings and Maxwell Anderson, who set them down on paper. The debate over the authenticity of the Cobb–Wilson interview was inaugurated by Jerold S. Auerbach in the *Journal of American History*, 54 (December 1967), pp. 608-17, with a reply from A. S. Link in the same journal, 55 (1968), pp. 231-5. See also Bertram D. Wolfe, *A Life in Two Centuries: an Autobiography*, New York [1981], pp. 149-51.

40 The text of the 'War proclamation' adopted at the St Louis Convention appears in full in the Lusk Committee report, *Revolutionary Radicalism: its History Purpose and Tactics... Report of the Jount Legislative Committee Investigating Seditious Activities...* , 4 vols, Albany, NY, 1920, 1, pp. 613-18.

41 David A. Shannon, *The Socialist Party of America*, p. 101.

42 Sinclair's resignation statement was published in the *Masses*, September 1917, accompanied by an unusually reasonable response from Eastman. Such calm exchanges between members and ex-members of the party were rare indeed in the summer of 1917.

43 The resigners in 1912-13 included Eastman, Walling, Boudin and Walter Lippmann. See Theodore Draper, *The Roots of American Communism*, New York, 1957, pp. 47-8.

44 David Montgomery, *The Fall of the House of Labor*, pp. 377-8.

45 Arthur and Barbara Gelb, *O'Neill*, London [1962], pp. 328-9.

46 Hicks, *John Reed*, p. 239.

47 Reed to Bryant, 5 July 1917, John Reed Papers, Houghton Library, Harvard University. This letter has been widely (and partially) quoted and analysed: see Hicks, *John Reed*, p. 239; Rosenstone, *Romantic Revolutionary*, p. 272; Gardner, *'Friend and Lover'*, New York [1982], pp. 78-9.

48 Sigmund Freud, '"Civilized" sexual morality and modern nervous illness' (1908), *The Pelican Freud Library*, 12, *Civilization, Society and Religion*, ed. Albert Dickson, trans. James Strachey, Harmondsworth [1985], p. 45.

49 Recounted by Reed in 'Militarism at play', *Masses*, August 1917.

50 Reed, 'One solid month of liberty', *Masses*, September 1917.

51 *Ibid*.

Chapter 5

1 Bourne quoted in Bruce Clayton, *Forgotten Prophet: the Life of Randolph Bourne*, Baton Rouge and London [1984], p. 230.

2 Randolph Bourne, 'The war and the intellectuals', *Seven Arts*, June 1917.

3 Quoted in David R. Francis, *Russia from the American Embassy April, 1916-*

November, 1918, New York, 1921, p. 109.

4 Reed, 'The fall of the Russian Bastille', *New York Times*, 25 March 1917.

5 Reed and Louise Bryant, 'The Russian peace', *Masses*, July 1917.

6 Stuart I. Rochester, *American Liberal Disillusionment in the Wake of World War I*, University Park and London [1977],pp. 134-47.

7 Reed, 'One solid month of liberty', *Masses*, September 1917.

8 Reed to Sally Robinson, undated letter [probably October 1917], and letter to Boardman Robinson, 17 September [1917], John Reed Papers, Houghton Library, Harvard University.

9 Reed to Sally Robinson, 3 September [1917], John Reed Papers, Houghton Library, Harvard University.

10 See Leonid I. Strakhovsky, *American Opinion About Russia 1917-1920*, Toronto, 1961; Christopher Lasch, *The American Liberals and the Russian Revolution*, New York [1962]; and Peter G. Filene, *Americans and the Soviet Experiment, 1917–1933*, Cambridge, Mass., 1967.

11 Francis, *Russia from the American Embassy*, p. 157.

12 Albert Rhys Williams, *Journey into Revolution: Petrograd, 1917-1918*, ed. Lucita Williams, with a Foreword by Josephine Herbst, Chicago, 1969, p. 36.

13 Negley Farson, *The Way of a Transgressor*, London [1935], p. 209.

14 Francis, *Russia from the American Embassy*, pp. 165-9.

15 Williams, *Journey into Revolution*, p. 26.

16 In the *Liberator*, July 1918, Reed accused Soskice of sending other correspondents' stories to the *Manchester Guardian* under his name, and then refusing them the right to send their own material. Neither Hicks or Rosenstone mention this accusation, nor does it appear in Williams's memoirs. In his capacity as Kerensky's secretary, Soskice played a significant role in the Committee on Civic Education in Free Russia, funded by William Boyce Thompson.

17 Bessie Beatty, *The Red Heart of Russia*, New York, 1918, pp. 16-18; Williams, *Journey into Revolution*, p. 29; Bertram D. Wolfe, 'The Harvard Man in the Kremlin Wall', *American Heritage*, 11 (February 1960), p. 100; Draper, *The Roots of American Communism*, New York, 1957, p. 119 (forgetting, however, about Reed's visit to Russia in 1915); Hook, *Marxism and Beyond*, Totowa, NJ, 1973, p. 131; Krupskaya quoted by James D. White, 'Early Soviet historical interpretations of the Russian Revolution 1918-24', *Soviet Studies*, 37 (July 1985), p. 336; White's article suggests that Trotsky was Reed's chief source for *Ten Days*, which was little more than 'a product of early Soviet historiography of the Russian Revolution' (p. 338). This is a flawed

argument, made without reference to Reed's writings about the Revolution which preceded *Ten Days* (and also which preceded publication of Trotsky's *The History of the Russian Revolution to Brest–Litovsk*, 1919).

18 Williams, *Journey into Revolution*, p. 93.

19 N. N. Sukhanov, *The Russian Revolution 1917: a Personal Record*, edited, abridged and translated by Joel Carmichael, London and New York, 1955, p. 571.

20 Radek quoted in Arthur Ransome, *Russia in 1919*, New York, 1919, p. 27.

21 John Reed, *Ten Days That Shook the World*, with a Foreword by V. I. Lenin and and Introduction by Granville Hicks, New York [1935], pp. 36, 50-1. This edition retains the pagination of the first edition of 1919. All further references to *Ten Days* will appear in the text.

22 M. Philips Price, *My Three Revolutions*, London [1969], p. 82.

23 M. Philips Price, *My Reminiscences of the Russian Revolution*, London [1921], p. 143; *My Three Revolutions*, pp. 84-5.

24 Williams, *Journey into Revolution*, pp. 108-11, 121.

25 *Ibid.*, pp. 106-7.

26 Leon Trotsky, *The History of the Russian Revolution*, trans. Max Eastman, 3 vols, London [1967], 3, p. 217. This translation was first published in London in 1932-33.

27 Williams, *Journey into Revolution*, p. 122.

28 See Robert C. Tucker, *Stalin as Revolutionary 1879-1929: a Study in History and Personality*, New York, 1974, ch. 9, 'The politics of revolutionary biography'.

29 Robert V. Daniels, *Red October: the Bolshevik Revolution of 1917*, New York [1967], p. 215.

30 The formal pattern of imagery is discussed in Eric Homberger, *American Writers and Radical Politics, 1900-1939: Equivocal Commitments*, London [1986], pp. 105-15.

31 Albert Rhys Williams, *Through the Russian Revolution*, with a biographical sketch of the author by Joshua Kunitz, New York, 1967, p. 99.

32 Daniels, *Red October*, pp. 210-11.

33 Williams, *Journey into Revolution*, p. 41.

34 *Ibid.*

35 Reed to Sinclair, 6 November 1918, Sinclair Mss, Lilly Library, Indiana University.

36 E. H. Carr, *A History of Soviet Russia: the Bolshevik Revolution 1917-1923*, 3 vols., London, 1953, 3, pp. 19-20.

37 See Reed's 'How Soviet Russia conquered imperial Germany', *Liberator*,

January 1919.

38 John W. Wheeler-Bennett, *Brest–Litovsk: the Forgotten Peace March 1918*, London, 1963 ed. , pp. 351-2; he quotes Reed as a source for the Bureau's activities on p. 94.

39 Williams, *Journey into Revolution*, p. 224.

40 Marcel Liebman, *Leninism Under Lenin*, trans. Brian Pearce, London [1975], p. 223; Bessie Beatty, *The Red Heart of Russia*, pp. 339, 440, 442.

41 Edgar Sisson, *One Hundred Red Days 25 November 1917-4 March 1918: a Personal Chronicle of the Bolshevik Revolution*, New Haven, 1931, pp. 256-9.

42 Arno Dosch-Fleurot spoke to Reed in the Tauride Palace immediately after Trotsky had offered him the Consulship. He thought it wrong for Reed, for it would land him in jail. 'Perhaps it is time some one went to jail', Reed replied. 'it may be the best thing I can do to advance the cause.' See Dosch-Fleurot, 'World man tells of Reed in Russia', *New York World*, 19 October 1920.

43 James K. Libbey, *Alexander Gumberg and Soviet-American Relations 1917-1933*, Lexington, Ky. [1977], p. 38.

Chapter 6

1 Military Intelligence Division (G-2), *Surveillance of Radicals in the United States, 1917-1941*, 35 reels of microfilm, Frederick, MD, n. d. Items cited by date. The material on Reed appears largely in reel 4.

2 Edgar Sisson, *One Hundred Red Days*. . . , New Haven, 1931, p. 286-7.

3 See George Theofiles, *American Posters of World War I*, New York, n. d.

4 Steffens to Reed, 17 June 1918, *The Letters of Lincoln Steffens*, ed. Ella Winter and Granville Hicks, 2 vols, New York [1938], 1, p. 429.

5 This memorandum apparently has not survived. The passage quoted appears in a letter from Bullitt to House, 20 May 1918, quoted in Beatrice Farnsworth, *William C. Bullitt and the Soviet Union*, Bloomington, 1967, p. 189 n. 48. Reed used something of the same language in 'The latest from Russia', *Liberator*, February 1919: 'A Government composed of "moderate" Socialists could only be supported by foreign bayonets, and then with difficulty'. See also *The Papers of Woodrow Wilson*, ed. A. S. Link *et al.*, 48 (13 May-17 July 1918), pp. 144-5.

6 'Bolsheviki foes of all imperialism', *New York Call*, 2 May 1918.

7 Norma Fain Pratt, *Morris Hillquit: a Political History of an American Jewish Socialist*, Westport, Conn, 1979, pp. 139-40.

8 '5, 000 hear Reed tell of Soviet government. . . ', *New York Call*, 15 May 1918, pp. 1-2.

9   Reed, 'Recognize Russia', *Liberator*, July 1918.

10 Reed, 'The case for the Bolsheviki', the *Independent*, 13 July 1918. See E. H. Carr, *A History of Soviet Russia: the Bolshevik Revolution 1917-1923*, 3, London, 1953, p. 38.

11 George Kennan has examined Trotsky's approach to Robins in detail in his *Soviet-American Relations, 1917-1920*, 1, *Russia Leaves the War*, Princeton, 1956, pp. 486-516.

12 Amos Pinchot to Wilson, 24 May 1918, *Papers of Woodrow Wilson*, ed. A. S. Link *et al.*, 48 (13 May-17 July, 1918), pp. 146-7.

13 E. P. Costigan to Wilson, 29 May 1918, *Papers of Woodrow Wilson*, 48, pp. 197-8, and Wilson's reply, p. 208.

14 See the exchanges between Hapgood, Eastman and Reed in the *Liberator*, July and August 1918; and Reed's letter to Sinclair, *Upton Sinclair's*, August 1918.

15 Reed, 'With Gene Debs on the fourth', *Liberator*, September 1918. Debs's response to this article was expressed in a letter to Reed on 21 September 1918 (Houghton Library, Harvard University): 'It is the bigness of you to which I am indebted for this flattering testimonial which, coming from the heart of John Reed, touches me more deeply than can be told in words'.

16 Reed, letter in the *Liberator*, September 1918.

17 Floyd Dell, *Homecoming: an Autobiography*, New York [1933], pp. 327-8.

18 Max Eastman, *Heroes I Have Known: Twelve Who Lived Great Lives*, New York [1942], pp. 218-19.

19 Benjamin Gitlow, *I Confess: the Truth About American Communism*, with an Introduction by Max Eastman, New York [1940], pp. 23-4.

20 *Ibid.* , p. 24.

21 *Ibid.* , pp. 70-4.

22 Transcript of Memorial Meeting in memory of Jacob Schwartz, 25 October 1918, Alexander Berkman Collection, Tamiment Library, New York University.

23 Reed, 'The second day', *One Year of Revolution: Celebrating the First Anniversary of the Founding of the Russian Soviet Republic. . . November 7, 1918*, Brooklyn, 1918, pp. 12-14.

24 Max Eastman, 'John Reed and the Russian Revolution', *Modern Monthly*, 10 (December 1936), p. 17.

25 Selig Perlman, *A Theory of the Labor Movement*, New York, 1928.

26 David A. Shannon, *The Socialist Party of America: a History*, New York, 1955, p. 129.

27 Reed, 'A new appeal', the *Revolutionary Age*, 18 January 1919.

28 *Bolshevik Propaganda: Hearings Before a Subcommittee of the Committee on the Judiciary. . . Persuant to S. Res. 439 and 469*, Washington, 1919.

29 Gertrude Atherton, 'Time as a cure for Bolshevism', *New York Times*, 16 March 1919, 7, p. 3.

30 Gitlow, *I Confess*, pp. 15-16. See also Ira Kipnis, *The American Socialist Movement, 1897-1912*, New York, 1952.

31 See David A. Shannon, *The Socialist Party of America*, ch. 4.

32 Stephen F. Cohen, *Bukharin and the Bolshevik Revolution: a Political Biography 1888-1938*, New York, 1975 ed. , p. 43.

33 The meeting is described in Bertram D. Wolfe, *A Life in Two Centuries: an Autobiography*, New York [1981], pp. 182-3, who was not himself present.

34 Reinstein, quoted in the Lusk Committee report, *Revolutionary Radicalism*, 1, pp. 428-9. Further references included in the text.

35 Robert E. Park, 'Public opinion and social service' (1918), reprinted in Park, *Society*, Glencoe, Ill. [1955], p. 143.

36 Wolfe, *A Life*, p. 189.

37 Gitlow, *I Confess*, p. 26.

38 Shannon, *The Socialist Party of America*, p. 132.

39 Theodore Draper, *The Roots of American Communism*, New York, 1957, p. 156.

40 Robert K. Murray, *Red Scare: a Study of National Hysteria 1919-1920*, Minneapolis, 1955, p. 75.

41 Cummings to his mother, 9 May 1919, *Selected Letters of E. E. Cummings*, ed. F. W. Dupee and George Stade, London, 1972, p. 70.

42 Letter from the Socialist Party to Reed, 9 May 1919, bMS Am 1091 (813), Houghton Library, Harvard University.

43 Pratt, *Morris Hillquit*, pp. 139-46.

44 Reed, 'Why political democracy must go', *New York Communist*, 15 May 1919.

45 Reed, 'Bolshevism? proletarian dictatorship and democracy', bMS Am 1091 (1222), Houghton Library, Harvard University.

46 See bMS Am 1091 (1224), Houghton Library.

47 Reed, 'Bolshevism? proletarian dictatorship and democracy'.

48 Reed [draft answer to heading I], bMS Am 1091 (1219), Houghton Library.

49 Reed [draft answer on heading III], bMS Am 1091 (1222), and [draft answer on heading VIII], bMS Am 1091 (1225), Houghton Library.

50 Reed, 'Bolshevism? proletarian dictatorship and democracy'.

51 *Ibid.*

52 David Williams, 'The Bureau of Investigation and its critics, 1919-1921: the

origins of federal political surveillance', *Journal of American History*, 68 (December 1981), pp. 560-79; Richard Gid Powers, *Secrecy and Power: the Life of J. Edgar Hoover*, London, 1987.

53 Military Intelligence Division (G-2), *Surveillance of Radicals in the United States, 1917-1941*, reel 33, frames 586-8.

54 Gitlow, *I Confess*, p. 35.

55 *Ibid.* , pp. 37-8.

56 Detailed accounts of the events in Chicago appear in many books on the Socialist Party. The following account has relied primarily upon Gitlow, Shannon and Wolfe. The wider context is best suggested in James Weinstein, *The Decline of Socialism in America 1912-1925*, New York, 1967, ch. 4. The manifesto adopted by the Socialist Party in Chicago is quoted in full in Lusk, 1, pp. 618-24. In 1935 Granville Hicks sent his draft papers upon Reed and the Left Wing to Lewis Corey, who, as Louis Fraina, was among the most prominent survivors of the momentous events of 1919. Corey had long since parted company with the Communist Party and the Comintern, but his long letter to Hicks of 30 December 1935 in the Butler Library, Columbia University, which amounts to a close commentary upon personalities and events as well as a criticism of Hicks's book, deserves to be far better known.

57 Gitlow, *I Confess*, p. 39.

58 Ruthenberg's role in the events of 1919 encapsulate the mystifying complexities of the Socialist Party's disintegration: he voted to swing the Left Wing behind the call of the language federations for a Communist Party convention, and took his place among the delegates who were determined to form a Communist Labor Party (CLP). His main contribution to their deliberation was to attempt delaying the formation until the other convention had met. He saw the CLP delegates as a desirable counterweight to keep Hourwich and the language federations under control.

59 Quoted Virginia Gardner, *'Friend and Lover': the Life of Louise Bryant*, New York [1982], p. 173.

60 Wolfe, *A Life*, p. 206.

61 Reed, Russian Notebook, bMS Am 1091 (1335), John Reed Papers, Houghton Library, Harvard University.

62 Angelica Balabanoff, *My Life as a Rebel*, London [1938], pp. 268-9.

63 Goldman to Stella Ballantine, 28 January 1920, quoted in Alice Wexler, *Emma Goldman in Exile: from the Russian Revolution to the Spanish Civil War*, Boston [1989], p. 25.

64 Emma Goldman, *Living My Life*, 1 vol. ed. , Garden City, NY [1934], pp.

739-40. Goldman's first account of this meeting appears in her *My Disillusionment in Russia*, Garden City, NY, 1923, pp. 15-16. Hicks's account of Reed's meeting with Goldman (p. 378) omits his extravagant language; and omits Balabanoff's comments altogether.

65 Goldman, *My Disillusionment*, p. 37.

66 Balabanoff, *My Life*, p. 269.

67 Reed, Russian Notebook, bMS Am 1091 (1321), John Reed Papers, Houghton Library, Harvard University.

68 Goldman, *My Disillusionment*, pp. 37-9.

69 Theodore Draper, *The Roots of American Communism*, New York, 1957, p. 241.

70 Eadmonn MacAlpine [Account of Reed's arrest in Finland, written for Louise Bryant, Paris, 1934], bMS Am 1091 (1143), John Reed Papers, Houghton Library, Harvard University; Max Engmann and Jerker A. Eriksson, *Mannen I Kolboxen: John Reed och Finland*, Helsingfors [1979], English summary pp. 227-31.

71 Virginia Gardner, *'Friend and Lover': the Life of Louise Bryant*, pp. 184-5.

72 *Ibid.* , p. 188.

73 Emma Goldman, *My Further Disillusionment in Russia*, New York, 1924, p. 24.

74 *M. N. Roy's Memoirs*, Bombay [1964], pp. 369-71. Roy's pages devoted to Reed are among the most erroneous and misleading ever to have been written about him.

75 *Second Congress of the Communist International. Minutes of the Proceedings*, 2 vols, London [1977] ed., 1, p. 46 and 1, p. 82. Further references to the minutes will be included in the text.

76 'A letter from Alfred Rosmer to Max Eastman', *Modern Monthly*, 10 (August 1937), p. 12. On the trades union theses, see Stanley W. Page, *Lenin and World Revolution*, New York, 1959, pp. 179-81; Warren Lerner, *Karl Radek: the Last Internationalist*, Palo Alto, 1970, pp. 102-3.

77 *M. N. Roy's Memoirs*, p. 391.

78 Balabanoff, *My Life as a Rebel*, p. 270. The story as told in her *Impressions of Lenin*, trans. Isotta Cesari, with a Foreword by Bertram D. Wolfe, Ann Arbor, 1964, pp. 74-5, adds the Ukraine offer to the account in her autobiography, but omits the sanitorium.

79 Balabanoff, *My Life as a Rebel*, pp. 262-8.

80 Benjamin Gitlow, *The Whole of Their Lives*, New York, 1948; reissued Boston and Los Angeles [1965], p. 32.

81 *Ibid.*, p. 16.

82 Reed made this comment apropos the proposed offer by Trotsky of the Soviet Consulship in New York in early 1918. Arno Dosch-Fleurot, 'World man tells of Reed in Russia', *New York World*, 19 October 1920.

83 Draper's discussion of this question in *The Roots of American Communism*, pp. 284-93, remains persuasive. New evidence on this question since the publication of Rosenstone's book, which largely follows Draper, consists of notes made of interviews with Bryant in Riga in May 1921, and summarised in a letter from Colonel Mathew C. Smith, Military Intelligence Division, to J. Edgar Hoover at the Department of Justice, dated 10 June 1921. The relevant passage from this letter: 'She stated confidentially that her husband, John Reed, was carried away by Communism when he first went to Russia, but that she believes that, if she could have been with him, he would never have gone to the extremes that he did. She stated, however, that he was much disappointed with what he found in Russia and that she believes this is what brought on his illness. He was so imbued with the idea of Communism, but when he got really in touch with the Russian situation, he found so few Communists and so many who used Communism as a means to get comfortable positions, extra food, homes, etc. that he was disappointed.' Military Intelligence Division (G-2), *Surveillance of Radicals in the United States, 1917-1941*, 35 reels of microfilm, Frederick, MD, n. d., document 10058-94, 10 June 1921. Disappointment is perhaps a somewhat tame word for what Reed felt about what he saw in Russia, but the interest of this material is its date. It is by several years the first indication of Reed's 'disillusionment' and supports Gitlow's retrospective claim in *The Whole of Their Lives* (1948) that Bryant had told him such a story in 1921. For many years Hoover was personally responsible for blocking Bryant's requests for passports.

84 Alfred Rosmer, *Moscow Under Lenin*, trans. Ian H. Birchall, with an Introduction by Tamara Deutscher, New York [1972], pp. 87-9. First published 1953. Rosenstone did not consult Rosmer's book for his biography of Reed.

85 Louise Bryant, 'Last days with John Reed', *Liberator*, February 1921.

Bibliographical note

Reed's main publications:

Insurgent Mexico, New York: D. Appleton and Co., 1914.
The War in Eastern Europe, New York: Charles Scribner's Sons, 1916.
Ten Days That Shook the World, New York: Boni and Liveright, 1919.
Daughter of the Revolution, ed. Floyd Dell, New York: Vanguard Press, 1927.
The Education of John Reed: Selected Writings, New York: International Publishers, 1955.
Adventures of a Young Man. Short Stories from Life, Berlin: Seven Seas, 1966.
Collected Poems, ed. Corliss Lamont, Westport, Conn.: Lawrence Hill and Co., 1985, based upon Leo Stoller's masters thesis completed at Columbia University in 1947.

The John Reed Papers at the Houghton Library, Harvard University, remain the central resource for any reassessment of Reed's life and writings. His letters appear in the archives of many of those who were his friends: including the Walter Lippmann papers at Yale, Lincoln Steffens's at Columbia, Max Eastman's and Upton Sinclair's at the University of Indiana, Bloomington. His letters to Mabel Dodge and Andrew Dasburg were destroyed. Granville Hicks's biography, *John Reed: the Making of a Revolutionary* (1936), and Robert Rosenstone's *Romantic Revolutionary: a Biography of John Reed* (1975) remain of considerable importance. Hicks's book is less candid and less reliable than Rosenstone on certain sensitive political issues. Much of what has been written about Reed is anecdotal and biographical. Of particular interest are Walter Lippmann, 'Legendary John Reed', *New Republic*, 26 December 1914; Louise Bryant, 'Last Days With John Reed', *Liberator*, February 1921; Mabel Dodge Luhan, *Intimate Memories*, 3, *Movers and Shakers* (1936); Angelica Balabanoff, *My Life as a Rebel* (1938); Benjamin Gitlow, *I Confess* (1940) and *The Whole of Their Lives* (1948); Max Eastman, *Enjoyment of Living* (1948) and Albert Rhys Williams's *Journey into Revolution: Petrograd 1917-1918* (1968).

There have been significant reappraisals of Reed's circle since the publication of Rosenstone's book in 1975. Martin Green's *New York 1913: the Armory Show and the Paterson Strike Pageant* (1988) is a *tour de force* of cultural criticism. New biographies of Louise Bryant (Virginia Gardner, *'Friend and Lover': the Life of Louise Bryant*, 1982), Walter Lippmann (Ronald Steel, *Walter Lippmann and the American Century*, 1981), Bill Haywood (Melvyn Dubofsky, *'Big Bill' Haywood*, 1987), Mabel Dodge Luhan (Lois Palken Rudnick, *Mabel Dodge Luhan: New Woman, New Worlds*, 1984), Emma Goldman (Alice Wexler, *Emma Goldman: an Intimate Life*, 1984) and Max Eastman (William L. O'Neill, *The Last Romantic: a Life of Max Eastman*, 1978) have altered our sense of Reed's place in the Greenwich Village milieu. There have been new biographies of diverse people on the margins of Reed's story, such as Alexander Gumberg, Reed's great enemy among the Russian–American community in Petrograd in 1917 (James K. Libbey, *Alexander Gumberg and Soviet–American Relations 1917-1933*, 1977). A. S. Link's edition of the papers of Woodrow Wilson have, in the volumes published since 1975, contained some interesting material on Reed. An important new source for the understanding of Reed is the recently declassified government surveillance reports on his activities from early 1918.

Of the various things written specifically on Reed, Jim Tuck's *Pancho Villa and John Reed: Two Faces of Romantic Revolution* (1984) is of particular interest. Among the few serious discussions of *Ten Days That Shook the World* is James D. White, 'Early Soviet historical interpretations of the Russian Revolution 1918-24', *Soviet Studies*, 37 (July 1985). Although I think White is incorrect in his reading of Reed's work, his article suggests several promising lines of inquiry.

Index

Index

Index